# Policing Northern Ireland

# Policing Northern Ireland

## Conflict, legitimacy and reform

**Aogán Mulcahy**

**WILLAN**
PUBLISHING

Published by

Willan Publishing
Culmcott House
Mill Street, Uffculme
Cullompton, Devon
EX15 3AT, UK
Tel: +44(0)1884 840337
Fax: +44(0)1884 840251
e-mail: info@willanpublishing.co.uk
website: www.willanpublishing.co.uk

Published simultaneously in the USA and Canada by

Willan Publishing
c/o ISBS, 920 NE 58th Ave, Suite 300,
Portland, Oregon 97213-3786, USA
Tel: +001(0)503 287 3093
Fax: +001(0)503 280 8832
e-mail: info@isbs.com
website: www.isbs.com

First Published 2006

Paperback
ISBN-13: 978-1-84392-072-4
ISBN-10: 1-84392-072-7

Hardback
ISBN-13: 978-1-84392-073-1
ISBN-10: 1-84392-073-5

British Library Cataloguing-in-Publication Data

A catalogue record for this book is available from the British Library

Project managed by Deer Park Productions, Tavistock, Devon
Typeset by TW Typesetting, Plymouth, Devon
Printed and bound by TJ International Ltd, Trecerus Industrial Estate, Padstow, Cornwall

# Contents

# Acknowledgments

This book emerged from a PhD dissertation in the School of Justice Studies (now the School of Justice and Social Inquiry) at Arizona State University. My sincere thanks to my supervisory committee – Michael Musheno, Gray Cavender and David Goldberg, and Peter Manning who served as an external committee member – for their support, encouragement and sound advice throughout. I also gratefully acknowledge a Dissertation Assistance Award from the National Science Foundation (#9512675).

While conducting the research in Belfast, I incurred many debts. The Institute of Criminology and Criminal Justice at Queen's University Belfast was extremely hospitable, and I benefited from the advice and assistance of staff and students there, especially Mike Brogden, Keith Bryett, Brian Hollywood, Michael Kearney, Kieran McEvoy, Dave O'Mahony and Moira Magee. Not nearly enough I enjoyed the good company and sound insights of Carol-Ann Barr, Colin Burns, Charlie Fisher, Niall Ó Dochartaigh, Eoghan McTigue, Brid McKernon, Lisa Rodgers, Sandra Rodgers, Mike, Tanya, Maura, Andy, Eric and Jerome. Numerous others also helped in at various stages, including Neil Jarman, Robbie McVeigh and Ronald Weitzer. Ciaran Crossey and Yvonne Murphy in the Linen Hall Library in Belfast were extremely helpful.

I particularly want to thank the individuals who were interviewed for this project. Many of them endured more than anyone should, and their willingness to share with me their experiences and insights contributed greatly to my understanding of the issues involved in police legitimacy against a backdrop of political violence. While not all of them will agree with the analysis presented in the following chapters, I hope that I have presented their own views accurately. Their assistance was crucial to completing the research and I am indebted to them.

Maggie Beirne, Graham Ellison, Alice Feldman, Tom Inglis, Kieran McEvoy and Niall Ó Dochartaigh provided valuable feedback on all or portions of the manuscript, and did a lot more besides. Their observations and suggestions greatly helped in clarifying and strengthening my argument. Clearly, any remaining errors or dubious interpretations are entirely my own responsibility. The Committee on the Administration of Justice generously provided access to draft copies of their ongoing work on Northern Ireland's new policing institutions. Ian Loader provided welcome support and encouragement. At various stages, Steve Baron, Jim Thomas and Peg Bortner helped in more ways than they may know. Thank you all.

Some parts of this book are revised versions of work previously published, and I gratefully acknowledge permission to include that material here: *Policing History, British Journal of Criminology*, 2000, 40(1): 68–87, by permission of Oxford University Press; and *Visions of Normality, Social and Legal Studies*, 1999, 8(2): 277–95, by permission of Sage Publications. The National University of Ireland generously provided financial assistance towards the publication of this book.

Brian Willan and the staff at Willan Publishing deserve a special mention for seeing this project through in such a supportive, professional and agreeable manner. And did I mention their patience?

My ageing and infirm parents, Aidan and Sheila, helped throughout, with love, encouragement and, when that wasn't enough, hard cash. Alice Feldman knows more about policing in Northern Ireland than she ever wanted to (well, she would say that, wouldn't she . . .). I hope she thinks it was worth it.

# List of tables

# List of acronyms

| | |
|---|---|
| AIA | Anglo-Irish Agreement |
| CA | Community Affairs (branch of RUC) |
| CAJ | Committee on the Administration of Justice |
| CID | Criminal Investigation Division |
| CJR | Criminal Justice Review |
| CLMC | Combined Loyalist Military Command |
| CPLC | Community and Police Liaison Committee |
| CSP | Community Safety Partnership |
| DPP | District Policing Partnership |
| DUP | Democratic Unionist Party |
| FRU | Force Research Unit (British Army) |
| GFA | Good Friday Agreement |
| HMIC | Her Majesty's Inspector of Constabulary |
| ICP | Independent Commission on Policing |
| ICPC | Independent Commission for Police Complaints |
| ICTU | Irish Congress of Trade Unions |
| INLA | Irish National Liberation Army |
| IRA | Irish Republican Army |
| LVF | Loyalist Volunteer Force |
| NIAC | Northern Ireland Affairs Committee (House of Commons) |
| NICRA | Northern Ireland Civil Rights Association |
| NIO | Northern Ireland Office |
| NIPB | Northern Ireland Policing Board |
| OPONI | Office of the Police Ombudsman for Northern Ireland |
| PANI | Police Authority for Northern Ireland |
| PBR | plastic baton round |
| PCB | Police Complaints Board |
| PFNI | Police Federation for Northern Ireland |
| PSNI | Police Service of Northern Ireland |

| PUP | Progressive Unionist Party |
| RIC | Royal Irish Constabulary |
| RIR | Royal Irish Regiment |
| RTÉ | Radio Telefís Éireann |
| RUC | Royal Ulster Constabulary |
| SDLP | Social Democratic and Labour Party |
| UDA | Ulster Defence Association |
| UDP | Ulster Democratic Party |
| UDR | Ulster Defence Regiment |
| UFF | Ulster Freedom Fighters |
| UTV | Ulster Television |
| UUP | Ulster Unionist Party |
| UVF | Ulster Volunteer Force |
| UWC | Unionist Workers' Council |

# Part I
# Introduction

# Chapter 1

# The context of policing and legitimacy in Northern Ireland

In deeply divided societies where state authority is widely disputed, the question of police legitimacy dominates the social and political landscape. The absence of a prevailing consensus over constitutional arrangements ensures that state agencies face widespread dissension, opposition and resistance. This problem is compounded for the police given their embodiment of state authority and their centrality to its maintenance. Police involvement in state security and public order ensures that their actions are largely directed against those for whom the state is already viewed as illegitimate. Police actions in turn have the capacity to alienate large sections of the public, often adding fresh momentum to the dynamic of social conflict, and lending strong and compelling grievances to extant political opposition. Such a pattern is evident in the case of Northern Ireland where the disputed nature of the state, and the conflict to which this gave rise, created a legitimacy crisis for the Royal Ulster Constabulary (RUC) police force, while also posing fundamental concerns for its successor force, the Police Service of Northern Ireland (PSNI).

The human costs of the Northern Ireland conflict – 'the Troubles' – have been immense. Since the late 1960s through to the present day, more than 3,600 people have been killed and many more thousands injured in Troubles-related violence (Fay, Morrissey and Smyth 1999; McKittrick *et al.* 2004; Sutton 2001). The conflict has also witnessed a deepening of political division, economic devastation and social polarization. While this is the backdrop against which policing developed and operated, this is a symbiotic process: policing itself constituted a major axis of division, and shaped the social and political landscape within which it operated. Policing was perhaps the single most emotive, divisive and controversial aspect of the conflict. The peace process from the mid-1990s onwards seemed to offer scope for a radical reconceptualization of how policing in Northern Ireland would be conceived and structured. In the wake of the 1994 paramilitary ceasefires, a far-reaching debate on policing ensued. Incorporating issues of state, security and safety, and affiliation and identity, the debate on policing paralleled broader debates underway about the future of Northern Ireland. Resolving the 'policing question', by creating a police service that would attract the support of nationalists and unionists alike, was central to any political settlement.

This book analyses the dynamics of the police legitimation process in Northern Ireland. It examines how the police seek to generate, maintain and enhance their legitimacy, in the broad context of the political division and violence in Northern Ireland. The key legitimacy crisis that faced the RUC, and latterly the PSNI, arose from the disputed nature of the state. Accordingly, it is among those who view the state as illegitimate – nationalists and republicans[1] – that police legitimacy is most problematic, and it is relations between the police and those communities that are the focus of this book. I address these issues by examining the RUC's efforts to improve its standing among nationalists. First, what strategies of police *reform* were implemented throughout the conflict in an effort to remedy the crisis over the RUC's legitimacy? Second, what forms of representation did the RUC employ to promote itself, and otherwise portray itself in a manner that might attract public support? Third, what form did nationalist responses to these various initiatives take? What histories of policing were constructed and celebrated in nationalist communities, and how do these engage (or not) with the accounts celebrated in the RUC's official discourse? Finally, how would the peace process impact on issues of policing legitimacy, through the reform agenda outlined in the 1999 Patten Report, and the establishment and operation of the PSNI and other organizations in the new institutional landscape of policing in Northern Ireland?

The remainder of this chapter provides a historical backdrop to these issues, and situates the issue of police legitimacy within the broader criminological literature. I begin with a discussion of the relationship between police and state in Northern Ireland.

## Police and state in Northern Ireland

*Conflict and coercion: Northern Ireland and 'the Troubles'*

Since its formation in 1921–22 under the provisions of the 1920 Government of Ireland Act, the state of Northern Ireland has functioned, if not always through outright coercion, then certainly in the absence of consensus (Rose 1971). The clearest historical divisions in Northern Ireland relate to the legitimacy of the state. Unionists and loyalists[2] – overwhelmingly Protestant – assert that the state is a legitimate political entity that properly expresses the political outlook of the majority of the Northern Irish population. Nationalists and republicans – overwhelmingly Catholic – claim the Northern Irish state is a malign and artificial creation based on the political expediencies of imperial retreat, and dependent for its survival on the dominance of the unionist community.

As Irish nationalism developed from the 1916 Easter Rising through to the widespread hostilities of the 1919–21 war of independence, unionists voiced their commitment to Britain and expressed their willingness to fight rather than be subsumed into an independent Ireland. Britain's response was to partition Ireland into two states – the Irish Free State (which became the Irish Republic in 1949) comprising 26 of the 32 counties, and Northern Ireland comprising six counties in the northeast of the island in which unionists were concentrated. The nature and ethos of the state was by design explicitly unionist, but nationalists comprised one-third of its population. While this minority group was certainly governable, profound unionist suspicion of nationalists' disenchanted and potentially threatening presence within the state ensured that few steps were taken to accommodate them (Bew, Gibbon and Patterson 1996; O'Leary and McGarry 1996). From 1922 to 1972, Northern Ireland was governed by one political party, the Ulster Unionists. Proportional representation, more favourable to minority parties, was abolished in favour of the majority-friendly 'first past the post' electoral system. Local government boundaries were manipulated to establish unionist control in areas where nationalists formed a majority of the population, and housing provision and public sector jobs were heavily skewed in favour of unionists. In spite of these various measures – supplemented by a considerable array of coercive powers – the events that unfolded during the late 1960s demonstrated the inherent instability of a state whose legitimacy had never been fully established.

The Civil Rights Movement emerged in the 1960s to address these discriminatory practices. The demands of the Northern Ireland Civil Rights Association (NICRA) included an end to electoral gerrymandering, the repeal of emergency legislation and the abolition of the 'B' Specials (a part-time militia force). The initial civil rights demonstrations were low-key affairs, but the hostility they met from loyalists and the security forces (who tended to view the civil rights movement as a republican-inspired plot to undermine the state) greatly increased the momentum of the campaign. During the 1960s, the Unionist Prime Minister, Terence O'Neill, began promoting a more liberal and less exclusive unionism than that advocated by his predecessors. While this increased the expectations of nationalists, O'Neill had difficulty in delivering even the modest reforms he had advocated. As political demonstrations escalated into widespread disorder, violent clashes between nationalists and unionists increased. During the ensuing conflict the RUC and 'B' Specials were overwhelmed, and British troops were sent to Northern Ireland on 14 August 1969. Initially viewed largely as the defenders of Catholics from Protestant attacks, their role in support of the Northern Irish state soon became apparent. Republican paramilitaries[3] launched a ferocious campaign of violence, and the army and RUC focused their attention on the nationalist population. Stringent security measures such as internment (detention without trial) alienated nationalists still further from the state, strengthening their conviction that the state was incapable of reform and could only offer a security response to the deteriorating situation. Shortly afterwards, the British government stepped in: the Stormont parliament was suspended and direct rule from Westminster was imposed.

Successive political initiatives, from the 1973 Sunningdale Agreement to the 1985 Anglo-Irish Agreement, proved unable to generate a political solution. During the late 1980s secret talks took place between the nationalist Social Democratic and Labour Party (SDLP) and the republican Sinn Féin party, and in turn with the Irish government. The thrust of these discussions was to build the foundation for a political settlement that would resolve the conflict. In February 1993, the British and Irish governments published the Downing Street Declaration in which they outlined their position regarding Northern Ireland and the issues arising in any political settlement. Intense negotiation and speculation followed this, and on 31 August 1994 the IRA announced a ceasefire. Six weeks later, on 13 October 1994, the Combined Loyalist Military Command (CLMC, a body representing the main loyalist paramilitary organizations) also announced a ceasefire. After 25 years of violence, it seemed that the conflict was finally over.

Despite the grounds for optimism laid by the paramilitary ceasefires, the political divisions endemic in Northern Ireland soon reasserted themselves. Three strands of relationships formed the essence of the peace process: relations between nationalists and unionists in Northern Ireland; between Northern Ireland and the Irish Republic; and between Ireland and Britain. The concerns of the British government and the unionist parties immediately focused on the status of the IRA ceasefire, and assurances were sought that its 'cessation of hostilities' amounted to a 'permanent' ceasefire. None were forthcoming. Demands were also made for paramilitary organizations to decommission their considerable arsenals, but they refused outright. Following further stalled political negotiations, on 9 February 1996 the IRA announced that it had abandoned its 17-month-old ceasefire and would resume its campaign. That evening, a massive IRA bomb exploded in London's Canary Wharf, killing two people, injuring hundreds, and causing up to one billion pounds worth of damage.

Political negotiations dragged on, and the British government announced a date for an election for all-party talks. In July 1997 the IRA renewed its ceasefire. Discussions were now underway at a furious pace, and in April 1998 the negotiators produced the Belfast Agreement (known generally as the Good Friday Agreement) as a blueprint for a comprehensive political settlement. This proposed an elected assembly in Northern Ireland, all-Ireland bodies with executive powers, a council of the Isles to discuss matters relevant both to Ireland and the UK, and other measures such as the release of paramilitary prisoners. On 10 May 1998, in separate referenda in Northern Ireland and the Irish Republic, the agreement was ratified, one aspect of which was the establishment of an Independent Commission on Policing. In peace as during the conflict, there was no escaping the significance attached to policing.

## Securing the state: policing in Northern Ireland 1922–68

Up until the 1920s, the Royal Irish Constabulary (RIC) policed the island of Ireland. Following the partition of Ireland, it was replaced by the Civic Guards (renamed An Garda Síochána, 'the guardians of the peace') in the Irish Free State and by the Royal Ulster Constabulary in Northern Ireland. From the outset, the Northern Irish government conceived of the RUC as a paramilitary police force that would play a direct role in the maintenance of the state and its unionist character. In addition to the RUC, an auxiliary police force called the Ulster Special Constabulary (USC, or 'B' Specials) was set up. The legislative framework under which the security forces operated also proved contentious, especially the extensive powers available under the 1922 Civil Authorities (Special Powers) Act.

A committee established in 1922 to examine the organization of the new police force recommended that Catholic recruitment to the RUC should be proportionate to the Catholic population in Northern Ireland (which then stood at one-third of the total), and it called for 1,000 of the RUC's establishment of 3,000 officers to be allocated to Catholics, although these were to be recruited from within the RIC rather than from the population at large. The remaining 2,000 officers were to be recruited from the USC and from Protestant members of the RIC (Farrell 1983). Catholic recruitment never reached this level, peaking in 1923 when it reached 21.1 per cent, and from then on declining gradually, if steadily. In 1969, approximately 11 per cent of the RUC were Catholics, and, as the Hunt Report observed (Hunt Committee 1969: 29), of these 'the great majority are probably men whose fathers had served in the police.' Within the 'B' Specials, there was not a single Catholic (p. 40).

Although 50 years of one-party rule ensured that Northern Ireland was in many ways a comparatively tranquil society, the RUC's relations with nationalists remained problematic. Ellison (1997) notes that while former RUC officers who served during this period described relations with the broad Catholic community as 'generally very good' (p. 162), they nevertheless retained a strong interest in containing political dissent, even in the complete absence of paramilitary activity. Thus the police would 'keep an eye out – in a nice way mind you' (p. 162) on 'the politically motivated Catholic' or 'families that displayed an anti-police attitude' (p. 167): 'It was good crack in them days . . . like you'd maybe pull a few boys in and give them a bit of grief . . . or the Specials would give them a bit of a rub over when they met them out one night' (ex-RUC sergeant, quoted in Ellison 1997: 163). One celebrated case in 1957 involved Frankie Meehan who, when RUC officers stopped him and asked him his name, replied in Irish. For doing so he was arrested and detained without trial for seven months in Belfast's Crumlin Road jail (McCann 1980: 10–11). Criticisms of the RUC were generally dismissed by the Unionist government as 'sinister' attacks against the police 'which the entire law-abiding population of our country knows is doing a splendid job' (quoted in Weitzer 1995: 56). In truth, the force was doing entirely what its role entailed: broad service provision *and* the control of political dissent. Police hostility towards the burgeoning civil rights movement in the late 1960s generated enormous criticism, and inquiries into those events confirmed the precariousness of the RUC's relationship with nationalists. During periods of political calm, acquiescence with police authority was often evident, but during periods of crisis, the rapidity with which this could be replaced with widespread suspicion and outright hostility reflected the underlying difficulties facing the RUC.

## Policing and the Northern Ireland conflict

Although police forces are key state agencies in any political context, in Northern Ireland the RUC played a pivotal role in maintaining the security and integrity of the state. Two major consequences flowed from this. First, given the RUC's overt involvement in state security as well as its intrinsic character as a key state agency, nationalists' and republicans' rejection of the state's legitimacy implied a *de facto* rejection of the RUC's legitimacy. It required little extra effort to include opposition to the RUC under the umbrella of a general opposition to the state. Second, the importance of the RUC's security role gave it a wide licence in terms of the strategies it could pursue to achieve this. Because nationalists and republicans represented the most visible threat to the state, historically the RUC concentrated its resources on policing those communities. This offered vast scope for aggressive, paramilitary-style policing of nationalist communities, a feature exacerbated during times of violent conflict. The combination of these two factors ensured that even among those who did not reject their legitimacy on the basis of political principle, the police suffered a diminution of legitimacy.

This contested background may make it easy to exaggerate the depth of opposition to the RUC that existed, or fail to appreciate regional variations in its role. For instance, in areas that were relatively untouched by the direct impact of political violence, especially middle-class suburbs, 'normal policing' often operated. Based on ethnographic research in a relatively peaceful unionist community in Belfast, Brewer and Magee (1991: 265) found: 'The mundaneness of policing in Easton parallels that for police forces in liberal democracies; and the processes of reasoning and cognitive resources by which this work is accomplished are also common to policemen and women elsewhere.' It is also important to appreciate that political affiliation was not the only factor shaping the public's attitudes towards the police: class, youth and gender also had a strong impact (Ellison 2001; McVeigh 1994; O'Mahony et al. 2000). Furthermore, surveys revealed that a sizeable proportion of Catholics viewed the RUC as fair in their handling of 'ordinary crime', while a small but significant proportion of Protestants viewed the RUC's behaviour as unfair (Weitzer 1995).

While these research findings refute the assumption that nationalists and unionists were inevitably and invariably poles apart in relation to their views on and support for the RUC, it is crucial to appreciate the depth of divisions that did exist. The RUC was viewed with suspicion, hostility and active opposition by a sizeable minority of the population of Northern Ireland. Over the course of the conflict, 302 RUC officers were killed and over 9,000 seriously injured. Its officers wore flak jackets, were heavily armed, operated from heavily fortified stations, and in some areas officers never patrolled without army support and often did not respond to calls for service because of safety risks. Some RUC stations in border areas were supplied and serviced *entirely* by helicopter. Vast differences also existed in the levels of routine contact that residents of different communities had with the police. A survey in 1997 found that 49 per cent of 'Protestant small town' respondents, but only 1 per cent of respondents in 'Catholic lower working class urban' areas, knew an RUC officer 'to speak to' (O'Mahony et al. 2000: 79). Furthermore, whatever Catholic support did exist for the RUC plummeted in relation to counterinsurgency and public-order policing (Weitzer 1995).

Nevertheless, some authors argue that the problems facing the RUC, exaggerated or not, were successfully addressed during the conflict, particularly through the lengthy process of professionalization from the 1970s onwards (Doherty 2004; Hermon 1997; Pockrass 1986; Ryder 2004, 2000). As Ryder (2000: 12) stated: 'Today, a new, professional RUC stands, impartially and politically independent, between the two communities in Ulster.' Similarly, Weitzer (1990: 211–12) argued that the characteristics of neutrality and impartiality have filtered throughout the organization and are embedded in its ethos: 'The RUC rank and file, no less than the upper echelons, have embraced impartial and apolitical ideals.' While this conclusion may have accurately reflected the attitudes and predispositions of many individual officers, the force's structural role of ensuring state security inevitably brought it into conflict with those who rejected the legitimacy of the state. Even the tightest embrace of 'impartial and apolitical ideals' would have but a limited impact on police–community relations as long as other police functions counteracted this (Ellison and Smyth 2000; Magee 1991; Weitzer 1995).

The Report of the Independent Commission on Policing (the 1999 Patten Report) – which emerged from the 1998 Belfast Agreement political settlement – sought to disentangle policing from disputes arising from issues of state. Its framework for 'A New Beginning' attempted to resolve the policing question in Northern Ireland by elaborating a model of policing that could attract widespread community support. The huge controversy that accompanied the Report's findings and their implementation confirms that police legitimacy remains a matter of fundamental importance in Northern Ireland.

### The rationale for this book

While there is now a substantial literature on policing in Northern Ireland, this book is warranted on the basis of several factors. First, while researchers have produced robust and insightful accounts of the RUC, there have been few analyses of the *dynamics* of police legitimacy there. In some research, such as Brewer and Magee's (1991) work on 'normal policing' and Mapstone's (1994, 1992) analysis of the occupational culture within the RUC Reserve, the issue of legitimacy featured in only an implicit or indirect fashion. In studies that have addressed legitimacy more directly – including research on the historical development of the RUC (Boyce 1979; Farrell 1983; Ellison and Smyth 2000; Tomlinson 1980) and on accountability issues (Jennings 1990a, 1990b; Walsh 1988) – the focus has largely been on demonstrating the absence of legitimacy rather than considering the means by which it might be lost, maintained or enhanced. By highlighting the dynamics of the police legitimation process, both during the conflict and in the subsequent peace process, my goal is to highlight the fluidity and contingency of police legitimacy in a way that previous works have often neglected.

Second, given the immense significance and the massive scale of recent policing developments in Northern Ireland, there is a need to map these out and examine their implementation and impact. Many of the major works on policing in Northern Ireland were published either during the conflict (Brewer and Magee 1991), as the peace process was first unfolding (Weitzer 1995), or before the career of the Patten Report was fully apparent (Ellison and Smyth 2000). Others were written specifically as contributions to the police reform debate following the 1994 paramilitary ceasefires (Brogden 1998; McGarry and O'Leary 1999; O'Rawe and Moore 1997; Wright and Bryett 2000). Since the publication of the Patten Report in 1999, a substantial body of work has considered its recommendations and implementation (Beirne 2001; Hillyard and Tomlinson 2000; Kempa and Shearing 2002; McGarry 2000, 2004; Moore and O'Rawe 2001; O'Rawe 2003; Shearing 2000, 2001; Smyth 2002a, 2002b; C. Walker 2001; N. Walker 2003). These, however, have generally been succinct overviews of the Patten Report and/or its implementation, and for the most part their analyses have been overtaken by events. One of my aims is to expand on and update these initial assessments by providing a more sustained evaluation of recent developments and placing this in the broader historical context of police reform in Northern Ireland.

Third, while Northern Ireland's status as a 'divided society' may place it at some remove from debates about police reform in less overtly contested jurisdictions (Brewer 1991), the ongoing police reform programme there establishes Northern Ireland as an important example of efforts to reconstitute policing and police-community relations. Difficulties surrounding policing in divided societies are often of a different order to those in other jurisdictions – whether because of communities' degree of affiliation with or estrangement from the state, the sheer scale of the conflict or other factors (Brewer et al. 1996; Brogden and Shearing 1993; Enloe 1980; Weitzer 1990, 1995) – and due consideration must be given to the specificity of policing in different contexts. But fundamental issues such as accountability and police–community relations do provide a basis for considering aspects of police legitimacy across a range of different socio-political environments. Moreover, in a world increasingly characterized by the global flow of policies and practices, analysis of the role that Northern Ireland plays as a case study of police reform can shed light on broader processes of political transition and conflict resolution (Ellison 2005; Mulcahy 2005).

In addressing these questions, this book draws on three broad sets of data. First, between 1995 and 1997 I conducted over 80 formal interviews (and many more informal interviews) with a variety of individuals. This included some 20 RUC officers ranging from the rank of constable to senior officer level. I also interviewed several members or former members of the Police Authority for Northern

Ireland, and representatives of the Northern Ireland Office, the Independent Commission for Police Complaints and various other official or semi-official agencies. The remainder of the interviews were with representatives of political parties, interest groups, human rights organizations, people involved in the policing debate and a number of other individuals with relevant experience or knowledge of policing issues. This was supplemented by further interviews in subsequent years. The second major set of data I used was historical/archival in nature. This included police material (including annual reports, speeches, press releases and other official documentation); policy statements from a wide variety of organizations; coverage of the policing debate in the main Northern Irish newspapers and a variety of other periodicals; and other miscellaneous material. The third set of data comprised observational data from two years of living in Belfast and numerous trips there subsequently. As well as attending conferences, meetings and other policing-related events, I was also able to benefit from the fragments of many conversations and observations in bars, living rooms and other informal venues.

Having outlined the historical context of police and state in Northern Ireland, I now turn to the question of legitimacy, and the dynamics of the police legitimation process generally.

## The nature of legitimacy

Legitimacy involves the justification of a particular state of affairs in terms of a rationale that is accepted by a relevant social audience. To be legitimate is to be viewed as established on valid and justifiable grounds. According to Bourdieu (1977: 164), 'Every established order tends to produce (to very different degrees and with very different means) the naturalization of its own arbitrariness.' To analyse the legitimation process, therefore, offers scope for inquiring how one set of social understandings and relationships comes to dominate others and be viewed as the natural outcome of social development.

The problematic of legitimacy 'blossoms' once an 'appreciation of the conventional character of social norms and institutions becomes widespread' (Connolly 1984a: 2). During the enlightenment era, rationality gradually displaced the traditional means – God and Nature – by which authority structures were justified. This was particularly associated with Hobbes' quest for the 'reason of state': a justification that could establish a legitimate foundation for the modern nation state (Foucault 1991; Held 1989). However, to pose this question highlights the very need for legitimacy and brings it into the sphere of public discourse. Once the conventions that form the symbolic and routine manifestations of the state – traditions, rules, customs – are exposed as such, their claims to naturalness are shattered. They are stripped of their previously transcendental qualities, and revealed as human products. Accordingly, the basis of legitimacy claims may be challenged, and counterclaims may emerge offering a different convention in place of the one accorded legitimacy.[4]

The problematic of legitimacy, then, is that its conventional origins and character are at odds with its claims to naturalness. If awareness of a political regime's conventional basis is the issue, then the resolution to the problem may also lie there by actively seeking to erase this awareness – to overlook or even 'forget' its conventional character. In this sense, legitimacy requires a form of social and historical amnesia, whereby conventions are put beyond question by establishing them as part of normal everyday life, the natural order of things: in effect, when a particular class, grouping or perspective establishes 'hegemony' over social relations and social reality. Gramsci (1971) conceived of hegemony as the success of a particular group in having other social groups accept its social, political and cultural values. Furthermore, not only does a socially subordinate group accept the social and political leadership offered by another group, but it views such leadership as the natural state of affairs. Gramsci argued that power was exercised most effectively when it operated on the basis of consent rather than coercion, when a 'historical bloc' engaged in social leadership rather than overt domination, and its power was constituted as 'authority' rather than oppression (Anderson 1977; Bobock 1986; Cain 1983; Hall 1988, 1977). Hegemony occurs when a particular ideology or combination of ideologies 'tends to prevail, to gain the upper hand, to propagate itself throughout society – bringing about not only a unison of economic and political aims, but also intellectual and moral unity, posing all the questions around which the struggle rages not on a corporate but on a 'universal' plane' (Gramsci 1971: 181–2). Hegemony, then, is the construction of 'common sense', and it is this taken-for-granted quality that characterizes it as the realm we live in but do not think (Bourdieu 1977). This account of hegemony should not be taken to imply that it is a state of affairs which prevails without contest. Hegemony is best understood in terms of process rather than end state, as an effort to naturalize and normalize a particular state of affairs rather than a guarantee of its achievement. No discourse can claim to have such a totalizing impact on society that it is accepted without question. Instead, it is necessary to recognize the partial quality of this enterprise, its contingency and fragility, and the manner in which resistance and critique feature even in relation to the most seemingly all-encompassing discourses (Foucault 1990; Scott 1990, 1985).

Weber's (1946) discussion of political legitimacy remains a key point of orientation here. He identified three 'pure' types of legitimation of state domination: *tradition*, *charisma* and *legal-rationality*. Tradition is 'the authority of the "eternal yesterday" '; charisma, the authority deriving from qualities of an individual's leadership; and legal-rationality, the authority flowing from 'legality' and 'rationally created rules' (Weber 1946: 78–9). Weber's schema has had an enduring significance, but many writers have criticized its reliance on a 'thin theory of legitimacy' (Connolly 1984b: 224). By describing a political system as legitimate if it is believed it to be legitimate, Weber highlighted the diversity of power relations viewed as legitimate. His definition, though, relies primarily on a 'subjectivist' conception of legitimacy in so far as it largely amounts to providing a description of 'people's beliefs' (Beetham 1991; Coicaud 2002; Schaar 1984; Simmons 2001). In essence, it suggests that a social order is legitimate if it is viewed as legitimate, and that if it is viewed as legitimate, then it is legitimate. It fails to outline any systematic means for identifying and analysing the underlying features of a system of power relations that establishes them as legitimate or illegitimate, and encourages description rather than analysis of the *dynamics* of the legitimation process. By conflating *forms* of legitimacy with *belief in* legitimacy, Weber ignored the relationship between the norms on which a political regime is based, the specific ways in which these norms are justified to particular social audiences, and the manner in which those audiences may respond to them – whether by acceptance (of whatever degree) or rejection. In addition, his framework gives little scope for analysing a deterioration of political legitimacy or how remedial action may be taken to address this (Beetham 1991: 23), or for outlining the basis on which people would resist state domination (Allen 2004: 101–2).

To overcome the limitations of Weber's approach, Beetham (1991) suggested that three conditions had to be satisfied for a social order to be considered fully legitimate. 'Power can be said to be legitimate', he wrote, 'to the extent that (i) it conforms to established rules, (ii) the rules can be justified by reference to beliefs shared by both dominate and subordinate, and (iii) there is evidence of consent by the subordinate to the particular power relation' (pp. 15–16). In other words, a given social order must be established on the basis of the broad rules relating to governance current in that society, and those rules must be demonstrably justifiable to all the parties concerned, and must secure the expressed consent of the subjects of a particular power relationship.

This formulation raises a series of questions for this study. While normalization is the overall goal of the legitimation process, what elements underpin this process, and what are the dynamics between them? What occurs following a crisis in which the 'established rules' under which a regime operates are discredited, when those rules are no longer – if indeed they ever were – justifiable to the socially subordinate? What responses may be made to a situation in which expressed public consent for a particular power relationship is absent? In the aftermath of a legitimacy crisis, what strategies might function to remedy a fractured relationship or replace an irreparably damaged one? What forms of resistance, in turn, might emerge, and with what consequences? In the following section, I apply these concerns to the issue of police legitimation.

## The police legitimation process

Reiner (2000: 15) quotes approvingly from the end of Raymond Chandler's novel *The Long Goodbye* to capture the ubiquitous role accorded the police in modern society: 'I never saw any of them again – except the cops. No way has yet been invented to say goodbye to them.' Certainly, few writers dispute the material and symbolic importance of policing institutions in contemporary societies. Goldstein (1977: 1) locates the role of the police at the very heart of social relations, and suggests that the public looks to the police not only to deal with crime and disorder, but also 'to protect the very processes and rights – such as free elections, freedom of movement, and freedom of assembly – on which continuation of a free society depends.' Such a depiction of policing easily lends itself to a characterization of the police as the 'thin blue line' between order and chaos (Mark 1978) and as 'an inevitable fact of modern life' (Reiner 2000: 16). While particular policing arrangements may appear to be a historical constant by virtue of their embeddedness within national cultures, the stridency of their advocates or simply through the longevity of specific institutions, police organizations do not stand apart from the rest of society in a state of utopian equilibrium. Their legitimation is inextricably linked with the pursuit of normalcy and the naturalization of a particular set of social relations.[5] Three overlapping elements form the dynamic at the heart of the police legitimation process: *reform*, *representation* and the public *response* to these initiatives. I now consider each of these in turn.

### Reform

The general rationale for a reform initiative is that a policing system is perceived to be dysfunctional in some respect. While reform agendas are often characterized by disputes over issues of scale and scope, as well as their very necessity in the first instance, they typically address either individuals or groups within the organization, or the police organization itself.

Addressing aberrant behaviour on the part of individual officers or groups of officers – often characterized as the 'bad apples' who threaten to spoil the organizational barrel – has been a key dimension of this, with issues of misconduct and corruption featuring prominently in reform debates. Although the search for ways of controlling police behaviour has been extensive, the answers provided have been somewhat equivocal. The fact that most police officers wield significant powers, operate with low levels of direct supervision and high levels of discretion, and are socialized primarily through contact with serving officers, ensures that effective oversight mechanisms are notoriously difficult to implement (Punch 1983). Many commentators suggest that the persistent failure of many police initiatives is partly due to the resilience of police occupational culture (Bayley 1977; Chan 1997; Van Maanen 1978), and considerable attention has been given to the relative merits of internal and external mechanisms for controlling police behaviour (Barker and Carter 1994; Bayley 1977; Blumberg 1989; Chan 1997; Fyfe 1988; Goldsmith 1991; Jefferson and Grimshaw 1984; Punch 1983). Moreover, police organizations often appear unwilling or unable to ensure that their members behave appropriately. Sherman's (1978) analysis of reform efforts in four US police departments revealed that it usually took a major precipitating event – the 'mighty weapon' of 'scandal' – to mobilize reform efforts, a finding supported by research in other jurisdictions (Chan 1997; Punch 1985; Skolnick and Fyfe 1993). However, to characterize police culture as inherently subversive of reform efforts may misrepresent the nature of the occupational cultures of policing (Waddington 1999). Moreover, 'rule-tightening' and other efforts to change police culture (through training initiatives, the promotion of 'progressive' officers, etc.) are likely to have only a limited impact on police behaviour in the absence of changes to the wider social field within which the police operate (Chan 1997). As long as the 'key practice' (Cain 1979) of policing remains the maintenance of social order, both at the level of securing the state and in everyday settings, police attention is likely to remain focused on individuals and communities of disrepute (Choongh 1997; Lee 1981).

The second main focus of reform efforts – reform of the police organization or even the broader institutional framework within which it is situated – can arise from two conditions. First, it can develop from the shift, within a reasonably stable political framework, from one major mode of policing legitimation to another. This includes, in the US context, the transition from a politically oriented model of policing to a professional model and on to a community-oriented model (Goldstein 1990; Kelling and Moore 1988; Skolnick and Bayley 1986). It includes, in the UK context, the rhetorical commitment towards 'community policing' following the urban riots of the 1980s, as well as the growth of an 'audit culture' within policing following the Conservative government's emphasis on 'economy, efficiency and effectiveness' from the early 1980s onwards (Newburn 2003; Reiner 2000). It is also evident in the recent growth of private security and the mushrooming of 'plural policing' and partnership initiatives, reflecting profound changes in the governance of security (Bayley and Shearing 2001, 1996; Crawford 2003; Garland 1996; Johnston and Shearing 2003). The second context for macro-level reforms arises when an alternative basis for police legitimacy is required following a crisis in which the fundamental bases of policing in a given context have been undermined beyond recovery. It is most visible when a state of revolution or violent social upheaval has occurred. In those instances, the limitations of the extant model of police legitimacy are plainly visible, and it is usually imperative to establish a clear break with the past if the newly established model is to flourish, or at least avoid its own legitimacy crisis through association with the previous discredited regime (Brogden and Shearing 1993; Dixon and van der Spuy 2004; O'Rawe and Moore 1997; Shaw 2002).

### Representation

Representation involves the expression and communication of particular images of policing *by* the police (or other agencies seeking to enhance police legitimacy, such as central or local government), both for the consumption of the police themselves, as well as for a variety of wider public audiences. While 'image work' is fundamental to all aspects of policing, for analytical purposes it is useful to distinguish between police 'image-work' performed at different levels of policing, ranging from micro- to macro-contexts.

The first level involves presentation and representation in face-to-face interaction (Goffman 1959). Dramaturgical analysis highlights the distinction to be drawn between 'front-stage' and 'back-stage' activities. The former involve the cultivation of images that offer convincing accounts of police officers' competence and are oriented towards the public's consumption. The latter generally comprise activities occurring in intra-organizational settings, in which the participants and audience are already attuned to the realities of policing (Holdaway 1983; Manning 1997; Young 1991).

The second level is the manner in which police organizations have become progressively more involved in strategies of 'external communication' (Manning 1992) and promotionalism generally, through the expansion of public relations activities and other measures of 'official propaganda' (Altheide and Johnson 1980). Mawby (2002: 194) suggests that the nature and impact of police 'image work' is context specific, with the potential to 'enhance police legitimacy by contributing to police accountability through transparency and open communications. At other times image work is deployed as a means of coping with illegitimacy, legitimacy deficit and delegitimation'. Increasingly, police organizations have assumed a proactive and prominent role in circulating information on policing and related matters, whether in the role of 'risk communicator' in a networked society (Ericson and Haggerty 1997) or as 'authorized' commentators on the 'state of the nation' (Hall *et al*. 1978; Loader and Mulcahy 2003). Discrepant messages may nevertheless emerge, perhaps reflecting the respective viewpoints of staff organizations and senior officers (McLaughlin and Murji 1998).

Third, representation of policing can be examined in terms of its relationship to the nation, namely the extent to which it comes to be embedded in national cultures, often assuming an iconic status as exemplar of the nation. The English 'bobby' (Emsley 1992; Loader and Mulcahy 2003; McLaughlin 2005), the Canadian 'mountie' (Walden 1982) and the Irish 'guard' (McNiffe 1997) have all – in admittedly different contexts – served as 'condensation symbols' (Turner 1974) of national identity and incubators of national ideals.

For all this, policing remains shrouded in secrecy and mystique. At one level, this is reflected in the manner by which people's dispositions towards the police are embedded in wider cultural frameworks rather than in terms of clinical analyses of police effectiveness (Loader and Mulcahy 2003). Beyond this, some aspects of police work are constrained by the rules of criminal procedure, generating levels of non-disclosure that increase dramatically the closer these are to the central structures of power. Yet policing is simultaneously a highly public endeavour, with the public's knowledge and understanding of policing mediated through a vast array of 'cop shows', crime-reality television programmes and other cultural forms (Fishman and Cavender 1998; Sparks 1992; Wilson 2000). While these programmes often depict policing in a positive light, giving supportive images of individual officers, their frustrations and their failings, they generally reinforce the view that policing is, at its core, a crime-fighting enterprise. However, the police's ability to provide a comprehensive solution to crime is limited at best (Reiner 2000), leading to an underlying tension between public expectation and organizational capacity. This creates an 'impossible mandate' for the police (Manning 1997). On the one hand, it situates them as a 'core' feature of society with all that entails in terms of being imbued with public expectation, trust (or, in some quarters, mistrust). On the other, it leaves them perpetually susceptible to being 'found out', propelling them towards a ritualistic rendering of their activities in which their mandate is 'concealed in circumlocution' (Bittner 1980: 46), and in which the focus is heavily skewed towards the 'dramatic management of the *appearance* of effectiveness' (Manning 1997: 32; original emphasis). Conversely, the police may seek legitimacy through other discourses – such as 'policing by consent' – that highlight the *limited* capacity of the police and seek public support explicitly on that basis. As Mark noted: 'The real art of policing a free society is to win by appearing to lose' (Reiner 2000). In such ways, the material dimensions of policing are innately linked with the means by which these are represented and communicated.

## Response

Response is the third element of the police legitimation process, and it involves an examination of the nature and effects of public responses to police reform and representational strategies. This approach directs our attention away from an exclusive focus on the police (and, relatedly, away from intra-organizational measures of legitimacy), and towards the dynamic between the police and the policed.

In terms of theoretical orientations, key works on 'resistance' are particularly useful here. Foucault (1990, 1980) posits resistance as an inherent component of power relations, such that power everywhere engenders resistance. By addressing fissures and points of instability in any regime of truth, a focus upon resistance offers scope for the deconstruction of official constructions of events, and the 'insurrection of subjugated knowledges' that have been 'located low down on the hierarchy, beneath the required level of cognition or scientificity' (Foucault 1980: 80, 82). Foucault argues that 'is through the re-appearance of this knowledge, of these local popular knowledges, these disqualified knowledges, that criticism performs its work' (p. 82). Scott (1985) also examined 'everyday acts of resistance', describing them as the 'weapons of the weak'. He suggested that subordinates' 'public transcripts' of acquiescence to social elites often shields 'a "hidden transcript" that represents a critique of power spoken behind the back of the dominant' (Scott 1990: xii). As he put it: 'slaves and serfs ordinarily dare not contest the terms of their subordination openly. Behind the scenes, though, they are likely to create and defend a social space in which offstage dissent to the official transcript of power relations may be voiced' (p. xi). Points of crisis are often characterized precisely by the emergence of these hidden transcripts onto the public stage. Focusing on these hidden histories may shed greater light on the dynamics of police–community relations by offering an oppositional reading of events that privileges the experience of the subordinate over the rhetoric of the dominant, and that questions the 'consensual' basis of authority in liberal-democratic societies.

In recent years, the police have become much more attentive to the issue of public attitudes towards them. This partly reflects the mass mediated nature of modern society (Thompson 1990) and the consequent emphasis that police organizations place on effective communication and positive reporting (Manning 2003; Mawby 2002). It also arises from two material contexts. First, the managerial framework within which the police operate constitutes the public as 'customers' whose satisfaction and support are actively sought as a measure of police 'effectiveness' and performance. Accordingly, surveys on public attitudes towards the police have now become standard measures of 'customer satisfaction'. The second key factor underpinning the growth of interest in public attitudes towards the police is the material core of policing, and the impact that police–public interaction has on shaping attitudes towards the police. While it must be acknowledged that the link between individuals' experience of, and dispositions towards, the police is nuanced in several respects (Loader and Mulcahy 2003: chapter 4), public trust in the police is nevertheless reflected in the flow of information provided to the police, and this low-level information is crucial in enabling the police to detect and prevent crime (Reiner 2000). When the public's levels of trust in the police diminishes, that information flow is reduced and, with it, police effectiveness. To compensate for this, police often resort to more intrusive and abrasive measures, such as stop-and-search tactics, that in turn may lead to a further drop in public trust, leading the police to use increasingly aggressive strategies that further alienate the public. Under certain conditions, this may escalate into widespread disorder and violence (Keith 1993; Lea and Young 1993).

In an effort to maximize public support, the police may be especially responsive to 'signal' crimes, high-profile events that feature prominently in individuals' sense of risk and danger (Innes 2004). There is, however, a tension between the effects associated with these high-profile but often distant events, and events arising from face-to-face interaction with the police or what otherwise would constitute a specifically 'local' knowledge. For example, Keith (1993) found that in black communities in London attitudes towards the police were shaped far more by local events than by the highly publicized scandals that occasionally gained prominence. This suggests that frameworks for understanding policing have a strongly local component that may seriously affect the success or otherwise of a particular policing initiative. Related to this, the ways that people perceive the *nature*, rather than just the mode of *implementation*, of policing strategies they are confronted with may determine the impact of those strategies in effecting a concrete improvement in police–community relations. Thus community-relations policing activities may actually lead to a deterioration in public trust in the police if the community views these activities as little more than a façade, or perhaps even as an intelligence-gathering operation (Gordon 1987; Weitzer 1995).

## An outline of the book

The remainder of the book is divided into three sections covering, respectively: (1) the years of overt conflict, 1968–94; (2) the period from the 1994 paramilitary ceasefires to the 1998 Belfast Agreement; and (3) the period 1998–2005 with its sweeping changes to the institutional landscape of policing in Northern Ireland. While I have tried to follow this structure as closely as possible, discussion of some issues requires a more fluid approach and at some points of the argument I have had to step outside of this chronological framework.

Chapters 2–4 consider the dynamics of the police legitimation process during the years of the conflict 1968–94. Chapter 2 discusses the emerging crisis that the civil rights movement and the police response to it generated for the RUC, and it outlines and assesses the measures undertaken to remedy this situation. In Chapter 3, I consider the organizational memory of the RUC, specifically the ways in which particular depictions of policing were mobilized to play a privileged role in the force's representational strategies. Chapter 4 assesses relations between nationalists and the RUC during the conflict, particularly in light of the professionalization of policing from the mid-1970s onwards.

Chapters 5–7 cover the post-ceasefire situation, between 1994 and 1998. These three chapters mirror those in the previous section as closely as possible, covering issues of reform, representation and public response. Chapter 5 charts the wide-ranging debate about police reform that ensued following the paramilitary ceasefires. Chapter 6 examines the manner in which RUC officers and others articulated their conceptions of what normal policing would entail and where the force would fit in the widely lauded 'return to normality.' In Chapter 7, I analyse nationalist responses to the wide-ranging policing debate on police reform, particularly in terms of various resistance narratives that were at the heart of oppositional discourses on policing in Northern Ireland.

In the final chapters of the book, I outline changes to policing arising from the report of the Independent Commission on Policing (the 1999 Patten Report) established as part of the 1998 Belfast Agreement. Chapter 8 provides a detailed analysis of the Patten Report and its approach to police reform, while Chapter 9 examines the implementation of these various elements of the new landscape of policing arrangements and offers a preliminary assessment of the operation of these institutions. In the concluding chapter, I examine the lessons of Northern Ireland for other jurisdictions, and consider the role that police reform plays in processes of political transformation and conflict resolution.

## Notes

1 Although nationalists and republicans share a critical view of the Northern Irish state and favour a united Ireland (to various degrees), they differ in their preferred solution to this. Nationalists are primarily represented by the

moderate Social Democratic and Labour Party (SDLP), which is opposed to the use of violence for political ends and favours solely constitutional means of political change. Sinn Féin (meaning 'ourselves alone' in the sense of political independence) is the major republican party, and has close links with the IRA. Republicans view the state as untenable and its dissolution as a historical necessity, and generally view the conflict as a legitimate political struggle. See McGarry and O'Leary (1995) and Ruane and Todd (2005).

2 Unionists and loyalists favour maintaining the political union with Britain. The Ulster Unionist Party (UUP) and the Democratic Unionist Party (DUP) are the largest unionist parties, although in recent elections the DUP has made large electoral gains at the UUP's expense. During the peace process the Progressive Unionist Party (PUP) and Ulster Democratic Party (UDP) emerged to represent loyalists, although with only marginal political success (the UDP subsequently disbanded as a result). Loyalists are viewed as more extreme in their political views than unionists, and loyalist paramilitaries believe themselves justified in the use of political violence to maintain the integrity of the Northern Irish state. See Bruce (1994), Cochrane (2001), McGarry and O'Leary (1995), Ruane and Todd (2005) and Shirlow and McGovern (1997).

3 Loyalist and republican paramilitary groups trace their lineage back to the early 1900s when they emerged to fight, respectively, for and against Irish independence. While they made sporadic appearances during the subsequent decades, they re-emerged in the late 1960s and early 1970s as products rather than causes of the widespread violence. The largest loyalist paramilitary organizations are the Ulster Defence Association (UDA) and the Ulster Volunteer Force (UVF). Other, smaller, groups have also emerged, such as the Loyalist Volunteer Force (LVF), largely formed from UVF members opposed to the peace process (Bruce 1992; Taylor 1999). The Irish Republican Army (IRA) split in 1970 into its Official and Provisional wings. The Official IRA split again, with one branch forming the Irish National Liberation Army (INLA) and the other pursuing a more explicitly political course. The Provisional IRA (known as the 'Provos', or simply 'the IRA') is the largest republican group, although in the 1990s factions opposed to the peace process broke away to form the Real IRA and the Continuity IRA (Bowyer-Bell 2000; English 2003; Taylor 1997).

4 From the social contract foundations of the modern state in which legitimacy was related to the pacification of a given territory, in later periods state legitimation came to be based on welfare provision in particular. This rendered the state vulnerable to changes in the socio-political environment that undermined its expertise or competence in such spheres (Habermas 1975), particularly through the advent of the 'information age' in which networks of power and influence often function either above or below the level of the state (Castells 2000).

5 In relation to the public police, challenges to police legitimacy inevitably raise broader questions about the nature of the political regime within which it is enacted and which it sustains. The rapid and massive growth of the private security industry and the emergence of new policing arrangements that blur the traditional distinction between the public and private sectors of policing – developments generally characterized as the advent of 'plural policing'

(Crawford 2003) – certainly give rise to new considerations here. But even though the state may not be directly involved in the operational side of such policing, it nevertheless retains the capacity to license and/or regulate it. In that respect among others, the legitimacy of plural policing is also an issue of state (Loader and Walker 2001).

# Part II
# Policing the conflict

## Chapter 2

# Crisis, rehabilitation and normalization: reform and professionalization of the RUC

During the late 1960s, the police response to the Civil Rights Movement and related events generated a major legitimacy crisis for the RUC. The 1969 Hunt Committee sought to address these concerns by rehabilitating the RUC and developing it into a 'normal' civil police force. The limitations of this policy led the British government to implement a raft of measures in the mid-1970s that together laid the framework for a new conflict management strategy. 'Police primacy' was at the core of this, and it entailed the RUC moving to the forefront of counterinsurgency policing, while also embarking on a major drive towards police professionalism, reflected in the tenets of impartiality, accountability, and 'policing by consent'. This chapter explores the origins and implementation of these measures. First, it examines the crisis of policing charted by the Cameron and Scarman inquiries, and the rehabilitation programme outlined in the Hunt Report. Second, it considers the emergence and nature of police primacy. Third, it analyses the means through which police primacy was consolidated.

## Crisis and rehabilitation

As the Civil Rights Movement gathered pace in the late 1960s, the activities of the RUC and the 'B' Specials contributed to the escalation of protest and demonstrations into riots. Against a volatile political backdrop, disturbances and riots developed into broader and more endemic violence. The state security forces were no longer able to contain the situation, and on 14 August 1969 the British Army was deployed in Northern Ireland 'in aid of the civil power'. In a further major step, official inquiries were held to examine the events of 1968/69, bringing the issue of policing to the fore. Police reform – which was *not* one of the Civil Rights Movement's initial demands – was now firmly on the political agenda (Ó Dochartaigh 2005; Ellison and Martin 2000).

### Charting the crisis: the Cameron and Scarman Inquiries

The Cameron Inquiry was appointed in March 1969 to report on the causes and nature of violence and civil disturbances in Northern Ireland between 5 October 1968 and March 1969. The Scarman Tribunal was established in 1969 to investigate the events of that summer (it reported in April 1972). Both inquiries had immense implications for police reform. As Scarman (1972: 14) noted: 'In a very real sense our inquiry was an investigation of police misconduct.'

Both inquiries made serious criticisms of the RUC and 'B' Specials. Cameron (1969: 72–4) criticized the RUC for 'unauthorized and irregular use of batons', indiscriminate use of water cannon on pedestrians for which there was 'neither reason nor excuse', 'assault and battery, malicious damage to property . . . and the use of provocative sectarian and political slogans', as well as 'further acts of grave misconduct among members of the RUC, including . . . serious allegations of assault'. The Scarman Report (1972) also made scathing criticisms of police behaviour, including the use of Browning machine-guns in Belfast (where their indiscriminate fire killed civilians), and especially the RUC's 'failure to prevent Protestant mobs from burning down Catholic houses' and the 'failure to take any effective action to restrain or disperse mobs or to protect lives and property' in riot areas (pp. 15–16). During the 1969 disturbances, Belfast witnessed what was at the time the largest forced population movement in Europe since the end of the Second World War.[1] The example of police standing by while families were forced out of their homes and entire streets were burnt to the ground had a devastating effect on nationalists' confidence – such as it was – in the state, and was seared into popular memory as incontrovertible evidence of partisan policing.

In spite of their criticisms, Cameron and Scarman strongly qualified their findings. In addition to praising the restraint and courage that characterized the actions of most officers (Cameron 1969: 73; Scarman 1972: 17), they found that insufficient numbers of personnel were available to police demonstrations effectively. In addition, poor leadership, inappropriate tactical deployment and lack of coordination between police units were all offered as mitigating factors in the explanation of RUC actions (Cameron 1969: 71–6). This qualification aside, there was no escaping the deep hostility that existed towards the RUC among nationalists. As Scarman noted, the police response to the Civil Rights Movement had created what he gravely termed 'the *fateful split* between the Catholic community and the police' (p. 15; emphasis added).

The inquiries also expressed concern about the impact these events had on the force's public image. Cameron noted that one consequence of the 5 October 1968 civil rights march in Derry 'was injury to the reputation of the RUC and the measure of confidence and support which they enjoyed in Northern Ireland' (p. 72). Of the allegations that officers had deliberately led civil rights marchers to Burntollet Bridge knowing that loyalists (including off-duty members of the 'B' Specials) were waiting there to attack them, Cameron concluded that this 'baseless and indeed ridiculous' claim 'could never have arisen at all if there had been such general confidence in police impartiality throughout the community as one would hope and expect to exist' (p. 75). Not for the last time, relations between nationalists and the RUC would be cast largely as matters of perception rather than reality. Reforms may have been deemed necessary, but the material basis for them was often over-shadowed by the need for measures that would improve nationalists' confidence in the police.

### Rehabilitation and reform: the Hunt Report

The Hunt Committee was appointed in 1969 to examine the 'recruitment, organization, structure and composition' of the RUC and 'B' Specials and, reflecting the urgency of the task, it submitted its report just six weeks after being established. The report identified the RUC's role in maintaining state security as *the* key issue to be addressed in this process. It argued that if relations between the RUC and nationalists were to be improved then the RUC must shed this role – 'which has understandably been regarded as of first importance' (p. 21) – and develop into a 'normal' civil police force. The most important recommendations were that the RUC should be relieved of its security role and be disarmed, and that the 'B' Specials should be disbanded and replaced with another force (the Ulster Defence Regiment). Hunt also proposed: the development of closer links with British police forces, the establishment of a representative police authority to which the police would be accountable, the creation of a community relations unit, a change of uniform, changes in complaints procedures, a dramatic increase in the RUC's size as well as the establishment of a reserve force. Most of Hunt's recommendations were accepted by the Stormont government, albeit under pressure from the British government (Callaghan 1973), and implemented in the Police (Northern Ireland) Act 1970.

All in all, what the Hunt Report proposed was a series of measures to demilitarize the RUC, by reshaping its role and image in ways that would extricate it from involvement in the conflict. The report described its recommendations as an effort to 'offer a new image' of the RUC 'as a civil police force' (p. 9). In the Northern Irish context, the 'normalization' espoused by Hunt meant anglicization, and the presence of that soothing cultural motif, the 'bobby on the beat', could be detected in the shadows of the report. By focusing on the establishment of an unarmed, civil police force, operating with the consent of the community, what Hunt had proposed was a decidedly English creation, one sharply at odds with the Irish historical experience in which the model of an armed, paramilitary-style police force developed particularly to enable the suppression of political dissension was the rule rather than the exception (Ellison and Smyth 2000).

While Hunt's proposals involved modernizing and 'tinkering' with the RUC rather than fundamentally reforming it (Tomlinson 1980; Ellison and Smyth 2000: chapter 4), the recommendations – particularly the disbandment of the 'B' Specials – caused outrage among loyalists. It was during loyalist riots in protest at the Hunt reforms that Constable Arbuckle, the first RUC officer to be killed during the conflict, was shot dead. Although the RUC was disarmed, it was forced to rearm in October 1971 in light of the rapidly deteriorating security situation. The benign vision of policing so well articulated in the Hunt Report foundered on the embedded conflict over the Northern Irish state, and its proposals turned out to be a 'false dawn' (Walker 1990). The reforms that might have placated nationalists were unacceptable to unionists, and those reforms that were introduced proved unable to satisfy nationalists or were overtaken by events as the conflict escalated dramatically in 1971/72.[2]

After an initial and brief 'honeymoon' period between the British Army and nationalists, relations deteriorated rapidly. The British Army's role in maintaining order inevitably meant maintaining the law and order agenda of a unionist state, moreover a state whose supporters were bitterly opposed to the prospect of a more politically assertive Catholic community. In the context of continuing civil rights marches, loyalist counter marches and increasing paramilitary activity, the army became more and more embroiled in conflict with nationalists. Aggressive arms searches, curfews and widespread allegations of misconduct had a hugely detrimental impact on nationalists' attitudes towards the security forces (Faul and Murray 1975; Kennally and Preston 1971; Ó Dochartaigh 2005; Taylor 2001). As republican paramilitaries dramatically increased the scale of their activities and the number of security incidents soared, the Northern Ireland government introduced internment on 9 August 1971 (consisting of the arrest and indefinite detention of those suspected of involvement in political violence). This merely exacerbated the situation, however, and levels of violence increased even further. At a banned anti-internment march in Derry on 30 January 1972 ('Bloody Sunday'), the British army shot dead 13 unarmed civilians (another marcher who was shot on that day later died from his wounds). By now the situation appeared beyond recovery. The British government demanded control over the security forces and, rather than rule without that power, the Northern Ireland government resigned *en masse*. The Northern Ireland parliament at Stormont, on the outskirts of Belfast, was suspended and 'direct rule' was imposed from Westminster. After 50 years of unionist rule, a British Secretary of State would now exercise ministerial responsibility for governance of Northern Ireland.

The ineffectiveness of the Hunt reforms was harshly exposed by the RUC's response to unionist protests over the 1973 Sunningdale Agreement. This agreement established a power-sharing executive for Northern Ireland and included provisions for a Council of Ireland which would address matters of common interest to Northern Ireland and the Irish Republic. Loyalists were adamantly opposed to the establishment of all-Ireland structures and organized the 1974 Unionist Workers' Council (UWC) strike in protest at this. The UWC 'rebellion' (Anderson 1994: 1) was an explicit effort to bring down the government and force new elections in Northern Ireland. By blocking roads, intimidating workers and disrupting key industries – notably by shutting down the electricity generating stations – the UWC effectively ended the power-sharing experiment.

The security implications of the strike were profound. With diplomatic understatement, former Secretary of State for Northern Ireland Merlyn Rees (1985: 109) observed that the strike 'revealed how much we depended on the army for basic security and the inability of the RUC to react quickly to events.' Other commentators were struck less by the 'inability' of the security forces than by their clear unwillingness to take decisive action against UWC barricades and intimidation (Anderson 1994). Despite the blatancy of the strike, only 71 arrests were made (Fisk 1975: 98) and widespread fraternization between members of the RUC and UWC protesters reinforced the image of a partial police force (Tomlinson 1980: 195), doing little to convince nationalists that the 'reformed' RUC was willing to defend their interests as much as it defended those of loyalists. As one officer noted: 'During the UWC strike the police deserved all the criticism they got. They stood back and let it happen' (quoted in Ellison and Smyth 2000: 88). The Chief Constable may have believed that 'it was to the RUC's eternal credit that not one man mutinied and joined the strikers' (Ryder 2000: 130), but that view in itself merely highlighted the gravity of the situation in terms of the long-term possibilities of police reform.

## The normalization of extraordinary policing: police primacy and 'the rule of law'

The stringent security measures introduced in the early 1970s confirmed nationalists' status as a marginal population within Northern Ireland, eroding what little hope they had that the state was being fundamentally reformed. Even the Hunt measures were considered badly compromised by the failure to establish sufficiently rigorous accountability mechanisms (Campaign for Social Justice in Northern Ireland 1972; Central Citizens' Defence Committee 1973; Faul and Murray 1975; SDLP 1975). Given this sustained criticism of the RUC, it was clear that a new initiative was needed which could yield improvements not only in the police's effectiveness against paramilitary organizations, but also in its relations with nationalist and republican communities. These various factors forced a major rethinking of security strategy in Northern Ireland, prompting significant changes in the respective roles of the army and the police. The overarching frame for these initiatives was, according to Merlyn Rees, 'the rule of law', specifically 'enforcing the recognized law of the land in the recognized courts' (Hansard, 14 June, 1976, col. 46). This amounted to a reversal of previous 'emergency' measures to quell the conflict. Internment (detention without trial which was introduced in 1971) and 'special category status' (introduced in 1972 and akin to prisoner-of-war status) were the key targets of this return to the 'rule of law': the former because of the political criticism arising from its suspension of *habeas corpus* and allegations of brutality during interrogation (Boyle, Hadden and Hillyard 1980; Compton 1971; McGuffin 1973, 1974; Parker 1972), and the latter because of the legitimacy it bestowed on paramilitary organizations (Gardiner 1975; McEvoy 2001; Mulcahy 1995).

In January 1976 Rees established a Ministerial Committee on Law and Order to consider long-term strategies to ameliorate the situation. The committee met until the summer of 1976, and its report (*The Way Ahead*) is credited with laying the foundations for the policy of *police primacy*. In its simplest terms, police primacy meant that the army, which since its deployment in Northern Ireland in 1969 had assumed primary responsibility for operational security matters, would instead play a largely supporting role. The RUC in turn would expand its role and assume primary responsibility for operational security matters. In terms of police organization, it involved such measures as: the creation of regional crime squads to target paramilitary organizations; a greater focus upon intelligence; a further dramatic increase in the RUC's size; and improved training and equipment (see, generally, Dewar 1996; Ellison and Smyth 2000; Rees 1985; Taylor 1980). These changes enhanced the RUC's capabilities to counter the activities of republican and loyalist paramilitary organizations. As a consequence, the force increasingly resembled an army of sorts, resulting in a profound tension between the increase in its capacity to 'take on' paramilitaries and its simultaneous claim to be a 'normal' civil police force (see, for example, RUC Annual Report for 1976: ix).

It is important to appreciate the immense significance of these measures, for they reflected a decisive shift in security policy, not least in terms of the professionalization of the RUC. If the Hunt reforms signalled an effort to secure the *normalization of policing* in Northern Ireland, then resort to 'the rule of law' reflected a broader initiative directed towards the *normalization of the conflict* itself. The real strength of these developments was their integration into a broad, coherent strategy. Professionalization, after all, implied a neutral solution to a technical problem. As such, it contributed to wider understandings of the conflict as criminal rather than political and best addressed through the ordinary criminal justice system rather than through the emergency measures – which were often counterproductive and always politically embarrassing – on which the government had relied during the early 1970s. Moreover, this invocation of the rule of law was entirely consistent with wider counter-insurgency strategies. As one of the foundational military texts on this subject noted:

> The law should be used as just another weapon in the government's arsenal, and in this case it becomes little more than a propaganda cover for the disposal of unwanted members of the public. For this to happen effectively, the activities of the legal services have to be tied to the war effort in as discreet a way as possible. (Quoted in Ellison and Smyth 2000: 74).

Increasingly, paramilitary suspects would be charged with criminal offences, tried in criminal courts and, if convicted (and the great majority were – see Boyle *et al.* 1980), spend their sentences in prisons rather than internment compounds. Under the related policy of *criminalization*, 'special category status' was no longer made available to those convicted of paramilitary offences after 1 March 1976. All those subsequently convicted of 'scheduled' (political violence-related) offences would be treated as ordinary criminals and housed in the Maze Prison instead of the internment compounds previously used.[3] The RUC's role in this was to obtain the evidence with which prosecutions could be mounted, and its activities in this regard soon began to cause problems for republican paramilitaries. The numbers of individuals arrested, charged and convicted increased steadily during the late 1970s, forcing the IRA to re-examine its organizational structure (English 2003; Taylor 1997). The regime of interrogations, though, was also causing difficulties for the RUC. Allegations of brutality began to surface regularly, and an Amnesty International investigation (1978) and the Bennett Inquiry (1979) brought sufficient negative publicity that such practices – administratively sanctioned or not (Taylor 1980) – declined dramatically.

From the outset, British military commanders were opposed to police primacy and were sceptical that the RUC was adequate to the task of taking the lead against paramilitary organizations (Hamill 1986; Taylor 2001; Urban 1992). The army favoured a more vigorous counter-insurgency approach, based on the lessons it had learnt from its involvement in various recent colonial campaigns. Despite conflict over the respective roles of the police and army, by 1980 Chief Constable John Hermon (who in 1979 had succeeded Newman) could state that police primacy was halfway achieved (Hart 1980). There remained areas, particularly along the border and in parts of Belfast, where police primacy was meaningless: the danger was such that the RUC played a very limited role and the army retained primary responsibility for security matters. In some locales, this situation persisted up until the 1994 paramilitary ceasefires. The seeds for the future, though, had been sown. Reliance on the rule of law and the normalization of the security situation did have significant material consequences, but it was also a far-reaching discursive artefact. Although the increase in the RUC's size as well as its reorganization were visible manifestations of police primacy, other developments shaped the conduct of policing and public representations of it. For example, there was a decisive shift in the security forces' media depictions of the conflict, as the language of counter-insurgency gave way to that of law and order (Curtis 1984; Miller 1994a, 1994b).[4] Thus police primacy implicated the RUC in a discourse that simultaneously characterized it as a 'civil' police force even as its officers were given extensive powers, heavily armed and trained in counter-insurgency policing techniques.

## Consolidating police primacy

Although police primacy involved an increase in the RUC's militarization, greater effectiveness against paramilitaries and in public order situations was only part of the equation. If policing was to become the foundation of the British government's conflict management strategy, then the RUC's legitimacy deficit among nationalists and republicans had to be addressed. This required a shift towards the professionalization of policing in terms of impartiality, accountability and consent (Mulcahy and Ellison 2001). The force's official discourse now came to reflect these themes, and the Annual Reports in the late 1970s and early

1980s increasingly were fortified with references to 'the rule of law', accountability and so on. In this respect they were nothing less than manifestos for the professional model of policing. In the 1983 Chief Constable's Annual Report (p. ix), Hermon noted that RUC professionalism 'must rest alongside genuine service to the community and enlightened membership of the community.' These measures were clearly focused on improving RUC effectiveness and efficiency, but they were also directed towards increasing its legitimacy. In demonstrating the steps it had taken to reform itself, the force claimed the public support it believed it was now due. As Hermon stated in calling for public support for the RUC, 'Law and order is the responsibility of all' (RUC Annual Report for 1981: xiv).

The development of a professional policing ethos was reflected in a variety of symbolic organizational measures. The publication of the RUC's *Professional Policing Ethics* in 1988, the RUC's *Strategic Statements* from 1990 onwards, the RUC's *Statement of Purpose and Values* in 1992 and the *RUC Charter* in 1993 demonstrated an awareness of and commitment to required standards of behaviour among police officers, as well as efficient use of resources throughout the organization. Reflecting the notion of 'service delivery' characteristic of 'new managerialism', these steps echoed broader moves towards the deployment of the concepts and techniques of corporate management in the realm of social control. Using terminology that is now commonplace in relation to policing, the RUC's *Strategic Statement 1992–1995* noted that 'it is important that every avenue is tested to ensure that "the needs of the customer" are catered for' (1992a: 2). Although these policy statements in themselves contained few novel items, the very fact of their introduction sent a clear message of intent on the part of the RUC's senior management and suggested that significant steps had been taken towards the professionalization of the force.

The goal of police primacy, therefore, was to effect concrete as well as symbolic changes in the social relations of policing. The trajectory of the RUC's development was not just towards the goal of targeting paramilitaries more effectively, but extended to a broad conception of professionalism in which policing was (1) impartial, (2) accountable and (3) based on public consent. In the remainder of the chapter, I examine the steps taken to implement these three components of the doctrine of professional policing.

## Impartiality

Given that the force had historically been aligned with unionism, demonstrating impartiality inevitably meant a more rigorous policing of that community. Once police primacy was introduced, the RUC did not have long to wait for an opportunity to test its commitment to impartial policing. In May 1977, a loyalist strike was again organized, this time to protest at the 'inadequacy' of official security policy and to demand that devolved government be re-established in Northern Ireland. Although a crucial factor behind the strike's ultimate failure was the absence of wholehearted unionist support for it, the RUC did take a more determined line of action than it had adopted during the 1974 UWC strike. A strong police presence at power stations was crucial in ensuring that electricity supplies were uninterrupted, and after eleven days the strike crumbled. According to Hermon (1997: 108), the police approach to the strike epitomized the impartiality at the heart of professional policing in Northern Ireland: 'A clear signal – if one were needed – had gone out from the RUC that, even though its members were predominantly Protestant, it would not kowtow to Protestant extremists and their paramilitary allies.'

A far more fundamental test of the RUC's impartiality arose from the Anglo-Irish Agreement (AIA), signed on 15 November 1985 by the premiers of Great Britain and the Irish Republic. This gave the Irish government a consultative role in the affairs of Northern Ireland and established a secretariat at Maryfield (outside Belfast) that would liaise between the two governments and also provide a forum for regular intergovernmental conferences on appropriate matters, including policing. The AIA was intended to prop up the SDLP's 'constitutional nationalism' that was being undermined – to the great alarm of the British and Irish governments (Fitzgerald 1992) – by the electoral gains that Sinn Féin had made following the 1981 hunger strike and its decision to contest local and parliamentary elections in 1983. Although Sinn Féin's electoral success *did* subsequently decline for several years, unionists saw the AIA as a fundamental erosion of the sovereignty of Northern Ireland and as nothing short of treasonous (Cochrane 2001).

Unionist outrage towards the AIA was soon reflected in criticism of the RUC. The RUC's willingness to face down anti-AIA protests shocked many staunch unionists and loyalists who were enraged that RUC officers 'were able to justify to themselves implementing a political decision against the will of the majority' (Ken Maginnis, UUP Security Spokesperson, quoted in Weitzer 1995: 114). Despite extremely violent loyalist protests in 1985 and 1986, the RUC continued to 'hold the line' (Hermon 1997), but at considerable cost to its relations with the unionist community. In 1986, there were over 500 attacks on RUC officers' homes as well as intimidation of their families, and 120 families were forced from their homes (RUC Annual Report for 1986: x). The distance that the RUC generally maintained between itself and the unionist community certainly did 'a great deal to enhance the RUC's reputation for professionalism' (Brewer and Magee 1991: 141). The manner in which the

RUC policed a unionist 'Day of Action' in March 1986 in protest against the AIA was also significant. There were several loyalist gunfire attacks on RUC officers, as well as 132 complaints of 'police inactivity' for failing to take robust steps against loyalist demonstrators. Nevertheless, for Hermon (1997: 193), this represented 'the turning point: it marked the emancipation of the RUC from the yoke, whether real or imagined, of unionist/loyalist influence.'

RUC independence from political influence was a major theme of the drive towards police professionalism. The frequency of unionist criticisms that RUC policy was now being part-driven by the Irish government (through the AIA Maryfield secretariat) seemed to add weight to the RUC's claims of independence from unionist influence. As loyalist violence during the 1990s escalated to new levels, and for the first time began to overtake republican paramilitaries in terms of the numbers of people killed, official statistics also reflected a greater proportion of loyalist paramilitaries arrested and charged by the RUC (RUC Annual Reports for 1992, 1993 and 1994). Hermon's statement that there were in fact three religious groups in Northern Ireland – Protestants, Catholics *and* RUC officers – was but the clichéd expression of the new set of social relations purportedly taking hold within Northern Ireland. As the RUC increasingly drew criticism from unionists *and* nationalists, 'getting it from both sides' was viewed as conclusive proof of impartiality in action (Hermon 1997; Holland and Phoenix 1996; Ryder 2000). The vast majority of RUC officers continued to be drawn from unionist backgrounds, and bubbling underneath the public transcript of official commitment to impartiality were many instances of police misconduct, as well as a variety of controversial policing policies that clearly operated to the detriment to nationalist communities (Amnesty International 1994; Committee on the Administration of Justice (CAJ) 1992, 1993; Helsinki Watch 1991, 1992). Moreover, as Ellison and Smyth (2000: 162) note: 'It is a rather curious barometer of legitimacy that depends on the ability to antagonize both sides of the community in equal measure.' Nevertheless, the social distancing that police professionalism entailed paid clear dividends in terms of the RUC's claims of impartiality. Criticism from 'both sides' may have shaken the age-old certainties – held by unionists and nationalists alike – that the RUC was in essence a unionist police force, but in so far as it reflected an official commitment to police each community equally, it was merely the Northern Irish application of Robert Mark's famous dictum of police legitimacy: 'winning by appearing to lose' (Reiner 2000).

## Accountability

Few aspects of policing in Northern Ireland were as contentious as the adequacy of accountability mechanisms to deal with allegations of police misconduct. This section considers the two main forms of oversight during the conflict: police complaints procedures and the Police Authority for Northern Ireland.

## Complaints procedures

From the start of the conflict, government inquiries repeatedly noted nationalist demands for an independent police complaints system (Cameron 1969; Diplock 1972; Gardiner 1975; Hunt 1969; Scarman 1972). The 1970 Police Act did establish procedures for recording and investigating complaints, but RUC officers retained the responsibility for investigating their colleagues. Following the Black Committee's (1976) recommendations, the Police Complaints Board (PCB) was established and became operational in September 1977. However, its powers were of an extremely limited order, and mainly consisted of the ability to review completed investigations and recommend that officers be charged with a criminal offence in cases where the RUC Deputy Chief Constable (in charge of complaints) had recommended that none be brought. During the ten years of its existence, the PCB overturned significantly 'less than one per cent of the cases it reviewed' (Weitzer 1995: 188). In 1988 the Independent Commission for Police Complaints (ICPC) was established to replace the PCB. The ICPC was empowered to supervise the actual investigations into complaints, not just review the completed investigation. It was also directed to supervise investigations into all complaints involving death or serious injury, as well as events in which no complaint has been made but for which an investigation might be in the public interest. The ICPC, however, had no independent power of initiative in this, and could only exercise its power when called to do so by either the Chief Constable, the Secretary of State or the Police Authority for Northern Ireland.

Running throughout official commentaries on the investigation of complaints against police officers was the constant claim that those procedures were more stringent and rigorous in Northern Ireland than in Britain (Bennett 1979; Black 1976; RUC Annual Reports for 1976 and 1977; Diplock 1972; Gardiner 1975). This abstract privileging of procedure over outcome, a core element of the liberal legal tradition, was persistently used to discredit complainants, and moves to amend the complaints procedures were always undertaken with the stated goal of improving public perceptions of the complaints system rather than its effectiveness. It was the effectiveness of the complaints procedures, however, that was the most persistent issue raised in public debates over complaints, particularly in relation to emergency legislation. During the early 1970s, substantiated complaints against the police were rare events indeed. Denis Faul and Raymond Murray (1975: 7), two Catholic clergy who were closely involved in documenting allegations of misconduct by the security forces, noted that between 1 January 1970 and 31 January 1975, 1,345 allegations of assault were made against RUC officers. Of these 1,345 cases, prosecutions were made in 31 cases, resulting in 8 convictions (and none of these were in relation to emergency legislation), amounting to prosecutions being brought in 2.3 per cent of cases and convictions being secured in 0.6 per cent of cases.

Although the ICPC's powers exceeded those of the PCB, this did not have a noticeable impact on the complaint substantiation rate. Between 1989 and 1992, the ICPC considered 9,145 cases of which 16.9 per cent (1,554) were complaints made by people arrested under emergency legislation (the Emergency Powers Act or the Prevention of Terrorism Act). Although 'a fact difficult to believe' (Dickson and Millar 1990: 90), the ICPC was not able to substantiate a single one of these 1,554 complaints, whether due to insufficient evidence, the complainant's refusal to cooperate with the investigation, or some other reason. The general substantiation rate was about one per cent, while for emergency legislation-related complaints it was 'to all intents and purposes zero' (O'Rawe and Moore 2000: 279). Complaints against the police in Northern Ireland were far less likely to be substantiated than complaints made against officers in British police forces (Weitzer 1995). In addition to concerns over the lack of independence and the strikingly low substantiation rate, many of the most contentious aspects of RUC activities could not be addressed through the complaints procedure, as they concerned policy decisions rather than the actions of individual officers. RUC decisions in relation to public order events, such as the use of plastic baton rounds (and their precursors, plastic bullets), were but one example of this. These various factors ensured that the complaints system, extensive though its procedural elements might be, largely failed to yield substantive accountability, or at the very least convince a sceptical public that full accountability had been achieved.

## The Police Authority for Northern Ireland

The Police Authority for Northern Ireland (PANI) was formed in 1970 following the recommendations of the Hunt Report. Under the provisions of the 1970 Police Act, its function was 'to secure the maintenance of an adequate and efficient police force' (section 1.2). Promoted as a key mechanism for securing police accountability, it was one of the major initiatives designed to improve police–community relations. It was required to keep itself informed of how complaints against the police were dealt with, and it was given the power to compel the Chief Constable to refer a case to a tribunal if the complaint was thought to affect the public interest.

PANI was a major failure. It never secured the confidence of nationalists, had no more than a token influence on police policy and proved reluctant to use the limited powers available to it. PANI representatives did claim credit for changing RUC policy concerning paramilitary funerals, expanding the scope of police–community liaison throughout Northern Ireland and contributing to the RUC's Code of Conduct (Weitzer 1995: 184). Even if this minimal input is acknowledged (and some PANI members I interviewed did not view it as having achieved a *single* worthwhile goal throughout its existence), the limitations of PANI's impact on policing and police–community relations was starkly highlighted during the mid-1970s when persistent allegations emerged that paramilitary suspects were being mistreated while in police custody, claims supported by doctors appointed by PANI (Taylor 1980).

Some members of the Authority – Jack Hassard and Donal Murphy in particular – repeatedly sought to raise this concern with the RUC, but senior officers were extremely reluctant to provide any information concerning the manner in which complaints were being dealt with. PANI could require the Chief Constable to submit reports to the Authority (1970 Police Act, section 15(2)), but this power was severely diluted by the Chief Constable's ability to refer any such request to the Secretary of State if he/she thought that disclosure of the information was not in the public interest or was not needed for PANI to discharge its duties. PANI's limited role as a watchdog was evident in a striking episode described by one if its former members:

> We had called for a report on assaults and after waiting for a long time, the Chief Constable eventually came along to deliver the report. So he opened the report, read out a list of statistics at phenomenal speed – it was like speed reading, you wouldn't think people could talk that fast – and of course no one could make sense of any of what he was saying, he was just reading out a bundle of numbers. Then he closed it, said he had fulfilled his statutory obligation to the authority, and walked out. He didn't even leave us a copy of the report. Can you imagine that? And this is the body he is supposed to be accountable to? (Fieldnotes)

When PANI members attempted to examine individual complaints files, some of these were not made available while others were provided but with some information withheld, including names being blacked out (Taylor 1980). Furthermore, it appeared that PANI's statutory duty to keep itself informed of the manner in which complaints were dealt with *did not* extend to the power to examine police files (Black 1976: 18). The one case that PANI did refer to a tribunal (the Rafferty case) collapsed when confronted with a High Court ruling that the tribunal lacked the power to compel witnesses to give evidence (Ryder 2000: 200–2; Walsh 1988: 94; see also Black 1976). PANI requested legislation to strengthen its tribunal powers, but the government never authorized this change (Irish Congress of Trade Unions 1981: 7–9). Hassard and Murphy eventually resigned from PANI in 1978 in frustration at the official inaction towards the assault allegations (Ryder 2000: 200).

From the outset, PANI was widely viewed as 'an integral part of the establishment' (Taylor 1980: 47). In 1986, the IRA targeted it, issuing a statement threatening to kill PANI members, and subsequently killing two of them as well as a member of PANI's support staff (Weitzer 1995: 182). Beyond this security threat, concerns over PANI's effectiveness were directly related to a lack of confidence in its ability and willingness to hold the RUC to account. This was most evident in the refusal of significant political groups to participate in the authority. Under PANI's original membership structure, places were specifically reserved for an SDLP nominee and for a representative of the Irish Congress of Trade Unions (ICTU). Hassard had been an ICTU nominee, and the ICTU decided in 1981 that it would no longer nominate representatives onto PANI, specifically due to the limited powers available to the authority and the political irrelevance of their representative on the authority. PANI's credibility was further diminished by the SDLP's continued refusal to participate in it;[5] by 1975 an SDLP policy statement on policing was already calling for a 'new police authority' with 'much wider representation' (1975: 1). According to one SDLP representative: 'It is a body that had the power to investigate any alleged RUC abuse over the years and has never done so; and we think that is now testimony to the purpose of the PA as a body and the application of its members over the years' (interview).

### Police-community relations

#### Community affairs and neighbourhood policing

Following the Hunt Committee's recommendations, the RUC established a Community Relations branch in 1970, renamed the Community Affairs (CA) branch in 1993. CA policing normally took two major forms: officers assigned to particular neighbourhood beats with the goal of fostering relationships with local residents; and broader activities oriented towards improving police–community relations generally.

While CA activities in many police forces are poorly regarded by other officers and dismissed as 'soft policing' (Chan 1997; Holdaway 1983; Keith 1993), the security situation and political divisions in Northern Ireland brought a particular dynamic to community policing. In republican (or other 'high-risk') areas, the danger of attack meant that community police on patrol resembled more 'an armed convoy' than the reassuring sight of police officers integrated into the community. Brewer and Magee (1990: 115) described the surreal nature of 'community policing' in those circumstances:

> Two neighbourhood men walking their beat are accompanied by at least sixteen soldiers, sometimes also by another squad of soldiers providing cover for those who are protecting the police, by two or more Land Rovers from the British Army and the RUC, and an Army helicopter.

Beyond the threat of attack, many members of the communities with whom they sought to improve relations rejected their efforts outright. As one RUC constable observed: 'When you're talking to a young girl in her garden and you're just saying hello, and her father comes out and says "Don't talk to them." That's offputting, and it happens quite often, you get that a lot' (interview). Nevertheless, the determined application of police primacy was evident in the RUC hierarchy's commitment to establish neighbourhood patrols even among communities largely hostile to the force. While it demonstrated that 'normal' policing could operate, it showed how it could only be pursued through the most 'abnormal' of ways.

A further consequence of the conflict was that many of the RUC's CA activities in nationalist and republican areas were conducted very discretely, usually with great care being taken to avoid publicity. One CA sergeant described some of the preconditions involved:

> There was one school where the kids were going on a trip and the headmaster rang us and said that the bus had broken down and could we provide one? We said 'Sure, but how will we pick up the kids?' The teacher said 'We'll meet you somewhere outside the area, we'll walk there.' This was just so that people in the area wouldn't see the RUC having contact with the kids ... Again in that school, a teacher rang us up and said that there had been a man trying to get kids into his car, and could we come out and talk to the kids about the dangers of that stuff? So I went out there and talked to the kids. But I was in plain clothes and I never told the kids that I was a policeman, that was the deal. (Interview)

The security situation also intervened in other significant ways. The low-key approach that CA officers used left them vulnerable to attack: 'A few times we were caught out, and once or twice they killed a community affairs officer. But that was usually the way we did it' (CA sergeant, interview). Their activities were also susceptible to being undermined in various ways, whether by various security policing operations that provoked widespread criticism, or by being viewed as little more than low-level intelligence-gathering operations or public relations exercises (Ellison and Smyth 2000: 172; Weitzer 1995: 254–74).

Community policing in Northern Ireland as elsewhere was pitched at both a material and a symbolic level. While its symbolic dimensions were fundamental to police primacy, CA activities had the potential to generate significant material benefits for the RUC. This included a greater flow of information to the RUC and an erosion of support for paramilitary organizations as members of the public become less willing to tolerate paramilitary designations of officers as 'legitimate targets'. One officer highlighted the safety benefits of his work: 'Community affairs saves lives. I can think of six people, including myself, who are alive today because of community affairs' (interview). Notwithstanding such significant outcomes, the Northern Irish context exposes a serious limitation of the logic underlying community policing initiatives. Structural constraints, notably the inability of the RUC to establish community-oriented beat patrols in the areas where their legitimacy levels were low, undermined the success of these projects. Reflecting research findings from other jurisdictions, community policing activities in Northern Ireland were easiest to implement in the areas they were least needed; conversely, where the RUC's levels of public support were lowest, they were most difficult to implement and least likely to be effective. Nevertheless, the material benefits it yielded as well as the commitment it demonstrated to the overall goals of police primacy were in themselves sufficient justification to continue with such initiatives even in areas where their implementation was near impossible.

## Community and Police Liaison Committees

Community and Police Liaison Committees (CPLCs) were a further component of the RUC's efforts to establish better police–community relations (Weitzer 1992). Liaison committees originated in the council-based 'security committees' of the early 1970s. While they became more formalized after the 1973 reorganization of local government, they still operated on an *ad hoc* basis, without any overarching system of regulation or operational guidelines. Under the provisions of the Police and Criminal Evidence (NI) Order 1989, PANI became more involved in the structure and coordination of CPLCs, and by the mid-1990s it had established a significant network of CPLCs across most of Northern Ireland.

From the outset, nationalists viewed CPLCs as largely symbolic entities, devoid of any real power. The SDLP's official policy was to boycott them, and while some independent nationalist councillors did sit on CPLCs, this probably occurred in no more than a handful of cases throughout Northern Ireland. Sinn Féin also boycotted CPLCs. Community-based CPLCs may have remedied this situation by allowing republicans to sit on them in the guise of 'community representatives'; however, from PANI's perspective, an absence of republicans on CPLCs was not necessarily a bad thing. Speaking in 1996, one PANI official stated that: 'There are no Sinn Féin representatives on any CPLC, and to be honest, I'm not sure that we'd want them there' (interview).

At an organizational level, the failure to attract the support of Sinn Féin and the SDLP meant that it was not feasible to establish council-based CPLCs in areas dominated by those parties. As a result, membership of CPLCs established in those areas tended to be drawn from local organizations and community groups rather than from elected representatives: 'That's one reason that we're keen to get community organizations involved, because that way you're more likely to have nationalists as members of the CPLC' (PANI official, interview). A further cause for concern was the fact that, consistent with research in Britain (Morgan 1989), CPLCs in Northern Ireland had little impact on policing operations generally and were largely confined to the discussion of minor issues (Weitzer 1995, 1992). One PANI official described what he considered the 'relatively trivial' nature of much CPLC debate: 'dogs messing up footpaths, traffic, people's pet peeves'; another stated that 'sometimes when you look at the minutes of CPLC meetings, it seems that they're all about traffic problems, that they never discuss anything but traffic' (interviews). Indeed, their main effect appeared to be the strengthening of support for the police among committee members; voices of dissent rarely interrupted these 'cosy rituals' (Weitzer 1992: 241).

## Conclusion

The British government's initial response to the developing crisis surrounding policing in Northern Ireland from 1968 sought to rehabilitate the RUC by normalizing it in line with an English model of policing – an unarmed police force, operating with the consent of the public. In the absence of parallel developments in the political sphere, the impact of these measures was negligible. As the conflict escalated during the 1970s, the British government adopted a further strategy that entailed the normalization of its overall approach to the management of the conflict. Under the umbrella policy of the rule of law, police primacy situated the

RUC at the forefront of official attempts to control and contain paramilitary violence. The RUC's role was to demonstrate that the conflict was indeed a 'police' matter and to reconfigure it in the language and concepts of criminality rather than political violence. Police primacy operated through two interconnected strategies: development of the RUC's counter-insurgency capabilities to a high degree, and adherence to a model of professional policing with its commitment to impartiality, accountability and close links with the community. The impact these measures had on the RUC's legitimacy was uneven and often contradictory, as the apolitical discourse of professionalization was always vulnerable to challenge given the disputed political framework within which it was enacted. Among nationalists, for instance, its counter-insurgency activities often overwhelmed its activities in other more mundane spheres, such as community relations (Weitzer 1995). Before considering the impact these issues had on nationalists' attitudes towards the RUC, I first examine the role that the RUC's organizational memories played in the legitimation process.

## Notes

1 Between July and September 1969, 1,505 of Belfast's 28,616 Catholic households and 315 of Belfast's 88,379 Protestant households were displaced as a result of the violence. Proportionately, Catholic households were almost 15 times more likely to be displaced than Protestant ones (Scarman 1972: 247–8).
2 It is crucial to appreciate that from the outset different strands of opinion circulated within the security forces concerning how best to respond to the developing crisis. While some favoured an unambiguously tough 'law and order' approach, others were anxious to pursue a more conciliatory approach and prevent an escalation in levels of violence. For a discussion of how this dynamic played out in the events leading up to Bloody Sunday, see Ó Dochartaigh (2005).
3 Prisoner protests against this policy culminated in the 1981 hunger strikes during which ten republican paramilitary prisoners starved themselves to death. Although the hunger strikes failed, the 'special status' of paramilitary prisoners was acknowledged in the day-to-day management of the prison (McEvoy 2001). Ironically, prisoners who had received special category status prior to March 1976 were allowed to retain it until 1991, when the last of them were quietly released (Mulcahy 1995). For analysis of the Irish government's implementation of a similar 'criminalization' policy, see Findlay (1985, 1984).
4 Ryder described how army briefings changed to reflect this new approach. Incidents that previously would have been reported as 'shots were fired at a foot patrol in Belfast' now were reported as: 'There was an attempt to murder members of an army foot patrol in Belfast' (quoted in Miller 1994a: 82).

5 In 1994 Francis Rocks, an SDLP councillor, publicly stated that he intended to assume the PANI seat reserved for the SDLP. Facing imminent expulsion from the party for publicly flouting its official policy, he resigned from the SDLP but took up the PANI position as an independent nationalist councillor. Soon afterwards, his car and home were vandalized.

# Chapter 3

# Policing history: the organizational memory of the RUC

The major reform strategies adopted and implemented by the RUC had as their goal the normalization of policing in Northern Ireland. The process of professionalization underlying this broad drive was ostensibly prospective in outlook, whereby the gradual improvement of police efficiency and conduct would yield future gains in public acceptability and support. However, such material practices – and the related hopes concerning their impact – were not the only terrain on which the drama of police legitimacy was enacted. Running alongside the more hard-headed concerns about impartiality and accountability were a set of representational practices which also formed part of the RUC's repertoire of legitimation strategies. In this chapter I consider the nature and role of such representational practices by focusing on the organizational memories that comprise the RUC's official discourse. I argue that while the RUC viewed a preoccupation with the past as obstructive to the cause of improving police–community relations, it relied heavily on the organizational memories that comprised its official discourse as a strategy of legitimation. This official discourse consisted of the RUC's preferred vision of itself; it was how the RUC sought to present itself and to be known by others. By establishing a coherent, plausible and *bounded* frame of understanding, the RUC, like other organizations, attempted to present itself as legitimate, both by confounding alternative and subversive narratives and by asserting the supremacy of its own account (Manning 2003, 1992). This involved the performance of a social and organizational reality that was deemed likely to attract support and thwart criticism. These organizational memories articulated the force's vision and understanding of its own history and coalesced around three particularly significant themes: commitment and sacrifice; community support; and accountability. Before proceeding to a discussion of these, I first consider the role accorded to history in Northern Ireland.

## History, memory and legitimacy

A preoccupation with the past is commonly viewed as a trait peculiar (in both senses of the word) to the Irish. One need look no further than to government reports on the administration of justice in Northern Ireland for evidence of the perceived significance that history has there. The Hunt Report (1969: 11) stated that: 'Historical factors are important ... the memory of the early years is still fresh in many minds ... The more recent occasions [of disturbances] are fresh in everyone's minds.' The Diplock Committee (1972: 9) claimed that 'in Northern Ireland memories are very long', while the Gardiner Committee (1975: 8) also observed that 'In Northern Ireland memories are long'. These official proclamations are consistent with popular conceptions of the role and significance of history and memory in Ireland, North and South (Walker 1996). According to this view, the whole of Irish society is awash with memory, so much so that people 'live in the past'. Symbols, memorials and other vestiges and invocations of the past are ubiquitous. Note, though, that this generally is intended as a criticism rather than a compliment. Ireland does not benefit from a 'glorious heritage'; instead it suffers from a bad case of history, as manifested in the regular outbreaks of its most visible symptom, memory. The past is depicted as dangerous, and as requiring regulation rather than celebration. Apprehension concerning the availability and deployment of memory largely derives from two related factors.

First, an 'obsessive' preoccupation with the past is considered anomalous in the modern world. Societies that 'have lost the use of their future-oriented compass' (Booth 2001: 777) are viewed as 'primitive': quaint perhaps, but too attentive to the lure of 'ancestral voices' (O'Brien 1994) and primordial passions to be fully rational.[1] Small wonder that Merlyn Rees (1985: 2), a former British Secretary of State for Northern Ireland, claimed that: 'An understanding of Ireland defies mere facts.' Second, memory is seen as an impediment to progress. As Stewart (1989: 16) famously claimed: 'To the Irish ... the past is simply a convenient quarry which provides ammunition to use against enemies in the present. They have little interest in it for its own sake.' Here, the concern is that constructive debate is deferred indefinitely due to the scope for further conflict and recrimination provided by history. Consistent with this view is the need to regulate the past. Accordingly, the cause of progress requires that the past be set aside, discarded or, best of all, forgotten.

Commentators on policing in Northern Ireland are well attuned to the supposed significance of memory, and its potential for derailing efforts towards political progress and undermining contemporary initiatives. This was the view of the Gardiner Committee which claimed that 'past oppression [by the security forces] serves to colour present experience' (1975: 8). In a similar vein, the Bennett Committee, which in 1979 conducted an official inquiry into RUC interrogations, noted that the past was a 'problem' to the extent that previous interrogation regimes[2] 'left behind a legacy of mistrust [that may] help to make credible allegations which are not in fact true' (Bennett 1979: 51). The logical outcome of this argument is that the past inhibits conflict resolution and the process of conciliation.

Within this approach, memory is portrayed solely as a negative force – what is needed is less of the past, not more. Without too much exaggeration, dredging up the past is considered analogous to exhuming corpses, and the past – like the dead – should be let lie. Such an understanding of the role that history and memory play is, to say the least, simplistic and, given the RUC's own reliance on history, disingenuous. Moreover, to draw on the past is hardly a necessarily destructive act. Memory and commemoration involve often overlapping functions and effects, including celebration, atonement and the construction and deconstruction of identity (Connerton 1989; Gillis 1994; Halbwachs 1992; Portelli 1991; Samuel 1994), themes much in evidence in Northern Ireland (Jarman 1997). The strategic use of memory is also a factor in the construction and presentation of coherent, compelling images that key social audiences may view as valid, sincere and authentic. As Fentress and Wickham (1992: 128) note, 'Almost all political rhetoric depends on the past as a legitimation device.' The significance of historical representation is evident in debates on research surrounding policing in Northern Ireland.

## Policing history: knowledge production and policing in Northern Ireland

While much research on Northern Ireland has been accused of partiality and bias, research on policing in Northern Ireland has been uniquely controversial, and commitment or opposition to the RUC is generally assumed to lurk beneath façades of academic objectivity. Indeed, Breathnach (1974: 27) suggests that objectivity is especially difficult in the context of writing about policing in Ireland: the 'inscrutable political background behind all police . . . is the reason why police science has not appealed to the Irish writer, and is best understood by trying to imagine a Northern Catholic attempting to write an impartial and non-incriminating history of the RUC.' Certainly, Farrell's (1983) history of the early years of policing in Northern Ireland gives a sense of some of the immediate difficulties this raises. In the book's preface, Farrell recalls 'the fear and intense dislike the "Specials" aroused in the Catholic community in which I grew up' (p. v).

Other researchers, however, have expressed sentiments quite the opposite of this. Mapstone (1994: xii), in the preface to his book on the RUC Reserve, acknowledges the difficulties of researching controversial subjects and describes his own position: 'My commitment to the RUC therefore dominates the perspective of this book. I was impressed by the dedication and commitment of part-time police officers, who were often the unsung heroes of the force.' Ryder's (2000) book on the RUC is the closest one available to an official history of the force, and one of its striking features is that it includes an account of the death of every RUC officer who died as a result of political violence. His account of the RUC, written with the explicit intention of providing 'an interim version' (p. xv) of its history, is also written from a viewpoint deeply sympathetic to the RUC: 'In writing this book I have been motivated by a limitless admiration for the valiant men and women of the modern RUC. They represent all that is best about the good people of Northern Ireland and they are truly the cement that holds the divided society together' (p. xv).

Generally, the RUC was keen to control the information available to researchers, whether through the provision of tours or orientations for visiting journalists, unattributable briefings or through its press office (Miller 1994a, 1994b).[3] The force was traditionally reluctant to grant permission for research to be conducted on it and its officers. It is striking that the first major research project to receive official support from the RUC was one that addressed its 'normal' policing role (Brewer and Magee 1991). The publication in the *Irish News* newspaper of portions of Ellison's (1997) doctoral thesis revealing the sectarian attitudes of some officers brought claims that he had concocted the research.[4] Other researchers investigating potentially controversial subjects such as police–community relations were denied official access to the RUC (Hamilton, Moore and Trimble 1995; Weitzer 1995). Although this did not prevent some authors (e.g. Weitzer 1995) from interviewing members of the RUC, it clearly inhibited the development of a more complete understanding of policing activity in Northern Ireland.

## The production of absent history

The RUC's interest in seeking to influence popular understandings of its role and development was pursued through a number of 'bureaucratic propaganda' avenues (Altheide and Johnson 1980). These include annual reports, press releases and other organizational products. Further expressions of official discourse are found in the reports of various committees of inquiry and PANI reports, and in statements made by RUC officers in various official settings. Despite the huge amount of material published by various official sources on the RUC, the question of history receives a curious treatment in these sources. What is so striking about this is the silence surrounding the RUC's historical role.

The RUC's official memory of itself was tightly bounded. The thousands of pages that comprised the entirety of the Chief Constable's Annual Reports – from the first report in 1970 to the final report in 2001 when the RUC was reconstituted as the PSNI – offer immense detail, but little context or background. In fact, it is only in the first report in 1970 that any historical detail at all was provided. This section, which comprises a little over one page of the first report (RUC Annual Report for 1970: vii–viii), notes that since its inception the RUC 'played a dual role in the policing of Northern Ireland', providing 'a service of law enforcement similar to other police forces in the United Kingdom' while also carrying out 'the added responsibility of protecting the Province from subversion from within as well as from outside Northern Ireland' (noting that this 'necessitated the carrying of firearms' and the use of 'military-type weapons and equipment'). The report goes on to outline the specific events which precipitated the dramatic changes in policing and security that were unfolding in 1969 and 1970. What the report does *not* do, however, is outline the context of those specific events. The reader is informed that, because of disturbances that were 'sweeping the province' the RUC was overwhelmed and the British army was deployed and assumed primary responsibility for law and order, the Hunt Committee was established and its recommendations implemented. Observers might argue that it is not the function of annual reports to offer historical analyses of events, that their focus is more immediate and is largely limited to the year under review. However, even when one turns to official documents with an explicitly historical focus, one finds a similarly abrupt treatment of the past.

Included in an 'Information Pack' which the RUC information office distributed to journalists and others throughout the conflict was a three-page document entitled *The Royal Ulster Constabulary: A History in Brief*.[5] This report described various aspects of the RUC's history, including the dual role of law enforcement and state security maintenance it traditionally performed, the outbreak of serious disturbances in 1968 and 1969, the reforms outlined in the Hunt Report, and the role of the RUC Reserve and the UDR/RIR. However, the only mention made of developments since the early 1970s is the advent of the policy of police primacy in 1976 and of the reorganization of the force divisional and subdivisional structure in 1983. The report also mentions the substantial number of officers killed and injured during the conflict, and describes how the size of the force was increased on several occasions. What the report does not provide is any sense of why or how those officers came to be killed and injured, and of why a disproportionately large police force of over 13,000 officers was required to police a population of 1.5 million inhabitants. The reader is offered no sense of why there is a conflict to begin with.

Similar questions are raised by the document, *The Royal Ulster Constabulary Museum: A Guide to the Collection* (1995). This handsome publication provides a wealth of detail about the historical development of policing in Ireland, the social conditions in which officers lived and worked, and other matters. What is curious is that while events from the nineteenth century are discussed in detail, the treatment given to the period of the Northern Ireland conflict is comparatively brief: a total of eight paragraphs comprising approximately three-quarters of a single A4-sized page (p. 21). This section mentions the disturbances that gave rise to the conflict (one paragraph), the recommendations of the Hunt Report (one paragraph), the deaths of the first RUC officers killed in the conflict (one paragraph), the imposition of direct rule (one paragraph), increases in the size of the RUC 'because of the terrorist campaign' as well as changes to its divisional structure (one paragraph), the casualties suffered and awards received by RUC officers (one paragraph) and the range of activities undertaken by RUC officers (one paragraph). The final paragraph dealing with events post-1968 is reflective in tone:

> Whilst it is impossible to predict the future, one can certainly hope that the vital role of policing will cease to be a political issue in Northern Ireland and become, more appropriately, one in which the entire community supports the RUC and participates with it in protecting everybody from criminal activity.

The slippage that characterizes the RUC's historical perspective is well illustrated by this final sentence. It appears on the heels of a narrative that gives a detailed historical account of the establishment and development of colonial policing in Ireland in the form of the RIC, and that also notes the paramilitary character of the RUC since its establishment and the persistent political violence it has faced. Although the document as a whole gives some sense of the immense and persistent difficulties surrounding policing in Ireland, this conclusion avoids any serious consideration of why this is so.

## The organizational memory of the RUC

As the above section suggests, 'history' often played a minimal role in police discourse, perhaps reflecting a sense that to invoke the past opened up huge potential for discord and recrimination. In other respects, however, specific understandings of the past featured prominently in how the RUC conceived of itself, and how it depicted itself to others. In the following section, I examine three elements of the RUC's 'organizational memory' that were key components of its assertions of legitimacy. These are: (1) moral appeals emphasizing the commitment, bravery and sacrifice of the police; (2) claims of widespread community support; and (3) assertions of accountability as expressed in its vindication in the face of scandal.

### Legitimacy as commitment: sacrifice and bravery

One of the most visible aspects of the RUC's organizational memory highlighted an implicit moral claim. By drawing on the flesh and blood costs endured by its officers, the RUC's official discourse cast the force as a long-suffering and heavily victimized organization or, in Hermon's words, as 'an extraordinary body of men and women bearing an extraordinary responsibility on behalf of the community' (PANI 1988: 2). In other societies, the dangers facing the police were associated with troubling features of police subculture (Skolnick 1993). In Northern Ireland, however, the fact that these sacrifices were willingly made and that RUC officers performed their duties in full knowledge of the dangers they faced were used to establish an ethical dimension to their activities and to cast the broader organization in heroic terms. These extreme human costs were used to demand a response from the community, namely support for the RUC. This was reflected in the themes of sacrifice and bravery that pervaded the RUC's official discourse.

In the Chief Constable's Annual Reports, the presence and prominent location of the 'Roll of Honour' is significant. This comprised a list of RUC officers who were killed in the line of duty during the course of the preceding year. Generally, it was the first page of text of each report, and this strategic position inevitably shaped how the following pages were read. The continuous reference to an officer's death as 'the ultimate sacrifice' is also significant. While it reinforces notions of a sacrifice that is willingly undertaken, and situates the RUC at the pinnacle of a moral hierarchy, it evokes further images. First, it implies innumerable other sacrifices that are surpassed only by death but which are still routine, unheralded and exact a heavy toll. Secondly, to euphemize death in this way calls to mind and celebrates the ritual elements of ceremonies surrounding death, while also establishing the frequent character of violent death that faced RUC officers. The risks facing the police were also highlighted in the many references to the bravery of RUC officers that punctuated the Annual Reports, particularly through mention of the medals and awards received by members of the force.[6] In later years, this information was placed in the body of the report, but throughout the 1970s a section called 'Honours and Other Awards' was placed in each report immediately following the 'Roll of Honour', emphasizing the bravery and sacrifice that characterized the RUC.

Overall, between 1969 and 1998, 302 RUC officers were killed as a result of the security situation, and approximately 9,000 seriously injured.[7] In addition to these casualties, Ryder (2000: 498) notes that up to 70 officers committed suicide during the conflict. While this figure is largely absent from official statements on the RUC's sacrifice, presumably to avoid any controversy or distress it might generate, it is not unreasonable to assume that these deaths were closely linked to the stress associated with policing in Northern Ireland and so should form part of a general audit of the human costs of the conflict. Even after the 1994 ceasefires, the RUC's 'savage sacrifice' (PANI Annual Report for 1995: 7) continued, as republican paramilitaries and loyalists killed a further five officers. Additionally, an officer who had been shot and badly wounded during an attack on an RUC station in May 1973 died in March 1995, having being in a continuous coma for the 22 years from when he was injured (RUC Annual Report for 1995: 7).

Memorials to RUC officers who were killed were present in many RUC stations, and in this sense the RUC's sacrifice was reflected in the physical, material structures of policing itself.[8] The most prominent of these memorials was the 'Book of Remembrance' which lists the names of RUC officers killed in the line of duty (one volume lists those killed during the conflict, a second lists those killed prior to the Troubles). Unveiled in 1979 by Princess Alexandra of Kent, this memorial was prominently situated in a display cabinet at the entrance to RUC headquarters in Belfast. These memorials persisted into the ceasefires and in 1996 the PANI chairperson unveiled a plaque dedicated to the officers stationed at Grosvenor Road in Belfast who were killed during the conflict.

A further element of this discourse relates to the funerals of RUC officers.[9] Police funerals the world over are imbued with notions of sacrifice and danger, of being on the 'front line' and of making 'the ultimate sacrifice'; they are one of the most vivid aspects of police symbolism (Manning 1997). In Northern Ireland, however, the funeral of an RUC officer assumed an even greater significance, partly due to their frequency and predictability, but also in terms of the solidarity and dedication that each funeral came to symbolize. When appointed Chief Constable in 1976, Kenneth Newman:

> found himself attending the funerals of seven murdered officers in his first month in office. No wonder he often remarked that as chief constable of the RUC 'the funeral dirge gets ground into your soul'.

Attending funerals was one of the most harrowing and routine duties for any RUC chief but it was an important factor, especially for an outsider to the close-knit RUC circle, in removing the remoteness between the officers at the top and those on the ground. (Ryder 2000: 143–4)

When Hugh Annesley took over as Chief Constable of the RUC, Ryder also noted that he 'was less than a month in office when he attended his first RUC funeral' (2000: 390). The fact that this was the 'first' of the presumably many police funerals Annesley could expect to attend portrayed it as an initiation into an inevitable ritual that expressed the sacrifice and the bravery of the RUC, emphasized its solidarity and cohesion in the face of attack, and confirmed its determination to continue even after the deaths of so many of its members. Hardly surprisingly, RUC officers often stated that they hoped the day would come when they would no longer have police funerals to attend:

We've seen recently the funeral of Constable Seymour dying after 22 years and you've seen the dedication of his family in looking after him for all of that time. So the sacrifice is just inestimable . . . We all hope that a police funeral that we attend is the last police funeral that we attend. (Ronnie Flanagan, 'Policing in Northern Ireland', RTÉ Interview, 9 March 1995)

I had hoped, when I took office, that I would be the first Federation Chairman who would not have to follow the cortege of a colleague murdered by terrorists. For almost two years it looked as if I would have that comfort. It was not to be . . . (Les Rodgers, speech to 1997 PFNI Annual Conference)

Following the paramilitary ceasefires of 1994, these themes of bravery and sacrifice were again emphasized. In this context, though, RUC commanders suggested that this sacrifice was instrumental in realizing peace:

The people of Northern Ireland and the nation as a whole owe an everlasting debt of gratitude to the police officers and service personnel who did their duty honourably and bravely, with exceptional commitment and dedication . . . They gave their lives and suffered injury in the just cause of peacekeeping. The loss to the bereaved families and the suffering of the maimed can never be fully assuaged: but they can draw solace and meaning from the sure knowledge that peace was only made possible because of such sacrifice. (Chief Constable's Annual Report for 1994: 11)

This view that peace prevailed only because of the RUC's commitment refuted any possible characterization of officers' sacrifices as empty or futile gestures and instead attributed to them incalculable worth. Such police symbolism would be a prominent feature of the police reform debate following the 1994 paramilitary ceasefires (see Chapter 5).

### Legitimacy as community support: private approval and hidden endorsement

While levels of community support are a major concern for police in any jurisdiction, in Northern Ireland it was one of the pivotal issues in the debate on the RUC's legitimacy. Certainly during the conflict there was abundant evidence of substantial public hostility to the police, including public protests and overt conflict between the force and members of some communities (Ellison and Smyth 2000; Weitzer 1995). In spite of such evidence, however, the RUC maintained that it attracted far more support than these indicators might suggest. Indeed, one of the primary ways that the RUC asserted its legitimacy was in terms of the 'hidden support' it received.

The RUC persistently argued that paramilitary organizations maintained control over certain communities through violence and intimidation directed at members of those very communities, and that it was primarily intimidation that accounted for the low numbers of Catholics within the force (Northern Ireland Affairs Committee 1998; cf. Ellison and Smyth 2000; McGarry and O'Leary 1999). Accordingly, expressions of anti-RUC sentiment were viewed as the work either of a few vocal individuals and groups who received hugely disproportionate amounts of media coverage or of people too fearful to act otherwise; even though these latter individuals may actually have supported the RUC privately, they were intimidated into behaving otherwise. Therefore it was only when individuals were able to express themselves in private settings, when they were hidden away from the intimidating presence of their neighbours or of paramilitary members in their community, that their 'true' feelings may be expressed. As RUC officers routinely observed, in those circumstances the public's 'private' communication with the police was overwhelmingly positive.

This reliance on people's privately expressed views was evident when opinion surveys were conducted on policing issues, and these were incorporated into the Annual Reports. Sitting in their homes, able to express their opinions without fear of recrimination or intimidation, a substantial majority of people expressed support for the RUC. The 1987 Annual Report illustrates the satisfaction deriving from this confirmation of the tenets of official discourse:

> Despite all the difficulties, it was most encouraging in 1987 to note the outcome of an independent public opinion survey. In general the

majority of people interviewed (72%) thought the police did a 'good job' or were satisfied with their contact with the RUC. Interestingly, this was comparable with identical surveys of police/public contact in Britain. (RUC Annual Report 1987: xviii)

Other evidence of community support for the RUC was in the form of letters from members of the public. During the early 1970s, the Annual Reports even included a short section devoted to this entitled 'Letters of Appreciation'. As the Chief Constable noted in the 1972 Annual Report (p. 12): 'It is most gratifying to me to find so many members of the public taking the trouble to acknowledge police effort notwithstanding the turbulent state of the province.'

The epitome of hidden community support involves anecdotal evidence from policing at street level, and may be characterized as *behind closed doors* support. In their most elaborate forms, these accounts add a rich texture to the support found in survey findings: even in the most staunchly republican areas, while members of the public might chastise officers in public, once the scene switches to a private setting the former critics of the RUC apologize for their remarks, explain that they felt obliged to make them for the benefit of their neighbours, and express their own support for the RUC.[10] A retired officer gave a vivid description of one such event that occurred during a period of IRA activity in the late 1950s:

> I was patrolling down one street in a Republican area in the dead of night. It was pitch black, pouring rain, and I stood into a doorway to take some shelter. Behind me, the door opened silently, and a woman's voice said, 'Constable, we're glad you're here.' Policemen were going into houses in that area and the mother or father would swear at them and say to them that they didn't want to see them. And then when they'd get them inside and close the door, they'd say 'Will you have a cup of tea, Constable. Sorry I had to say that.' I'm not saying it's all rosy and all pure like that, but there was a very massive dimension to that. (Interview)

Examples of closed-doors-support during the Troubles provide similar descriptions of this aspect of police community relations. Officers may have acknowledged that there remained difficulties between nationalists and the RUC, but fear of intimidation remained the dominant barrier preventing closer relationships between locals and the police:

> . . . often people would be different *behind closed doors*. They couldn't afford to seem to be friendly, not to be shouting abuse at the RUC. But behind closed doors, things were different, not different in terms of them throwing their arms around you, but different in terms of

being neutral, being less tense. And that was the case with the vast majority of people in West Belfast. (RUC chief inspector)

Well, I policed Ardoyne, and it was a very difficult area, a sound base for terrorist groups in there and it was a very active area. But again there was a terrible lot of decent people in there, in fact most of the people were decent. All they wanted to do was get on with their lives, and when you got into their houses and actually got into their houses and actually spoke to them *behind closed doors*, you got this from them, the true feelings of people crying out for a bit of peace. But people were afraid to be seen to speak to you prior to the ceasefire, they wouldn't have openly spoken to you. A few would, most of them wouldn't. (RUC superintendent)

A variation on this theme includes 'success stories' in which people who were initially suspicious of the RUC were given an opportunity to witness just how service-oriented the police were. A chief inspector described the sentiments contained in a letter from a woman whose opinion of the RUC, formed in ignorance, was changed on the basis of the kindness they extended to her:

This letter was from a woman on the Falls road who hadn't spoken to a police officer in 20 years, because she'd been told that they were all Billy's or Jimmy's from the Shankill Road and they were basically there to force her to do things she didn't want to do, to keep her down, to keep her in her place. Then her house was burgled, nothing much was taken but some sentimental things were damaged, and an old clock was broken. So one of the officers there, his name was Seán, he knew another officer who could fix clocks so he brought it to him and he fixed it and brought it back to the woman. She sat and cried her eyes out because she'd been told for 20 years that these people were here to hammer them down and keep them in line. They weren't, they were there to help. (Interview)

### Legitimacy as accountability: vindication in the face of scandal

Complaints against the police were a persistent feature of the conflict, and were readily acknowledged in numerous official reports into aspects of the criminal justice system. Some senior judicial figures minimized this concern by asserting that the existing complaints procedures were entirely adequate, and that the public's concerns about their adequacy – while understandable – were baseless (Diplock 1972; Gardiner 1975). Demonstrating accountability was a key plank of the RUC's efforts to enhance its legitimacy, particularly with the advent of police primacy and the manner in which this established police professionalism as the mainstay of the government's conflict management strategy. In the late 1970s, however, the scandal surrounding allegations that RUC officers assaulted paramilitary suspects during interrogation threatened to undermine the force's claims of professionalism and adherence to the rule of law (Taylor 1980). Even though the allegations of assault in Castlereagh RUC station and the other holding centres resulted in a highly critical report by Amnesty International (1978) and the resignation of two members of the Police Authority (discussed in Chapter 2), claims of accountability remained a core dimension of the RUC's official discourse (e.g. Hermon 1997; Newman 1978; Ryder 2000). Here I use official accounts of these events as a case study to consider the manner in which accountability – expressed here as vindication in the face of scandal – came to play such a prominent role within the RUC's organizational memory.

With the introduction of police primacy in the mid-1970s, the RUC assumed primary responsibility for policing the conflict. The phasing out of some emergency measures meant that internment was no longer available as a basis for detention. In that context, securing the conviction of paramilitary suspects in criminal trials assumed a heightened import-ance, and confessions made during interrogations played a major part in this process. As allegations of assault by RUC officers escalated into a major scandal, the force's response highlighted two issues in particular. First, it stressed the organization's commitment to accountability by focusing on the numbers of officers assigned to the investigation of complaints:

> The Complaints and Discipline Branch at Headquarters now con-sists of a total of 14 special full-time investigators . . . with additional investigators being called in as required. There are more senior officers in this branch than there are in the anti-terrorist Crime Squads and this fact is surely proof of our determination to ensure that justice is done . . .

The mention of the size of the Complaints and Discipline Branch is interesting, given that while the number of officers investigating com-plaints might be taken as evidence that complaints are being taken seriously, there is no immediate link between this fact and, say, the rate at which complaints are sustained. The RUC's stated 'determination to ensure that justice is done' – however commendable – is one thing, translating this into accountable policing is quite another. The second element of the RUC's response was the negation of the material basis of the complaints, and this was outlined in a section entitled 'False Allegations':

It is naturally a matter for concern that there are so many allegations of assault on persons in police custody or associated with arrests. Having already illustrated the stringency of our investigations into such complaints, I feel bound to point out that terrorist organizations have adopted a deliberate policy of manufacturing allegations or contriving incidents, including self-inflicted injury. Their purpose is to discredit the police or cast doubt on statements of confession when cases are tried in court.

It is absolutely right that police conduct and the system of investigating complaints should be capable of withstanding close scrutiny. On the other hand any society which allows its police force to be unjustly discredited is creating a serious threat to its own well-being. It is my considered view that leaders of public opinion have a responsibility to consider very seriously the wisdom of publishing or broadcasting one-sided versions of allegations without awaiting the results of thorough investigation and the completely impartial decision by the Director of Public Prosecutions to whom all such cases must be referred. The RUC cannot object to justifiable criticism but it is not in the interests of any community that confidence in its police force should be undermined unfairly or irresponsibly. (RUC Annual Report for 1976: ix–x)

This general approach was a persistent feature of the RUC stance on the interrogations scandal. As the Chief Constable stated on another occasion, the allegations of assault during interrogations were 'criticism of the vilest possible kind', particularly in light of the contribution that CID officers made to national security:

The Force generally is deserving of great credit for its performance in combatting terrorist activity and not the least of this credit must go to the CID who have the responsibility for investigating serious crimes and interviewing terrorist suspects. The nature of their work lays them open to danger day after day and exposes them to criticism of the vilest possible kind. It is beyond question that detectives must conform to the highest standards of conduct. Nothing less would be tolerable or acceptable. But it has to be asked how much the public appreciate the tremendous burden which is borne by the CID on their behalf. (RUC Annual Report for 1978: vi)

Although allegations of ill-treatment had been made on a regular basis for several years (Faul and Murray 1975; Ryder 2000; Taylor 1980), it was not until a highly critical Amnesty International report was published in 1978 that a committee of inquiry under Lord Bennett was set up.

Crucially, although hardly surprisingly, the terms of reference for the Bennett Inquiry did *not* include any assessment of allegations of assault; instead the report focused on identifying measures which would ensure that interrogations were conducted appropriately. Nevertheless, when the Bennett Report was published in 1979, it questioned the thoroughness of complaints investigations: 'We have to consider the possibility that the questioning by the officers investigating complaints may not be as searching or persistent as it should be.' Bennett also observed that a finding that a complaint was unsubstantiated 'must continue to be read as a term embracing a range of circumstances ... This must be understood when reading the statistics' (pp. 116, 139). Allegations of ill-treatment continued to be made subsequently, but the numbers of complaints made dropped significantly. As RUC officers acknowledged, the use of that particular strategy against paramilitary organizations had been undermined beyond recovery, at least at previous levels of incidence (irrespective of whether or not it constituted an organizationally sanctioned practice). According to Taylor (1980: 326): 'The Bennett report was a damaging document, given the RUC's insistence over the last two years that the safeguards for persons in custody and the complaints investigation procedures were among the most rigorous in the United Kingdom. Bennett washed such assertions away.'

The report made detailed recommentations concerning the establishment of improved safeguards for prisoners. However, and in no uncertain terms, the committee identified the RUC itself as the primary beneficiary of these changes. It noted that allegations of prisoners being assaulted during interrogations hampered the activities of other sections of the force and undermined public confidence in the RUC. They also made false accusations more plausible. Accordingly, the major benefit of increased safeguards for prisoners would not be the better protection of prisoners from their interrogators, but the better protection of the interrogators from the false allegations of the prisoners. As Bennett noted:

> It is apparent that any misconduct by an individual member of the force concerned with the interrogation of prisoners affects the reputation of the force as a whole in the community, makes more difficult and dangerous the work of his comrades in the streets, and so defers the day of the return of peace in the community. It strengthens the propaganda campaign and provides ammunition for the enemies of society who are adept and experienced in inventing allegations against the police, even without any justification. We have seen evidence that established that this is their declared purpose. One of the purposes of this inquiry is to review police practices and procedures in the interrogation of prisoners so as to

ensure as far as possible that ill-treatment of prisoners cannot take place. If this purpose can be achieved, and can be shown to be achieved, it will make difficult, if not impossible, the task of those who seek to discredit the police by inventing false allegations of ill-treatment. (1979: 7)

Furthermore, in spite of the supposed 'critical' thrust of the Bennett Report, it is worth noting that while it lists 64 'principal conclusions and recommendations', only one of these states that prisoners were injured while in police custody. Even there, the report refrains from explicitly stating that the prisoners were ill-treated by the police: 'Our own examination of medical evidence reveals cases in which injuries, whatever their precise cause, were not self-inflicted and were sustained in police custody' (p. 136). Thus could Roy Mason (then Secretary of State for Northern Ireland) maintain that: 'The Bennett Report has not said that ill-treatment has taken place' (Taylor 1980: 324). In fact, only one month after the publication of the report, Mason told the RUC officers assembled for the annual passing out parade that 'the people of the Province can rest assured that the policing of the Province is in excellent hands. The RUC have come through with great courage and great integrity' (quoted in Tomlinson 1980: 189). Newman resigned as Chief Constable in the autumn of 1979 and was replaced by Hermon. The 1979 Annual Report is the last report to refer to the interrogations scandal. It simply states:

The month of March saw the publication of 'The Report of the Committee of Enquiry into Police Interrogation Procedures in Northern Ireland' – the 'Bennett Report' – and during the year considerable progress was made towards implementing those recommendations accepted by the Secretary of State. (p. 12)

Following this, the issue disappears from the RUC's official discourse. With accountability 'established' in the record and the RUC 'vindicated', the issue is closed.

## Conclusion

This chapter has argued that while the RUC's official discourse nominally viewed a preoccupation with the past as detrimental to police–community relations, organizational memories featured prominently in its own discourse of legitimacy. RUC commanders clearly recognized that beneath the gloss of the force's official representation there operated a widespread and coherent 'unofficial discourse' that was attuned to the street-level realities of policing in Northern Ireland, and acknowledged them in the daily practices of RUC officers.[11] In this discourse, minor deviations from force regulations were frequent and acknowledged. Rather than being ever-vigilant, some RUC officers slept on duty (Brewer and Magee 1991: 195–6), while others phoned in sick in order to finish putative plumbing jobs (p. 37). Occasional references were made to the major scandals that have rocked the RUC, and officers sometimes acknowledged that there may be firm grounds to these allegations. For example, one undercover RUC officer interviewed by Ellison had no doubt that high-level clearance had been given for the killing of paramilitary suspects (Ellison and Smyth 1996: 195). Such vivid examples of concern over the RUC's actions would, however, remain entirely absent from the RUC's official discourse of sacrifice, community support and accountability.

While the invocation of police symbolism plays a key role in legitimation processes generally (Loader and Mulcahy 2003; Manning 1988, 1997, 2003; Walden 1982), for police organizations shrouded in controversy, the significance of promoting a discourse of normality and beneficence is greatly increased. However, it may be worth considering the extent to which such imagery disrupted – rather than enhanced – police efforts to improve relations with nationalists. Simply put, the RUC's memory of itself stood in stark contrast to the memories of it held by many individuals in nationalist and republican communities, and, importantly, many unionist and loyalist areas also (Ellison and Smyth 2000; Weitzer 1995). This is neither to suggest that such a preoccupation with history was a feature of the RUC alone, nor that the history promulgated in the RUC's official discourse was factually inaccurate. The point is that this history diverged significantly, if not entirely, from that experienced and remembered in many areas of Northern Ireland. The ardour with which the RUC's organizational memory was celebrated jarred with these alternative accounts of policing history in Northern Ireland. After the 1994 ceasefires these discrepant readings of the RUC's history would form a major part in the reform debate, not least in ensuring that police reform became one of the most contentious issues, even in the absence of widespread violence. First, though, in the following chapter, I outline the main elements of nationalists' and republicans' understandings, experiences and assessments of the RUC's role and activities during the conflict.

## Notes

1 Such an approach is fully consistent with colonial discourse's juxtaposition of tradition and modernity. The colonized were generally characterized as

politically immature and oriented to the past rather than the future. The colonizers, by contrast, were portrayed as future-oriented, and as makers rather than victims of destiny (Lloyd 1993; Memmi 1990; Spurr 1993). Elements of colonial discourse continue to assert themselves in 'cultural explanations' of the Northern Ireland conflict; see McGarry and O'Leary (1995), Miller (1998) and Ruane and Todd (2005).

2 The interrogation regime in question involved sleep deprivation, continuous 'white' noise, being forced to stand for prolonged periods of time and other measures (see Compton 1971; McGuffin 1974; Parker 1972). The Irish government subsequently bought a case against the British government, and in 1978 the European Court of Human Rights found that while this treatment did not constitute 'torture', it did amount to 'inhuman and degrading treatment' (Ní Aoláin 2000).

3 In other cases, controversial material has been inaccessible to researchers. Farrell (1983: vii) described how the Public Record Office denied him access to certain cabinet papers, although these documents were made available to researchers sympathetic to unionism. Other files were withdrawn altogether from public inspection (p. 310).

4 Ellison had, in fact, been given official permission to conduct interviews. Following the controversy surrounding his research, the RUC amended its procedures for providing access to researchers. During a meeting I was asked to attend with members of the force soon after Ellison's research had been made public, I was asked to sign a contract which would give the RUC ownership of the data (including the interviews I had conducted prior to that), copyright over the data and a veto over any public dissemination of the research findings, whether through the media or any other outlet. The reason for this, one officer told me, was to prevent embarrassment to the RUC arising from researchers 'running away off to the newspapers' with their findings. I was also advised that I would not be allowed to conduct any further interviews with officers unless I signed it. After consulting with my PhD supervisors, I declined to do so.

5 During the peace process this document was replaced by *The RUC* (undated) that largely focused on the force's response to the ongoing reform debate. Despite its contemporary focus, it quotes approvingly from a *Daily Telegraph* article that described the RUC as 'the thin green line that stopped Northern Ireland from sliding into a Bosnian-style abyss, and suggests that 'collectively the RUC deserves the Nobel Peace Prize for its heroic efforts over the past 30 years' (p. 1).

6 An RUC Museum (1995: 21) publication noted that: 'Awards since 1969 include 16 George Medals (the highest award for civilian bravery), 103 Queen's Gallantry Medals, 111 Queen's Commendations for Brave Conduct and 69 Queen's Police Medals.' In the midst of the controversy surrounding the Patten Report, the RUC was awarded the George Cross, the only collective other than Malta to receive such an award.

7 Sutton (2001) notes that a further 18 ex-RUC officers were killed during the conflict. See http://www.cain.ulst.ac.uk/sutton/index.html. An Interpol study in 1983 found that the risk factor for the RUC was the highest of any police force in the world, twice as high as the next most dangerous location, El Salvador (Ryder 2000: 2).

8 These included informal measures, such as the PFNI poster 'Our Murdered Colleagues'. In his autobiography, John Hermon (1997: 169) also noted that in one of his office desk drawers he kept a copy of the PFNI magazine *Police Beat* open to the page where it listed, with their pictures, the nine RUC officers who died during an IRA mortar attack on Newry RUC station in 1985.

9 For discussion of the role that funerals played in generating community cohesion in North Belfast, see Matassa (1999: 189).

10 On this point, see also Brewer and Magee (1991: 132), Ellison (1997), Mulcahy and Ellison (2001) and Weitzer (1995).

11 For 'insider' accounts of RUC culture, see Barker (2004), Gregory (2004), Hermon (1997), Holland and Phoenix (1996) and Latham (2001). For academic accounts, see Brewer and Magee (1991), Ellison (1997) and Mapstone (1994, 1992).

# Chapter 4

# Simultaneous surfeit and deficit: security policing, crime prevention and 'alternative justice'

The police reforms that lay at the heart of the RUC's drive towards professionalism – reflected in the principles of impartial and accountable policing – appeared to yield dividends over the course of the conflict, both in terms of officers' conduct and in greater public support for the police (Brewer and Magee 1991; Ryder 2004, 2000; Weitzer 1995, 1990). This was, however, an uneasy process, as the RUC's security role often clashed with its stated commitment to routine crime prevention activities (Ellison and Smyth 2000; O'Mahony *et al.* 2000; Weitzer 1995). In this chapter, I examine nationalists' attitudes towards the RUC, and consider the extent to which police professionalization was successful in gaining the support of the broad nationalist community during the Troubles. First, I analyse the findings of several major surveys on public attitudes towards the RUC. Second, I examine nationalist perceptions of the security policing measures implemented throughout the conflict. Third, I examine the impact that concerns over the policing of ordinary crime had on nationalists' attitudes towards the RUC, and finally, I examine the dynamics between these concerns and the emergence of a paramilitary-based system of 'alternative' justice.

## Public attitudes towards the RUC: the rewards of professionalization?

Weitzer (1995: 127) suggested that the process of professionalization underway throughout the conflict paid clear dividends in terms of improving standards of conduct: 'Officers are better trained, less politicized, more impartial and accountable, and more sensitized to their delicate position in the divided society.' In addition to yielding better policing, a further aim of this strategy was to secure the support of nationalists for the RUC. In this respect, according to Hermon (1997), the policy bore fruit. He claimed there was a 'quiet, steady improvement of RUC relations with the Catholic community throughout the 1980s' (p. 227), the period often characterized as the testing ground of the RUC's professionalism when it demonstrated its impartiality by 'holding the line' against unionist demonstrations following the Anglo-Irish Agreement. During the 1980s and 1990s several large-scale social attitude surveys addressed issues of policing and security, and their findings were often seized on as measures of the RUC's legitimacy among Catholics (RUC Annual Reports for 1987 and 1988). Hermon observed that 'the so-called alienation of the Police and the public is often a political manipulation of the facts.' Citing one survey that found that the majority of those who contacted the RUC were satisfied with the RUC response, and noting that the clearance rate for criminal activity compared 'more than favourably' with the rest of the UK, Hermon was adamant that this was due to public confidence in the RUC: 'How else could such results be achieved?' he asked (RUC Annual Report for 1988: xviii).

The use of survey data to assess levels of public support for the RUC is, however, problematic in several respects (Ellison 2000). For example, in the 1990 Northern Ireland Social Attitudes Survey data reported in Brewer's work, although 34 per cent of the respondents identified themselves as Catholics, only 17 per cent of the respondents described themselves as nationalists (Brewer 1993: 15). This suggests that the survey either over-sampled Catholics supportive of the status quo, or else respondents felt restricted in their responses. As these surveys were usually conducted through face-to-face interviews, Whyte (1990: 87–8) noted that they 'overstate moderate opinion' and that differences between Catholic and Protestant opinion on security measures were 'even greater than the polls indicate'. Moreover, much of the violence in Northern Ireland was concentrated in particular geographical areas. In areas left relatively untouched by the worst excesses of the conflict, it would not be surprising to find higher levels of support for the RUC.

Nevertheless, these survey findings seemed to support the view that the RUC's professionalism was paying dividends in attracting broad community support. In surveys conducted from the mid-1980s onwards, a majority of Catholic and of Protestant respondents considered the RUC to be doing a good job, and the difference between Protestants and Catholics was not great. Surveys in 1992/93 and 1993/94 revealed that an average of 69 per cent of Catholic respondents and 78 per cent of Protestant respondents considered the RUC to be doing a 'very good' or 'fairly good' job (NIO 1994a: table 4.4; 1995a: table 2.28). These findings

**Table 4.1** Public perceptions of police impartiality, 1986–94

| | 1986 | 1989 | 1990 | 1991 | 1992/93 | 1993 | 1993/94 |
|---|---|---|---|---|---|---|---|
| % of Protestants who think the RUC treat Protestants better than Catholics | 11 | 13 | 12 | 18 | 22 | 17 | 19 |
| % of Catholics who think the RUC treat Protestants better than Catholics | 56 | 52 | 54 | 48 | 55 | 48 | 50 |

*Source*: Data for 1986 adapted from Whyte (1990: 86); data for 1992/93 and 1993/94 adapted from the Northern Ireland Community Attitudes Survey (NIO 1994a, 1995a); and data for the remaining years adapted from McGarry and O'Leary (1999: 19), based on the Northern Ireland Social Attitudes Survey.

appeared to challenge the conventional republican criticism that the RUC was inherently oppressive, and to support the force's own self-declared stance that it largely operated with the public's consent. There is, however, considerable evidence that survey respondents drew a sharp distinction between operational issues and the broader question of RUC legitimacy. For example, while survey results suggest that a large overall majority of respondents found RUC officers polite and helpful (Brewer 1992, 1993; NIO 1994a, 1995a), Catholics were *far less* likely than Protestants to view the police as treating both communities equally. A poll in 1985 found that 47 per cent of Catholics thought the RUC was 'fair' or 'very fair', while 53 per cent of them thought it was 'unfair' or 'very unfair'. By contrast, 96 per cent of Protestant respondents thought the RUC was 'fair' or 'very fair' (*Belfast Telegraph* 6 February 1985; see also Whyte 1990: 86). Surveys from the mid-1980s onwards found similarly divided results when respondents were asked how they believed the police treated Protestants and Catholics (see Table 4.1).

Overall, clear trends emerged from these surveys. Catholics tended to rate the RUC higher than was often assumed, but they were consistently more critical and less supportive of the RUC than Protestants were, particularly in relation to how the police dealt with political violence and sectarian crime. In one respect, these findings supported the RUC's official discourse in terms of the hidden support it received from all quarters, at least in so far as issues of *effectiveness and efficiency* were involved – what might be termed a 'thin' conception of professionalization. In other respects, they highlighted the continuing difficulties in the

RUC's relationship with Catholics and nationalists. Despite a process of police professionalization underway since the beginning of the conflict, a significant proportion of Catholics continued to harbour deep reservations about the RUC, particularly in relation to issues of *impartiality and fairness*. Surveys consistently found that approximately half of Catholic respondents believed that the RUC treated Protestants better than Catholics (see Table 4.1). Perceptions of fairness were also reliant on the sphere of policing in question. For example, 67 per cent of nationalists and 94 per cent of unionists believed the police did a good job in tackling 'non-sectarian crime', while for 'sectarian' crime this dropped to 44 per cent of nationalists and 88 per cent of unionists (Brewer 1993). In the remainder of the chapter, I suggest that Catholics' attitudes towards the RUC reflected a simultaneous surfeit of security policing and deficit of normal policing.

## Over-policing and under-protection: a surfeit of security policing

Hunt's (1969) vision of civil policing seemed to offer a strategy through which police reform might secure greater nationalist support for the RUC. Strong measures were required given that Catholic support for the RUC 'virtually disappeared completely after the events of 1968/69' (SDLP 1975: 1). The full potential of these measures would only be realized through their determined application in operational policing. From the outset, however, the changes in accountability mechanisms arising from the 1970 Police Act proved sorely lacking in terms of controlling police misconduct. Not only did it fail to establish an independent police complaints procedure, but public concern was compounded by the failure to address the misconduct in 1968/69 that was already well-documented in the Cameron and Scarman reports (see Chapter 2). As Faul and Murray (1975) found, complaints procedures appeared remarkably ineffectual in the face of persistent well-documented allegations of police misconduct. The SDLP (1975: 2) claimed that, as a consequence: 'the RUC does not enjoy the confidence of the minority community. In some areas this is shown by physical rejection, but everywhere by the lack of trust.'

One reason for nationalists' continued lack of confidence in the security forces was the use of the British army as the primary policing agency during the early 1970s. Its actions – what Ó Dochartaigh (1997: 313) called the 'particular disaster of abrasive colonial "policing"' – proved enormously counterproductive, and soldiers' aggressive conduct in many of the defining controversies in the conflict – for example, the Falls Road curfew (1971), internment (1971) and Bloody Sunday (1972) – had an extremely detrimental effect on nationalist confidence in the

Table 4.2 Public attitudes towards security measures

| | Catholics agreeing (%) | Protestants agreeing (%) |
|---|---|---|
| House searches are used too little | 3 | 26 |
| House searches are used too much | 35 | 3 |
| Random searches of pedestrians are used too little | 6 | 32 |
| Random searches of pedestrians are used too much | 41 | 3 |
| Vehicle checkpoints are used too little | 9 | 34 |
| Vehicle checkpoints are used too much | 40 | 8 |
| Approve of 'shoot-to-kill' action against terrorist suspects | 7 | 61 |
| Approve of increased use of undercover intelligence operations | 25 | 90 |
| Approve of use of plastic bullets during riot situations | 9 | 86 |

Source: Adapted from Weitzer (1995: 137); based on surveys conducted in 1985 and 1990.

security forces and the state itself (McCann 1980). Through the RUC's re-establishment as the primary policing agency from 1977 on, the authorities hoped that a professionalized police force would be more successful in countering paramilitary violence while at the same time attracting the support of nationalists. However, the expanded role of the RUC proved controversial, not least for the many rank-and-file officers who bitterly resented their increasingly militarized role (Ellison 1997; Hermon 1997; Ryder 2000). This reconfiguration increased pressure on the force to obtain 'results' against paramilitaries, leading them to undertake many of the same activities that had proved so detrimental to the army's credibility among nationalists.

Nationalist support for the RUC was inevitably conditioned by police actions on the street. The threat posed by republican paramilitaries remained the major focus of security force activity, and most of the security measures implemented during the conflict were directed towards the broad nationalist communities from which republican paramilitaries originated and operated. Between 1971 and 1979 the security forces carried out 308,000 house searches, and 26,000 between 1980 and 1989 (Helsinki Watch 1991: 22). Although the number of searches diminished greatly over the years, they nevertheless had 'a profoundly alienating effect' (Weitzer 1995: 131) on those directly involved, as well as on the residents of the area within which a search occurred. In a series of interviews with teenagers and young children, Hamilton, Moore and Trimble (1995: 62) found that 22 of the 60 Catholic youths they interviewed had had their homes searched, and: 'Almost all of the respondents had known friends', neighbours' or relatives' homes being searched.' Among the Protestant youths they interviewed, 'house searching was virtually unheard of'. Perceived harassment by the security forces was a further source of antagonism. McVeigh's (1994: 101) survey of 18 and 19 year olds in Northern Ireland found that 51 per cent of Catholic respondents claimed they had been harassed by the security forces, compared with 16 per cent of Protestant respondents. The striking differences between Catholic and Protestant attitudes towards the use of these security measures is illustrated in Table 4.2.

Catholics were far more likely than Protestants to consider that house searches, random searches of pedestrians and vehicle checkpoints were used too much. While this was abundantly clear in relation to the use of relatively low-level security measures, differences between Catholics and Protestants were heightened in relation to the most serious measures. The plastic bullet question yielded the 'sharpest division' that Whyte (1990: 87) found 'on any question in any opinion poll held in Northern Ireland' (the poll was conducted after several Catholic children had been killed by plastic bullets). Catholics' low levels of approval for the use of these security measures reflected the fact that these had been directed largely against nationalist communities, whose loyalty to the state was uncertain and who therefore remained a 'suspect community' (Hillyard 1993; Ó Dochartaigh 1997). Concerns over excessive force, misconduct and the adequacy of accountability procedures were encapsulated in two serious scandals involving the security forces: allegations of a shoot-to-kill policy; and collusion between members of the security forces and loyalist paramilitaries.

### Shoot-to-kill

Allegations of unlawful killings by members of the security forces were recurrent features of the conflict. Between 1969 and 1993 the security forces (including the British Army, the UDR/RIR and the RUC) in Northern Ireland killed a total of 357 individuals, of whom 194 were *not* members of paramilitary groups (Sutton 2001). Although this constituted only a fraction of those killed by paramilitary organizations, over half of those killed by the security forces were unarmed at the time of their death; many of the killings involved suspicious circumstances; and in many cases civilian eyewitness testimony and/or forensic evidence directly contradicted the official accounts of events (Amnesty International 1994; Murray 1998; Ní Aoláin 2000; Rolston 2000). The majority of these deaths were attributable to British soldiers, but a series of killings in Armagh in 1982 raised concerns that sections of the RUC were operating a shoot-to-kill policy against suspected paramilitaries.

Within a one-month period in 1982, an SAS-trained RUC unit known as E4A shot dead six unarmed individuals in three separate incidents, five of whom were republican paramilitaries. A total of four RUC officers were charged with murder arising from these incidents. All were acquitted. During one trial, the judge praised the officers 'for their courage and determination in bringing the three deceased men to justice, to the final court of justice' (quoted in Taylor 1987: 33). It emerged from evidence presented during the trials that senior RUC officers provided the officers involved in the shootings with a cover story – that the encounter arose from random patrols rather than more directed surveillance – to present to the investigating RUC CID officers. The reason given for this was to protect the identity of a republican informer.

Due to the resulting public outcry, John Stalker, Deputy Chief Constable of the Greater Manchester Police, was appointed in May 1984 to examine the circumstances surrounding the killings. Following allegations of professional misconduct on his part, Stalker was removed from the investigation and was replaced by Colin Sampson (Chief Constable of West Yorkshire Constabulary) who assumed responsibility for concluding the RUC investigation and for the investigation into Stalker's conduct (the Stalker/Sampson Report remains unpublished). Stalker maintained he was removed from the investigation to prevent him from accessing information vital to his investigation. The 'shoot-to-kill' allegations could not have been more vigorously denied by the RUC Chief Constable, Sir John Hermon (1997). Nevertheless, Stalker (1988: 253) claimed that that 'The circumstances of those shootings pointed to a police inclination, if not a policy, to shoot suspects dead without warning rather than to arrest them.' In 1988 the Attorney General, Patrick Mayhew, decided that in spite of the evidence of a conspiracy to pervert the course of justice, it would not be in the public interest to prosecute the officers involved. In 1989, 18 RUC officers were reprimanded and one cautioned by the Chief Constable for their actions. Two superintendents involved in the cover-up retired from the force on health grounds (Ellison and Smyth 2000; Hermon 1997; Taylor 1987).

Following the scandal over the 1982 killings, the RUC's involvement in ambush-type operations greatly declined. RUC Special Branch officers retained command over surveillance and undercover operations, but from then on they were largely carried out by the SAS (Taylor 2001; Urban 1992). Several further contentious killings reinforced public opinion that paramilitary suspects were liable to be shot by the security forces rather than given an opportunity to surrender. Concern over such killings was compounded by the fact that criminal charges were rarely brought against serving members of the security forces, and when they were, the courts appeared extremely unwilling to convict them (CAJ 1993; Jennings 1990a, 1990b; Murray 1998; Ní Aoláin 2000; Rolston 2000).

## Collusion

During the 1980s, the issue of collusion between members of the security forces and loyalist paramilitaries came under sustained focus, particularly following the UFF killings of Pat Finucane (a defence solicitor) and Loughlin Maginn in 1989. In Finucane's case, RUC detectives had persistently claimed he was working for the IRA and had told his clients that he would be killed. The UFF also claimed that Maginn was an IRA member, and publicized details of his official security file to support their contention. Shortly after these killings, details from the security files of 250 individuals were leaked to the media or pasted on walls throughout Belfast (Amnesty International 1994: 23). John Stevens, a senior British police officer, was appointed to examine allegations of collusion.

Stevens proved unable either to trace the origins of 'many' documents found in the possession of loyalists or to determine the number of files that had been provided to loyalist paramilitaries. Nevertheless, he concluded that collusion 'is restricted to a small number of individuals and is neither widespread or instutionalized' (RUC 1990: 6). As a result of the 1990 investigation, 94 people were arrested, of whom 59 were charged resulting in 44 convictions. Approximately 30 of those arrested were UDR officers, of whom several were charged. No RUC officers were charged, although a report was submitted to the DPP concerning two officers in relation to whom no action was taken (Relatives for Justice 1995; Ryder 2000; Weitzer 1995). Although Stevens noted that the implementation of his recommendations would make the leaking of security files far more difficult, he also observed that 'in the present security climate' collusion 'may never be completely eliminated'. This would prove prophetic, as newspaper reports between 1990 and 1994 indicated that approximately 750 individuals were informed that their security files either were missing or had been discovered in the possession of loyalists (Relatives for Justice 1995: 4–6). Stevens was asked to conduct another inquiry in 1993 as a result of this, and he submitted his report to the DPP in February 1994. In March 1997, the Chief Constable stated that no RUC officer had ever had any formal disciplinary or criminal charges brought against him/her for collusion (Human Rights Watch 1997: 141).

By highlighting the role of Brian Nelson, Stevens also raised disturbing questions about whether collusion was actually sanctioned at a senior level within the security establishment. Nelson was a UDA intelligence officer who gathered information on potential targets. At his trial in 1992, it emerged that he had been recruited as an informer by the Force Research Unit (FRU) of the British Army in 1987. The army provided him with information on republican suspects, and his primary purpose was to ensure that the UDA did not conduct random sectarian assassinations, but instead to ensure that it focused its activities on known IRA members.[1] Nelson was also involved in procuring arms for loyalist paramilitaries from South African sources. Although the arms shipment was under surveillance by British Military Intelligence, Colonel 'J', an army intelligence officer, claimed that the surveillance broke down as the shipment reached Northern Ireland. Nelson subsequently stated that his army handlers had told him the shipment had been allowed through to protect his identity. This weaponry greatly increased loyalists' capacity to mount successful attacks and partly explains the dramatic increase in the number of people they killed during the late 1980s and early 1990s (Ellison and Smyth 2000: 142; Relatives for Justice 1995).[2] Following the publication of new material in a British Irish Rights Watch report in 1999, Stevens was asked to conduct a third inquiry. After further investigation into the murders of Finucane and Andrew Lambert (a Protestant student shot dead after being mistaken for a Catholic), Stevens concluded that 'there was collusion in both murders and the circumstances surrounding them' (Stevens 2003: 16). These issues would continue to haunt the debate about police reform through to the present day.

## Under-protection?

In addition to the general criticism that nationalist areas were policed much more vigorously than unionist areas, many nationalists suggested that this 'over-policing' was accompanied by 'under-protection'. Allegations that the RUC did not provide Catholic communities with sufficient protection against loyalist attacks were a feature of the conflict from the outset (Scarman 1972: 16). Collusion epitomized this criticism in extreme form, particularly through the Nelson trial revelations that individuals under threat from loyalist paramilitaries were not warned that they were in danger or otherwise protected. As Stevens (2003: 11) noted, one aspect of his investigation was 'to determine whether both sides of the community were dealt with in equal measure. They were not.'

One of the most common criticisms was that the RUC simply failed to address the problem of loyalist paramilitary attacks on nationalists with the same degree of rigour with which it addressed attacks by republican. A 1986 survey found that 74 per cent of Protestant and 82 per cent of Catholic respondents thought that the RUC 'try hard to stop Catholic attacks'. However, 86 per cent of Protestants but only 46 per cent of Catholics agreed that the RUC 'try hard to stop Protestant attacks' (Weitzer 1995: 86). This view was reflected in widespread accounts of occasions when, following a loyalist attack in a Catholic area, the security forces concentrated their activities on the area where the attack took place, rather than on the area to which the attackers had escaped

(Amnesty International 1994; Relatives for Justice 1995). There was also a persistent criticism that loyalist attacks on Catholics were treated with less urgency than they deserved, and that investigations into those events were often less than rigorous (Hillyard 1995; Stalker 1988). The relative ease with which loyalists could escape from nationalist areas following an attack, despite the enormous surveillance conducted of those areas, was sharply at odds with the extensive security checkpoints whose sole purpose seemed to be to monitor traffic from nationalist areas into the city centre rather than traffic between nationalist and loyalist areas (Murray 1998; O'Doherty 1992). Although loyalists represented an increasing proportion of the total number of individuals charged with security offences during the 1980s and 1990s, the widespread perception in many nationalist areas was simply that republican violence against the state was a far greater priority for the RUC than the safety of nationalists within that state. In 1984, an RUC chief superintendent claimed that loyalist violence 'is very much reactive' and that 'the Loyalist terrorist and para-military threat can at present be described as largely insignificant' (*Police*, November 1984: 30). The diaries of a superintendent in the RUC Special Branch reflected a similar view:

> The rising tide of loyalist violence meant that in 1993 and 1994 Protestant hit squads were killing more people than the Provisional IRA. But for the RUC the Provisionals still remained the number one threat, because of their potential to drastically heighten the level of violence and widen its scope. (Holland and Phoenix 1996: 309)

Nationalists' concern that they were being over-policed and under-protected inevitably compromised the gains the RUC made through its professionalization, but it was not just the issue of security policing that was contentious here. The police response to normal crime also impacted on relations between nationalists and the RUC.

## A policing vacuum? The deficit of 'normal' policing

Despite strenuous efforts by government to highlight the relatively low rate of crime in Northern Ireland (NIO 1989, 1996), concern about crime and safety were significant issues in many Northern Irish communities (Brewer *et al.* 1997, 1998; Matassa 1999; O'Mahony *et al.* 2000). Against the backdrop of high levels of social deprivation as well as the broader political conflict, the activities of petty criminals (known locally as 'hoods') were often the focus for major concern in specific areas. Much of this related to a perception that 'hoods' were impervious to risk, exemplified by the dangers associated with joyriding, which was an enormous concern in West Belfast in particular.[3] One aspect of joyriding, for instance, included 'sandbagging', in which the youngest person present in the car lay across the back window of the stolen car. If the car then drove through a security checkpoint and was fired on by the RUC or army, this youth would act as a 'sandbag' against the shots fired (Fisher 1995: 19). Other concerns were specifically related to complaints about the inadequacy of the police response to joyriding.[4]

In nationalist and republican areas of Northern Ireland concerns about crime were compounded by suspicion of, or hostility towards, the RUC. The term 'policing vacuum' (Brewer *et al.* 1997: 202–6) was frequently used to describe the widespread absence in republican areas of a broadly acceptable policing service. In such communities, attitudes towards the RUC were shaped and reshaped by the tension between security-oriented policing and the policing of 'ordinary' crime. Frequently, people's stated unwillingness to deal with or support the RUC partly rested on a belief that that it was an illegitimate force. This, however, was intertwined with the criticism that the RUC had neither the capacity nor the will to tackle the problems of crime and 'anti-social behaviour' in those areas, whether through antagonism towards the residents or because such policing was overshadowed by the RUC's security role (Brewer *et al.* 1997, 1998; Matassa 1999; O'Mahony *et al.* 2000). This, in turn, fed back into the view that it was an illegitimate force *because* of its lack of commitment to providing nationalists with an adequate policing service.

The claim that the RUC 'largely abdicated normal policing in troubled areas' (Helsinki Watch 1992: 34) was commonplace in republican areas. During one discussion I observed about the broad topic of a community-based justice system, a republican and former prisoner remarked: 'What's the point of calling the cops? They arrest someone for car theft, but they won't press charges if he'll keep an eye on someone.' A friend of his added, 'They never come, or they just make you into a tout' (fieldnotes). This highlights two of the major concerns raised about the RUC's response to non-politically motivated crime: that the police did not take crime in republican areas seriously, and when they did respond to crime, their responses were subservient to the broader security agenda, often leading to petty criminals being offered a 'deal' by the police in return for serving as informers.

### 'They never come anyway'

Responsibility for the 'policing vacuum' in nationalist areas was laid squarely at the feet of the RUC, whom nationalists and republicans alleged were unable and/or unwilling to provide an adequate policing service in those areas. This critique related to the delay surrounding the RUC's response to calls from the public, and was expressed in the commonly held view that there was little point in calling them as 'they never come anyway', or else the police response was delayed by hours or days (Brewer *et al.* 1997: 157–61). McWilliams (1995: 18) found that some nationalist women who had suffered domestic violence were reluctant to involve the police, but those who did 'reported that the police would not, or did not, come out to their homes'. Several women described the RUC's response: 'We are not going out there because it could be a set up, anybody could phone us up and tell us that.' Similarly, one Catholic priest I interviewed described an incident that highlighted the RUC's response to calls from the public when safety considerations might be at issue:

> I remember a young man being knocked down in Armagh in the street and he was killed. The man who killed him was a young UDR soldier, but he was in civvies. That was in a catholic nationalist area. Obviously the police had to be called, but they wouldn't come. Often they wouldn't come without great reinforcements because of danger. But it was pouring with rain, and the body was lying on the street, and you weren't allowed to lift the body. I got the young man [UDR soldier] away, I took him to a police station in case something happened to him; he was afraid himself. So the body laid there for a few hours and it was a terrible agony for the relatives. Finally, we said we have to take this body in. So, they [the RUC] never appeared at all. It was the same when you had break-ins or burglaries. They weren't coming for this, that or the other reason.

Not every area would involve such concerns about officer safety, and in middle-class suburbs or quiet rural areas (whether predominantly Catholic or Protestant) this issue might arise only rarely, if at all (Brewer and Magee 1991). However, in many areas, particularly staunchly republican areas, safety considerations had a massive impact on RUC responses to calls from the public.

The officers I interviewed were very aware of the criticisms raised against them in this respect, but regarded it as an inevitable consequence of the safety precautions they were obliged to take. The threat of being ambushed was not merely an academic concern, as RUC officers had hard experience of occasions when calls were elaborate set-ups, and there were many examples of officers being killed in these operations. One of the events leading up to the 'shoot-to-kill' allegations described earlier in this chapter involved a phone call – 'orchestrated' by the IRA to lure RUC officers to an ambush – reporting a stolen tractor battery. The three RUC officers who subsequently responded to the call were killed by a massive IRA bomb (Taylor 2001: 248–9). As one RUC inspector noted (interview):

People complain because we take so long to get to calls, but that's usually been because two weeks earlier the IRA called us up with the same story and were waiting there to kill us. There was a case where the home-help of an 88-year-old woman on Grosvenor Road rang us because the woman didn't answer her door. The IRA had taken the woman out so that the home-help would call us. And every case has to be treated like that. We checked up on the old woman. We checked up on the home-help, and she was who she claimed to be. We go around there, and there was a bomb by the back door. It didn't go off, though, luckily. Now, not every call is like that, but some are, and you don't know which ones are, so for every call you have to go through all these procedures.

As events such as these demonstrate, the delays or non-appearances that characterized the RUC's response inevitably were a source of deep antagonism with the public. However, when the police did eventually arrive, the convoy of vehicles that descended on the crime scene may often have inconvenienced the public still further:

The dangers the RUC faced in nationalist/republican areas meant that when you went in for anything, you had to surround yourself with guns. The army had to go in, the area had to be sealed off, everything had to be done at once. We couldn't be going back there later on to ask more questions, to gather more evidence. The aim was to go in in one trip, do all the work we had to, and then get out. That meant we'd be there for four or five hours, and co-ordinating with the army before we went in there meant that we couldn't respond immediately. (RUC inspector)

Most RUC officers did not dispute the validity of criticisms concerning the failure to provide comprehensive normal policing, and acknowledged that during the conflict ordinary crime was a low priority. For example, a member of the Drug Squad noted that: 'During the war years, few people from the police took an interest in drugs . . . so many of them weren't particularly sympathetic to the question of doing a drugs search or anything like that.' Nevertheless, the police firmly denied that responsibility for this state of affairs rested with them, or reflected poorly on them. Instead they argued that it was a regrettable but unavoidable consequence of the security measures they were forced to adopt: 'Of course people were pissed off with the police because we couldn't give them the service they wanted, but we just couldn't' (RUC inspector).

The claim that security risks prevented the RUC from better meeting the policing needs and demands of the public generally fell on deaf ears in republican circles (Fisher 1995: 38). As one former republican prisoner noted (interview):

Well, that's what they say, but look, there'd be people ringing up and saying the house has been broken into, or the car's been stolen, or anything at all, and they wouldn't come. Sometimes they wouldn't come for days. Sometimes they wouldn't come at all. But if someone called and said they'd seen someone carrying a gun, they'd have the whole area sealed off in five minutes. You see, they can respond to calls when they want to.

This view highlights a perception common among nationalists and republicans that the policing of those communities was, as one interviewee claimed, 'subservient to a political agenda'. In other words, the provision of policing was always viewed as secondary to the maintenance of the Northern Irish state. Safety considerations were acknowledged by people, but equally they noted how easily such considerations could be dispensed with when the state security imperative was raised. This view that the provision of policing services would always play a poor second fiddle to issues of state is reflected in republicans' critique that 'they're only looking for touts'.

### 'They're just looking for touts'

As with any police force, information-gathering was a major activity of the RUC. The overt security role played by the RUC gave it a special interest in the collation and analysis of information, both for the development of a population profile consistent with the demands of 'low intensity operations' (Kitson 1989) and for the cultivation of informers with a view to prosecuting their colleagues. Sutton (2001) notes that during the course of the conflict, 82 individuals were killed by paramilitary organizations – 66 by republicans and 16 by loyalists – on the grounds that they were alleged informers. The significance that the security forces attached to information-gathering was evident in a number of ways, including: the ever-present surveillance helicopters hovering above Belfast; the highly visible observation post on Divis Tower or other vantage points; the lengthy questioning that often occurred at security checkpoints; and the RUC policy in the early 1980s of using the evidence of 'supergrasses' (or 'converted terrorists' in official terminology) against other paramilitaries (Greer 1994; Hillyard 1997; Taylor 2001). All of this inevitably conditioned people's responses to the RUC, and provided a widely accepted and readily apparent backdrop against which to situate the 'informer' and establish its relevance for the RUC's response to crime.

Throughout the conflict, there were widespread allegations that the RUC offered immunity from prosecution to criminals who could provide useful information about paramilitary activities. The head of the RUC Drugs Squad described the difficulties of drug enforcement during the conflict, noting the impact that Special Branch had on determining what operations could be undertaken and which individuals could be investigated:

> The conflict made drug enforcement very difficult. To actually search a house in West Belfast was a major operation during the Troubles. You had to have maybe 20 uniformed police, the same number of soldiers. That took hours to organize. You had to get specific clearances from various groupings – Special Branch – within the force, because you had to make certain you weren't impacting on an operation that they were doing. And inevitably by the time you got there the information was dated by a number of hours or a day. Same with surveillance. During the Troubles, all surveillance was controlled by central groupings within the RUC. Again, it was controlled very much by the need to counter terrorism, terrorism was given the highest priority. So if we were doing a surveillance operation in Belfast and I got a call from Special Branch saying 'Could I stop the operation?' I had to do it, because a terrorist operation was developing from another part of Belfast or something. So you had to get clearance to do that, and they could just pull the plug whenever it suited – didn't have to give me an explanation or anything. Very frustrating. And it's inevitable that some people who are drug dealers are also of use to groupings within any organization who are interested in terrorism. So I had to get clearance to search houses and if there was a conflict of interest with informants, I inevitably lost out. It happened occasionally . . . and when it does happen it does cause a problem because people within the drug squad work out that that person is working for another group, and it was a bit disappointing. (Interview)

Special Branch's focus on combating paramilitary organizations could in this way actively undermine the agendas and priorities of other sections of the RUC, and this difference in role often was a source of conflict within the force (Ellison 1997; Ellison and Smyth 1996: 199; Ryder 2000; Stalker 1988; Taylor 1987).

While the RUC's efforts to cultivate informants within the ranks of paramilitary organizations was a constant source of controversy, its ongoing efforts to gather intelligence from residents in republican areas also had significant consequences for public confidence in the RUC's crime prevention role. Several interviewees described the general perception in republican/nationalist areas that informers were actively recruited by the RUC: 'You'd come across it all the time, someone who'd been lifted for the fifth night in a row and was always released right away' (republican community worker). Invariably this was perceived to operate to the detriment of the RUC's crime-fighting efforts, and was used to justify hostility and suspicion towards the RUC: 'They never tried to do anything about the problems that people here had with burglaries, or stolen cars . . . The RUC have never tried to solve the problem of crime, they've only tried to exploit it. They've done it to demoralize our communities and to recruit informers' (republican community activist). This view, while sustaining the deep opposition to the RUC already evident in those areas, had the added effect of reducing the willingness of people in those areas to involve the RUC in the problems that impinged on their lives (Brewer *et al.* 1997: 156–7). Thus McWilliams (1995: 19) noted that some nationalist women she interviewed about domestic violence were reluctant to report their victimization to the RUC due to the fear that their partners would be pressured into becoming informers.

## Policing *by* paramilitaries? 'Alternative justice' in Northern Ireland

The concerns raised by nationalist and republican communities about the RUC's response to crime and 'anti-social behaviour' were deeply felt. However, while individuals may have been able to articulate these concerns clearly, what was less clear was what should be done about them. Some individuals dismissed the RUC out of hand solely on the basis of political considerations. For others, criticism of the police reflected concerns not only over the force's legitimacy, but also over its willingness and capability to address crime and disorder. Even if some residents in a republican area were supportive of the RUC, they still may not have been in a position to use the police freely. The reputation of their area ensured that poor response times still applied (Brewer *et al.* 1997), and individuals in those areas may have been reluctant to involve the RUC through fear of intimidation from republicans (Kennedy 1995; Northern Ireland Affairs Committee 1998; O'Doherty 1998). These reasons – rejection of the RUC on political grounds and concern over its record of crime control – have been the primary impetus behind the resort to an alternative justice system, largely comprising a system of punishments implemented by paramilitary organizations.[5]

During the Northern Ireland conflict, several examples of alternative justice emerged, including a 'People's Courts' system established in some areas in the early 1970s and a system of community tribunals developed during the 1974–75 IRA ceasefire (Hillyard 1993; Morrissey and Pease 1982; Munck 1984, 1988). Alternative justice during the conflict generally involved a loose system of policing and punishment measures administered by paramilitary organizations (in the IRA's case, by its 'Civil Administration Unit') after a complaint had been made to Sinn Féin or one of the loyalist political parties. The form of punishment used has varied according to community responses and external political considerations. During the early 1980s, the IRA stated that it would move away from administering physical punishments. However, community pressure for tough action against local criminals apparently led to the number of assaults and shootings increasing from the mid-1980s (Hillyard 1993; Munck 1984). Similarly, in the early 1990s, the IRA announced that it would increasingly resort to expulsions as punishments in an effort to limit the criticism it received (Kennedy 1995: 79).

Within republican circles, paramilitary punishments were generally viewed as a form of policing – albeit one that many considered both ineffective and unconscionable. Among loyalists, however, paramilitary punishments were more closely related to organizational or personal interests. This broad distinction is supported by two main factors. First, the problems facing the police in loyalist areas, although often acute, were simply not of the same order as those they faced in republican areas. As such, there was not a corresponding niche in the policing market in which they could embed themselves. Second, loyalist paramilitary organizations are more regionally autonomous and tend to have a looser structure than their republican counterparts. As such, the problems of internal control were magnified for loyalist paramilitaries (Bruce 1992: 198; Helsinki Watch 1992: 43–4; McEvoy and Mika 2001).

Since 1973 the RUC has recorded punishment shootings and assaults carried out by loyalist and republican paramilitary groups. It is likely that these data significantly underestimate the extent of assaults that did not require hospitalization, and they also exclude various other forms of paramilitary punishments, such as expulsions and 'shamings', which, while coercive, do not directly involve physical violence. Between 1973 and the 1994 ceasefires, republican paramilitaries accounted for the majority of recorded punishment shootings and assaults (1,199 of the 1,563 shootings and 364 of the 610 assaults, comprising 61 per cent of all paramilitary punishments). Republicans carried out the bulk of shootings and assaults in the 1970s and early 1980s, but from 1986 to 1994 (with the exception of 1989) loyalist paramilitaries conducted more punishment shootings than republicans. A similar trend is evident in relation to paramilitary assaults, and in 1993 and 1994 the number of loyalist assaults surpassed that of republicans. The increase in loyalists' use of punishments was likely due to loyalists' diminished confidence in the RUC following the 1985 Anglo-Irish Agreement, feuding between loyalist organizations and a general upsurge in the activity of loyalist paramilitaries.

### Levels of support for alternative justice

Paramilitary organizations claim that they provide policing services to their respective communities, but this claim is often received with scepticism, if not outright hostility. Even staunchly republican and loyalist communities are deeply divided on this subject, and bitter protracted debates on paramilitary punishments are a persistent feature of community life in those areas (Kennedy 1995; see also Hayes and McAllister 2001). Within official doctrine, punishment assaults and the often shocking levels of violence involved were described as symptomatic of paramilitaries' pathology. According to the Chief Constable's Annual Report for 1984: 'Nothing less than broken limbs and battered bodies satisfies the power lust of the paramilitary godfathers who control such activities' (p. xiii). The RUC constantly argued that the influence of paramilitary groups derived overwhelmingly from coercion of the community, and that the system of punishments was an integral component of their repertoire of tactics to achieve this (see also O'Doherty 1998).

Common as this explanation was, it failed to recognize that involvement in an alternative justice system brought costs for paramilitary groups in terms of negative publicity and – for republican groups – in terms of the energy and resources it diverted away from the primary objective of opposing the state. The official explanation of punishment beatings also failed to explain the existence of significant levels of public support for them within some communities. As one republican community worker stated:

> The only reason there are punishment beatings is because there's a demand for them. It would be a public relations disaster for the IRA to be involved in something like that unless the public supported it. First and last, those things occur at the behest of the community. (Interview)

A republican man in his fifties recalled his surprise at his elderly mother's (and her neighbours') support for punishment beatings because they 'thought something like that was necessary'. As he put it: 'Most of the people in the area want hoods to be punished. They're old or poor or vulnerable and they've had enough of that sort of stuff. They want to see punishment beatings, and they want to see more of them, or as many of them as it takes to make them feel safer' (fieldnotes). A PUP spokesperson confirmed this view, explaining that he felt it necessary to tell the public 'to desist from asking paramilitaries, because that's what happens. They don't go trawling the streets, they don't go rapping on doors asking "Has anybody violated your property or person so that we can give them a good hiding?" ' Furthermore, despite the very vocal condemnation of paramilitary punishments in the RUC's official discourse, some individual officers acknowledged they were often administered to satisfy community demand:

You hear all this talk about it being a terrible thing to do and it's just the provos keeping their hold on their community, but when you talk to people, you find that a lot of them want to see something done about crime. The thing is, see, lots of people say that the hoods are being shot in the wrong place. Instead of shooting them in the legs, they should be shooting them here [pointing to the side of his head]. (RUC sergeant)

Some interviewees (republican and loyalist) also claimed that RUC officers occasionally advised victims of crime to approach paramilitary representatives, as they offered the best hope of achieving some form of redress in specific situations (see Helsinki Watch 1992: 37).

Residents in republican and nationalist areas were not necessarily under any illusions about the impact of paramilitary punishments. Many openly conceded that, as a strategy of crime control, it simply has not worked; others found it so morally repugnant that it could never be countenanced: 'it hasn't had any impact on reducing crime ... There's very few people who have been beaten or who were shot that have ceased their activity ... It's a judicial system that certainly hasn't worked. And that's aside from the moral issue' (youth worker).

## Conclusion

While police professionalization did appear to attract nationalists' support for the RUC's 'ordinary' policing activities (although this had never been the key source of division), when contentious aspects of policing are examined, levels of support began to diminish and the differences between Catholics' and Protestants' attitudes became extended and often extreme. As Whyte (1990: 88) noted: 'There is an even greater degree of disagreement between Protestants and Catholics on security policy than there is on constitutional questions. Security issues remain an unhealed sore.' The memories celebrated within the RUC's official discourse found little to resonate with in the oppositional accounts of policing outlined in this chapter. The nationalist experience of policing was, in terms of security policing and the policing of ordinary crime respectively, one of simultaneous surfeit and deficit. Moreover, it is important to appreciate that among nationalists this oppositional discourse of policing was not an empty ideological shell; rather it was seen as experientially based, grounded in lived reality and accepted as such. This clash of belief and experience was fully evident in the often-heated debate on police reform that developed following the 1994 paramilitary ceasefires, and to which I now turn.

## Notes

1 At Nelson's trial, Colonel 'J' – a military intelligence officer – stated that the army had passed on 730 intelligence reports to the RUC, involving threats to 217 people. However, the RUC stated that the information it received saved the lives of only two people. Although the army claimed that it had passed information to the RUC detailing the threat against Finucane, the RUC denied receiving any such information. The disparity between these accounts has never been resolved. Moloney (2003) suggests that the Force Research Unit partly used Nelson to ensure that the UDA did not target informers within the IRA, who in turn were used to support the pro-peace process camp within republicanism.

2 According to Sutton's (2001) database of deaths related to the conflict, in the seven-year period (1981–87) up to the receipt of this weaponry, loyalists killed 82 people. By contrast, in the seven-year period following it (1988–94), loyalists killed 224.

3 O'Mahony et al. (2000: 23) noted that in Catholic lower-working-class urban communities, more people (37.7 per cent of respondents) rated 'joyriding' a 'big' problem in their area than any other form of crime. See also Brewer et al. (1997: 131–2).

4 The police response to joyriding probably arose from several factors. First, police pursuits of joyriders were dangerous affairs for all concerned, and it is likely that concerns over the safety of the general public as well as the pursuing officers shaped the police response to this issue. Second, the primary patrol vehicles used by the security forces during the conflict were armoured landrovers, cumbersome vehicles not suited to car chases. Third, however, persistent allegations were made that joyriders were treated leniently by the police on the basis that they became informants.

5 The complexities of paramilitary punishments require more attention than it is possible to provide here. For more sustained treatment of these issues and their evolution, see the differing approaches taken by Feenan (2002), Knox (2002), McEvoy and Mika (2001) and Silke and Taylor (2000).

# Part III
# Policing the peace

# Chapter 5

# Police reform as peace dividend: the debate over the future of the RUC

Few issues generated the volume or intensity of debate that policing and police reform did in the post-ceasefire period. Momentum towards police reform had been gathering prior to the ceasefires, but the developing peace process brought into sharp relief the role that policing would play in any overall political settlement. In this chapter, I examine the dynamics and contours of the reform debate between the 1994 paramilitary ceasefires and the 1998 Good Friday Agreement. In the first section, I discuss the emergence of the debate and examine, in particular, the RUC's response to widespread calls for reform. Second, I examine the various official reform proposals and highlight their general focus on issues of organizational efficiency, in a logical extension of the normalization policy pursued through police primacy throughout the conflict. The final section considers the issue of community involvement in policing structures.

## Setting the parameters of debate

Police reform was viewed as one of the most significant dividends of the peace process. As the Chief Constable put it: 'Enduring peace will make possible a new era of policing' (Annual Report for 1994: 11). For the RUC, the ceasefires had immediate implications. Officers increasingly began to patrol without military support, and to use cars rather than armoured Land-Rovers. Most no longer wore flak jackets or carried sub-machine guns, although side-arms continued to be worn. Military activity was scaled back, and in many cases soldiers were confined to their barracks (see generally NIO 1995b). Other changes included an improvement in response times to calls for assistance and a substantial increase in the size and profile of the Drugs Squad and the Traffic Branch.

While these changes were widely welcomed, setting the parameters for debates about the scope of any changes in policing proved much more contentious. It was also immediately clear that the issue of police reform would be one of the most heated aspects of the post-ceasefire period; within days of the IRA's 1994 ceasefire, Sinn Féin president Gerry Adams had already called for a new police force (*Irish News*, 3 and 5 September 1994). Some events, such as PANI's consultation exercise (discussed below), featured prominently in the police reform debate, but community conferences – several of which were held in the months following the ceasefires – also functioned as a locus of debate on these issues (Ardoyne Association 1994, 1996; Fisher 1995; Kennedy 1995; see also O'Rawe 2003: 1029). These conferences frequently were vehicles for the articulation of local community concerns and, significantly, they were organized mainly in nationalist and republican areas, although loyalist representatives had an input in some of these. In character, they were decidedly 'popular' rather than 'official'. While they generally involved presentations from a panel comprising academics, community workers and political representatives, by far the most significant element of these conferences was the input from the audience, and the depth of feeling that policing aroused was evident in the passion of the speakers as well as in the acrimony of some exchanges. While the ceasefires offered scope for the development of non-militarized policing in Northern Ireland, they also opened the floodgates of public concerns relating to policing, providing what many communities viewed as a rare opportunity to articulate their experiences of and views on these issues, and to have, perhaps, an input in shaping the policing service they received.

While these conferences largely involved the articulation of nationalist and republican concerns, loyalists appeared increasingly willing to discuss policing matters. This reflected the emergence of the loyalist political parties – the Ulster Democratic Party (UDP) and the Progressive Unionist Party (PUP) – and their involvement in many grass-roots issues. It also reflected an easing of the loyalists' dilemma over whether to complain about police behaviour and risk undermining the RUC (and particularly its campaign against republican paramilitary violence), or to say nothing and endure what they viewed as inappropriate and/or excessive policing. If this dilemma had traditionally been resolved through silence or muted criticism, the ceasefires offered an opportunity for loyalists to cast this discretion aside. Days after the IRA ceasefire, a number of loyalist councillors met with a senior RUC officer to discuss 'their concerns about heavy-handed policing of loyalist areas following the IRA ceasefire' (*Irish News*, 9 September 1994; see also *New Ulster Defender*, December 1995: 5). The repeated presence of Billy Hutchinson, a PUP spokesperson, at some of the policing conferences demonstrated the increasing profile given to loyalist concerns in these issues, and underlined the existence of parallel concerns in loyalist and republican areas. As one PUP policy document noted (1995: 1):

> RUC actions and attitudes towards Catholic people has left a legacy of real bitterness and the Protestant community cannot hope to engage the Catholics in honest debate without an open admission of this reality (a reality not that hard to accept since the Protestant working-class often received similar attention from the RUC).

The issue of police reform gained enormous impetus from PANI's decision to conduct a 'community consultation exercise' on attitudes towards policing. This spurred many organizations – even those such as the SDLP which did not formally participate, describing it as an 'inherently flawed procedure' (1995: para. 18) – into developing formal policies on policing, and maintained the high profile of the police reform debate. Overall, community conferences, the relaxed security environment and the widespread belief that a permanent peace settlement would emerge from political negotiations combined to ensure that police reform remained one of the most high-profile issues in the post-ceasefire situation.

### 'Indecent haste': official responses to the calls for reform

Despite the prominence of policing issues on the public agenda, it soon was evident that while some visible aspects of policing changed fairly quickly to reflect the lesser risks that officers faced, the attitude of many RUC officers to the emerging policing debate was strikingly equivocal. It had long been recognized within the RUC that the advent of peace would pose significant difficulties for a police force primarily oriented towards countering paramilitary violence. In a 1980 interview, Chief Constable Hermon discussed the problems the RUC would face in that event:

> . . . if peace breaks out, the armed patrols, vehicles, and flak jackets would disappear overnight. But we'd have a stupendous job of reorienting the whole force to a community service role . . . [Many RUC officers] don't know what it's like to work eight-hour days on a regular basis, to live on a policeman's pay without overtime, to

deal with 'ordinary' crime and social problems. They would have to become almost an entirely different sort of policeman. (Quoted in Hart 1980: 30)

Some difficulties had their origins in the economic consequences that peace held for RUC officers. The average RUC salary before the ceasefires was approximately £33,000 (of which a large proportion was earned from overtime), placing police officers in one of the highest earning occupational categories in Northern Ireland. Peace meant an immediate reduction in overtime levels, a development that was exacerbated by the relatively high standard of living associated with RUC officers. According to one RUC superintendent:

Young people who put themselves in danger on a repeated basis felt they deserved to be well remunerated for that, and they were, because they worked long hours and got lots of overtime. So they accordingly lived that kind of lifestyle, big fancy house, smart car, smart car for the wife, kids at maybe private schools. And I think a lot of them now, because they're not getting big overtime, are having serious financial problems, which lead to domestic problems and welfare problems as well ... For a lot of them, they've over-extended themselves and I think it will cause serious, serious problems. (Interview)

In addition to the pay cuts involved, a permanent peace could only mean severe cutbacks throughout the RUC. A police force of over 13,000 for a population of approximately 1.6 million was a commitment that no government was anxious to finance. Leslie Rodgers, Chairperson of the Police Federation for Northern Ireland (PFNI, the official staff association representing all ranks up to and including chief inspector), expressed anxieties within the force: 'Although peace is wonderful and if it continues it's absolutely the best thing that's ever happened, at the end of the day it doesn't put bread and butter on the table if you're unemployed' (*War or Peace?* Ulster Television, 26 February 1996). Reflecting the widespread concerns throughout the RUC at these possibilities, one of the RUC's first organizational responses to the ceasefires was the establishment of a welfare unit to provide advice and counselling for officers (although such welfare problems failed to materialize to the extent feared).

Other factors also shaped the force's reaction to the reform debate, most notably the palpable sense of betrayal over the 'indecent haste' with which the issue of police reform gained such prominence. It seemed to many officers that barely had the ceasefires been announced when plans began to circulate of massive changes in the force. The policing debate was viewed as unnecessary and treacherous by many officers, given their belief that the sacrifice of their colleagues had been paramount in actually getting the paramilitaries to announce a ceasefire (Barker 2004; Holland and Phoenix 1996). What a peaceful environment should provide, therefore, was an opportunity to acknowledge and give thanks for the RUC's achievements. The debate was, in effect, threatening to snatch defeat from the jaws of a well-deserved victory. As the PFNI chairman, Les Rodgers, put it: 'We have successfully policed the troubles ... What we deserve now, what we have earned through paying a terrible price and what some would deny us, is the right to police the peace' (speech to the 1995 PFNI Annual Conference). In language not unsuited to a post-mortem, Rodgers further observed that: 'This force has been poked over, dissected and prodded for response in a way which my members have found unnerving, demoralising and distasteful' (speech to the 1996 PFNI Annual Conference).

RUC commanders were forced to confront the enormous concern within the force, particularly among rank-and-file officers who viewed themselves as fodder in the ongoing reform debate. A superintendent involved in an in-force *Fundamental Review of Policing* (discussed further below) stated that the RUC's hierarchy was very conscious of the potentially demoralizing impact of the review, particularly in light of the tremendous amount of debate then underway about police reform:

> There was that feeling that there was 'indecent haste', that was the word being used. I think we had to be extremely conscious of that, that was in the background, the indecent haste of change. Not in the spoken word, but in the subconscious, there was that feeling, 'Look at how quick people started to look at the organization' ... So we had to be conscious of that, a lot of people lost their lives, thousands injured. So yes, it was in the psyche. (Interview)

Another superintendent echoed this view, noting that particularly among front-line officers, 'there was great bitterness, and people felt let down' that reform rather than recognition dominated the debate. RUC commanders used various means of communication to inform officers about the review and to assuage their concerns, including a video featuring a statement from Ronnie Flanagan (who in 1996 replaced Hugh Annesley as RUC Chief Constable). While his comments illustrate the significance attached to assuaging concern and bolstering morale within the force, they also reveal a concern within the RUC to contain the policing debate within strict parameters and ensure the primacy of the RUC's own proposals for change:

It seems to me that during the past twelve months virtually every Tom, Dick and Harry has had his or her say on policing. Now is the time for the people who really know best, the policing practitioners, to have their say ... If we don't take this opportunity to shape the future of policing in our Province, there are plenty of other people who will grab the opportunity and try and impose a policing system upon us. Now is the time for you to help shape our future together.

Throughout the force there was a massive rejection of the calls for reform. On 15 November 1994, the RUC published a full-page article in the national newspapers comprising extracts from a speech Annesley had days earlier delivered to police recruits. While he acknowledged that changes would occur in the security infrastructure, he also noted that much of the debate about restructuring the RUC was 'inaccurate, ill-informed and shows little understanding of the operational and logistical realities of policing. Above all, it is entirely premature and, inevitably, damaging to the morale of this organization' (*Irish News*, 15 November 1994). The sacrifice of the RUC featured prominently in statements dismissing or minimizing calls for reform, and several commentators suggested that the heavy price the RUC had paid during the conflict should be reflected in any future changes to the force. The significance of the RUC's sacrifice was a feature of practically every major official statement on policing made during the post-ceasefire situation, as senior RUC officers stressed their confidence in the force. Many of these sentiments were summed up in Chief Constable Annesley's statement that 'I do not accept the change argument. I do not believe that there is anything inherently wrong with the RUC that needs to be changed. I do not accept that the organization is wrong and must be fixed. [The RUC is] an outstanding professional police service ... one of the best, if not the best in the world' (*Irish News*, 13 January 1995).

It would be difficult to underestimate the depth of feeling that the reform debate generated within the RUC. According to an editorial in the PFNI magazine *Police Beat*: 'The test of nerve for the RUC may not have been what we have been through but what we may yet face' (January 1995: 1). In an address to the PFNI's 1997 Annual Conference, the chairman highlighted 'the subject which causes my members more grief and anger than perhaps any other that I can remember – the debate on the role of the RUC within this community.' Given the high number of RUC officers killed and injured during the conflict, to suggest that the reform debate was the greatest threat the RUC had faced can only be described as an extraordinary response. It is easier, however, to understand this perspective once one appreciates that the rejection of reform demands often revolved around negative characterizations of reform proponents. Quite simply, critics were viewed as misguided at best, enemies at worst. From that perspective, to acquiesce in the reform process was to accept the claims made by the force's critics, memorably described in a 1991 *Police Beat* article as 'propagandists, carpists and manufacturers of pseudo-history' (quoted in Ellison 1997: 223). The RUC's response to the post-ceasefire debate overflowed with denunciations of reform proponents. As Deputy Chief Constable Blair Wallace (at the time, one of the candidates to succeed Annesley as RUC Chief Constable) put it: 'these people are politically motivated, unrepresentative, dubious barometers of public opinion and . . . the sort of people who speak loudest at meetings' (*Irish News*, 2 January 1995).

A key fissure in the debate involved competing definitions of 'reform'. PFNI Chairman Les Rodgers criticized the view that reform meant the 'abolition of the RUC', and instead advanced an understanding of reform 'shared by me and every one of the federated officers which I represent.' This conception of reform amounted to 'change – a process of adjusting to unfolding events and the anticipation of new circumstances' (Speech to 1997 PFNI Annual Conference). This focus upon 'change' rather than 'reform' implied an evolutionary and politically neutral approach. Moreover, its focus was solely on the removal of the security threat. Consider, for instance, how Flanagan and Annesley, respectively, described a 'fundamental' change in policing:

Fundamental change is already underway; fundamental change as I've described in terms of individual officers being able to operate without the fear or risk of threat and attack that they've had to operate under in the past; being able to operate with their own discretion in the application of the law. And that's fundamental change and it's something that we will continuously develop. (Flanagan, 'Policing in Northern Ireland', RTÉ interview, 9 March 1995: 10–11)

My idea of a huge change in policing is to get someone, say in Strabane, to answer a call and for a single man or woman officer to get into a Panda car, drive to the house, deal with the call and come back to the station. (Annesley, *Police*, July 1995: 29)

Soon after the ceasefires, visible changes were made to policing practices, especially in relation to security measures, and a major review (*A Fundamental Review of Policing*) was undertaken of measures that might both improve the quality of policing delivered by the RUC and underpin its changing role in a peaceful political environment. Crucially though, and consistent with the Federation's approach, these were generally portrayed by RUC command as organizational measures whose implementation would satisfy the call for reform, and they were constructed very much as 'quality management' measures or natural responses to a new environment rather than as responses to the demand for reform.

## The official agenda for reform

The post-ceasefire period witnessed an unparalleled flurry of reform proposals. While much of the debate on policing had a distinctly 'unofficial' air to it, being conducted largely through community conferences, the letters pages of newspapers and policy statements from various community-based organizations, an official agenda of reform was also underway. There were several distinct components to the official strands of the reform debate: *A Fundamental Review of Policing* conducted by the RUC; a review of the tripartite structure (comprising the Chief Constable, the Secretary of State for Northern Ireland and PANI); a community consultation exercise undertaken by PANI; and a review of the police complaints system undertaken by Maurice Hayes (a former ombudsman for Northern Ireland).

### The RUC: A Fundamental Review of Policing

The initiative which seemed to offer the promise of the greatest *concrete* changes in policing was the RUC's *Fundamental Review of Policing*. Overall, the review was conducted in view of the opportunities the political and security developments gave the RUC 'to consider the service it provided to the community and to assess what changes it might make to enhance the delivery of that service' by establishing what 'constitutes a high quality policing service and how that service should be delivered to the whole community in Northern Ireland' (p. 1). The review noted that an effective police service had to be 'responsive to the needs of the community at a local level' and that it 'must set and meet the highest standards of behaviour.' The review made a total of 189 findings in relation to several dimensions of policing, but only a short summary of the review was published. The recommendations made in relation to various dimensions of policing were as follows:

> *Service*: Community Liaison Committees should be developed fur-
> ther; greater use should be made of customer attitude surveys to
> determine areas of satisfaction and dissatisfaction with policing;
> there should be increased partnership with other agencies; and the
> role of neighbourhood police units should be promoted and
> redefined.
> *Structure*: The major structural changes the review proposed was
> that sub-divisions should become area commands, and that they

should have as their basis council boundaries/districts. The super-intendent in charge of each subdivision would have ultimate responsibility for the provision of policing in that area. The divisional tier of command also would be removed. Additional recommendations were that 'a new department should be developed responsible for oversight of the police service's links to the community' and, when the security situation permitted, that CID and Special Branch should be amalgamated.

*Establishment*: No changes in the RUC's establishment should occur until the security situation warranted it, but, given the large numbers of officers engaged in security duties, a peaceful environment would require reductions in these. The issue of reductions 'should be handled sensitively and in close consultation with the staff associations.'

*Systems:* There should be an increased reliance on good management systems, and sub-divisions should be provided with appropriate managerial, information technology, and budgetary support.

*Support Services*: Given government proposals to transfer responsibility for support services and day-to-day management of finances from PANI to the Chief Constable, directorates should be established to deal with personnel, finance, and technical services.

*Personnel Issues*: Initial targets should be set for Catholic recruits and female recruits, while selection should continue to be based on the principle of merit.

*Organizational Style*: Community awareness training should be further developed through all training programmes, a neutral working environment should be promoted, and a culture of continuous improvement should be promoted through the use of consultative, open and innovative working practices.

The review was conducted against the possibility of three possible scenarios involving different levels of paramilitary violence and threat, and full implementation of the recommendations would occur only in *Scenario 3*, a peaceful and stable environment. The ending of the IRA ceasefire in February 1996, when the research for the fundamental review was almost complete, required evaluation of these recommendations to determine which, if any, could be implemented in that changed environment and which would be shelved until a lasting peace was achieved. The review concluded that some recommendations could be implemented, but those relating to *structure*, *establishment* and *personnel* could not. The RUC also reinstated its security measures. Some changes made by the RUC remained intact, such as the increase in the Drugs Squad.

While the ambitious title of the review appeared to hold out the promise of unparalleled change, the review's scope was strictly *intra-*

*organizational*: it dealt with the internal structures and operations of the police organization rather than the social and political environment within which the police operated. Couched in the nominally neutral language of managerialism and service delivery, the review offered a carefully constructed image of how policing should be organized and managed in the context of a stable and peaceful environment. But it was the organizational focus of the review that demonstrated its limitations as *The Fundamental Review* made few concessions to the reform lobby. For example, the *sole* explanation it offered for the huge underrepresentation of Catholics within the force was 'intimidation' (p. 9; cited in McGarry 2004: 377). Management consultants aside, however, 'inefficient use of resources' had never been the primary criticism laid against the RUC. Those charges had focused on the force's role in contributing to the political domination of nationalists, and the militarized policing during the conflict the brunt of which had been borne by nationalists. One Sinn Féin councillor highlighted this point:

> They have conducted their affairs over the years as a paramilitary unionist force, and that cannot be erased. Obviously over the years when there's conflict, you can say 'yes, well of course, if they're under attack that makes it a different force . . .' But they've always been basically the same. They're more modernized now, they've better techniques, better equipment, but they've always conducted their affairs in the same way. They're much more sophisticated now, and I think it's right to say that they're one of the most professional forces in the world. But they're not a professional police force, they're a professional paramilitary unit. (Interview)

Policing had been one of the most contentious issues throughout the conflict. The difficulties surrounding it would not be resolved by the managerialist changes outlined in *The Fundamental Review*. There would be no new dawn of police–community relations until broader political structures, including those relating to accountability, had been addressed.

### PANI and the community consultation exercise

During the summer of 1994 PANI had been considering undertaking a major community consultation exercise in line with its statutory obligation to ascertain public attitudes towards the police, and the environment following the ceasefires gave an immense impetus to its activities. The appointment to PANI in July 1994 of a new chairperson, David Cook, and Chris Ryder, a journalist and author specializing in policing and security issues, was significant as both were especially keen on this proposal. It was also felt that Ryder's journalistic experience would help elevate the RUC's public profile. Elsewhere, though, the future role of PANI had been called into question; the 1993 Sheehy Report, for instance, queried the utility of a police authority in Northern Ireland. Perhaps in an effort both to address criticisms of its passivity and ensure the authority's survival, 1994 signalled the beginning of a more active and proactive role for it, at least until legislative proposals for changes to the tripartite structure were put in place.

Relations between PANI and Annesley had been poor. Cook noted that during his first meeting with Annesley, the Chief Constable informed him that he disagreed with the very principle of having a police authority (interview). He also described PANI as 'a well-intentioned bunch of amateurs' and stated that 'he would pay as much attention to a letter to the *Irish News* [newspaper] . . . as he would to the police authority' (Hamilton, Moore and Trimble 1995: 24). Furthermore, for some time PANI had been seeking information from the force concerning its efforts to improve Catholic and female representation within the force. According to one PANI representative, authority members were 'fuming' at the Chief Constable's failure to respond to their requests in the level of detail they had requested (interview). Under section 15(2) of the 1970 Police Act, Cook made a formal request for the information. The data were provided, but at the cost of angering many members of PANI who did not wish to become embroiled in the public controversy this generated. The RUC issued a press statement criticizing the move, and PFNI described it as a needlessly provocative gesture by PANI. Cook also generated further controversy by issuing a statement rejecting the Chief Constable's Annual Report, embargoed until the press conference at which Annesley unveiled the report (*An Phoblacht/Republican News*, 1 June 1995: 13). It came as no great surprise that Annesley's retirement statement made no reference to PANI.

The approach that Cook and some other PANI members favoured towards the issue of police reform was sharply at odds with the RUC's own approach. Just days before PANI announced its extensive community consultation exercise, Annesley suggested instead that a policing commission should investigate the future of policing in Northern Ireland (*Irish News*, 4 January 1995). Nevertheless, on 4 January 1995, PANI announced that it would conduct a community consultation exercise, seeking the views of the Northern Ireland public on how to ensure a police service that 'would be free to operate everywhere in Northern Ireland with the consent and co-operation of the entire community . . . delivering an impartial, professional and effective police service to the entire community.' The extensive consultation exercise involved: public advertising; information seminars; mass mailings to almost every postal address in Northern Ireland (over 600,000 addresses), to over 3,500 public and private organizations and to all RUC officers and civilian staff; a large public opinion survey (2,682 interviews); and a series of follow-up meetings with some of the 7,974 individuals and groups who initially had made written submissions.

Of the written submissions PANI received, the vast majority were supportive of the RUC and strongly opposed to major changes in its role and structure. Controversial issues were mentioned in only a very small proportion of submissions. On the basis of these submissions, PANI's public opinion survey asked about the levels of policing activity they wished to see directed towards the particular areas raised. Hardly surprisingly, they overwhelmingly favoured a higher police emphasis on crime prevention, more community policing and more police 'on the beat'. What was most striking was the salience of drugs: 42 per cent of all respondents (and 51 per cent of Catholics) viewed it as their first priority, with a further 26 per cent rating it as their second priority policing concern. In relation to issues of civility, helpfulness and fairness, some distinctions were evident between Protestant and Catholic respondents. Overall, 81 per cent of Protestant and 70 per cent of Catholic respondents viewed the police in their area as very or quite helpful when dealing with ordinary policing problems. The survey also found that 74 per cent of Protestants and 55 per cent of Catholics viewed the RUC as fair, while 16 per cent of Protestants and 32 per cent of Catholics viewed it as unfair. Issues relating to the RUC's symbolism (such as the force's name and flying the Union Jack flag over RUC stations) also highlighted deep divisions between Protestant and Catholic respondents.

Although it represented a distinct break from the past for an organization with such a legendary low profile, the consultation exercise itself was marked by various controversies. While the SDLP and Sinn Féin boycotted the process on the basis of its limited scope, many of the public meetings it held were picketed by republican protesters carrying 'Disband the RUC' signs. The republican perspective on it was described in *An Phoblacht/Republican News* (23 March 1995: 15):

> The Police Authority also asks what the community wants from their police force and helpfully provides its five options, managing in the process, like the entire flawed exercise, to totally miss the point – that the RUC is a partisan force in a divided society. The choices are:
>
> • Increased traffic policing;
>
> • More uniformed officers on the street;
>
> • Extra effort to deter drug abuse;
>
> • Greater emphasis on crime prevention;

- Expansion of community policing at local level.

But no mention of the urgent need for a police force the community can trust.

The consultation exercise was further tarnished by revelations of immense divisions between members of the authority, including proposals to publish majority and minority reports given the likelihood of failure to agree on a final report particularly due to disagreements over recommendations concerning the RUC's symbols and ethos. Cook and Ryder were accused by other authority members of dictatorial styles of conduct and of leaking proposals under discussion to the media, thereby undermining the input of other authority members. Following Ryder's hardly inaccurate description of PANI as 'more a performing poodle than an effective watchdog', motions of no confidence in Cook and Ryder were passed. After refusing to resign, both were dismissed by the Secretary of State.

Following the eventual publication of the report, Cook and Ryder claimed that it was a watered-down version of the one that PANI was closest to agreeing on while they were on the authority. Although there allegations were denied by other PANI members, there were significant differences between the draft report prepared by Cook and the final one published by PANI. As Cook and Ryder specifically noted, the authority had adopted a much more timid approach to the recommendations surrounding the ethos and symbolism of the RUC, but also in terms of stressing the very need for reform. The dismissal of PANI's two most reform-oriented members confirmed for many observers that it was unable and/or unwilling to step outside what was generally perceived to be its traditional role of passivity and subservience. PANI did subsequently embark on a series of measures to democratize its working practices, including opening its meetings to the public. Ironically, its first public meeting was barracked by republican protesters sharply critical of PANI's record. Caught between its desire to be a more active agent in policing debates and its own timidity, PANI found itself sidelined as other proposals emerged which would drive the reform debate.

### NIO proposals for the reform of policing structures

In March 1994, in a discussion document entitled *Policing in the Community*, the Northern Ireland Office (1994b) announced a re-examination of the structural relationship between the three parties responsible for political control and accountability of policing in Northern Ireland (the Secretary of State, the Chief Constable and PANI), on the basis that current arrangements created 'uncertain lines of accountability' and 'wasteful duplication of resources' (p. 8). In May 1996, the Secretary of State outlined proposals for legislation that built on the initial proposals outlined in that discussion document. He made clear that the upcoming political negotiations might well shape the eventual legislation (p. 5). Although he claimed that the proposed changes would 'strengthen' the tripartite structure of police accountability, the primary component of this exercise was organizational efficiency, especially through the application of the principles of 'total quality management' in objective setting, planning and the allocation of and responsibility for resources. The most notable aspects of the White Paper were the extension of the Chief Constable's managerial responsibility over policing resources, the introduction of costed policing plans for the implementation of identified policing objectives and PANI's loss of financial control over the RUC as it gained an input into the setting of local policing objectives.

The introduction of these measures promised improvements in financial and personnel management and in other areas, but how exactly they 'strengthened' the tripartite structure was far from clear. Their primary purpose appeared to be a clarification of the respective roles of the Secretary of State, the Chief Constable and PANI, and a rationalization of resource management. However, while these three parties were held to represent the interests of, respectively, government, the police and the community, it seemed that the likely outcome of these measures, consistent with the experience in England and Wales following the introduction of similar measures, would be a strengthening of government control at the expense of local community control. The historical trend in England and Wales has been towards a gradual increase in central government control over the police, whether through the advisory (yet rarely ignored) Home Office Circulars, or the diminished local accountability of police authorities (Jones 2003). PANI's input into policing would now be in terms of consultation over local policing plans, yet under the principle of operational independence the Chief Constable retained the option of deviating from these plans if conditions required this. Overall, then, these proposals strengthened only two parts of the tripartite structure. PANI remained, as ever, the poor cousin in this relationship.

### The Hayes Report: an 'independent' police complaints system?

Throughout the conflict, the police complaints system was one of the most contentious aspects of policing, and its prominence continued into the post-ceasefire policing debate. In November 1995, Maurice Hayes, a former ombudsman for Northern Ireland, was appointed to review the complaints system and recommend changes that would attract both public and police confidence in the system and offer an effective service.

His report was published in January 1997. Hayes located his review of the complaints system within the overall context of reform, and stressed that if the other contemporaneous reviews 'can be got right, arrangements for dealing with complaints become less important', because 'no complaints system, however sophisticated, will compensate for failure to reach a satisfactory resolution of the broader questions of structure, management and political accountability' (1997: v, 2). He noted that there was a 'lack of faith' in the current system and that criticisms against it included concerns over 'the length of the process, the low number of complaints found to have been substantiated and the small number of police officers who had been brought to court, or convicted, or even disciplined as a result of a complaint by a member of the public.' He suggested that the extremely low substantiation rate for complaints against the RUC 'can only reflect a less than totally effective complaints system or a more than perfect standard of police behaviour in all circumstances' (p. 5), particularly when set against the large amount of money the force paid out in settling civil actions brought against it.

According to Hayes, 'The main value which was impressed on me was independence, independence, independence,' and his recommendations reflected this. He proposed the establishment of a police ombudsman operating independently of the police who would have responsibility for investigating complaints made against the police. The ombudsman would have complete control over the complaints process, determine what constituted a complaint and the manner in which it would be handled, and be able to instigate an investigation of its own volition. The ombudsman also would be able to comment on police policies where it felt these had a bearing on behaviour that tended to generate complaints. As well as much greater use being made of informal resolution, a sliding scale of standard of proof would be introduced: the more severe the potential outcome, the greater the standard of proof required to substantiate a complaint. The report also recommended that time limits should be introduced, special attention should be paid to the deployment of mobile support units given their frequent involvement in public order situations, supervising officers should be disciplined if it is impossible to identify an officer under their command against whom a complaint was made, and an outcome category of 'substantiated, but officer(s) unidentified' should be introduced. The ombudsman would make recommendations to the Director of Public Prosecutions where criminal behaviour may be involved, and to the Chief Constable where disciplinary action might be required.

What was most striking about the Hayes Report was not the novelty of its subject matter. Demands for independent investigations into police complaints had been noted in *every* major official inquiry into policing in Northern Ireland, and was probably the most pressing concern advanced by nationalists throughout the conflict. As O'Rawe (2003: 1058) notes, Hayes 'frequently commented that if the government had spent £3.50 . . . to buy the CAJ publication on the issue, they could have saved themselves a lot of time and money.' Rather the report's significance was that the establishment of an independent complaints system – which previously had been noted only to be rejected as unnecessary – was, for the first time, articulated as a formal recommendation. Ultimately Hayes' thoughtful work was well received and the Police Act (Northern Ireland) 1998 included provisions for the establishment the Office of Police Ombudsman.

## The parameters of the reform debate

While the above proposals comprised the bulk of the official reform agenda, the overtly public or 'unofficial' debate on policing extended far beyond these measures. A series of PANI surveys addressed the level of public demand for reform. These found a consistent pattern highlighting a number of points (Table 5.1). While an overall majority (two-thirds or more) of Protestant respondents wanted the RUC to remain unchanged, only a minority of Catholics preferred that option (ranging from 28 per cent to 11 per cent, and reflecting the impact of events at Drumcree during the 1996 marching season – see Chapter 7). Significantly more Catholics than Protestants wanted the RUC reformed (the single biggest response category of Catholics, ranging from 38 to 52 per cent). Approximately one-third of Catholic respondents (compared to only 4 per cent of Protestants) wanted the RUC 'replaced' or 'disbanded' (although the difference between these two terms is not clear).

**Table 5.1** Public attitudes towards police reform

| Regarding the future of the RUC, do you think it should be . . . | 1995 | | 1996 | | 1997 (February) | | 1997 (October) | | 1998 | |
|---|---|---|---|---|---|---|---|---|---|---|
| | C | P | C | P | C | P | C | P | C | P |
| Allowed to carry on exactly as it is now | 28 | 71 | 13 | 61 | 11 | 68 | 18 | 70 | 15 | 65 |
| Reformed | 38 | 23 | 46 | 32 | 52 | 26 | 42 | 25 | 48 | 30 |
| Replaced by altogether new police force | 31 | 4 | 32 | 4 | 29 | 4 | 33 | 3 | 31 | 4 |
| Disbanded | 1 | 0 | 4 | 0 | 5 | 0 | 2 | 0 | 3 | 0 |
| Don't know/refusal | 2 | 1 | 5 | 2 | 4 | 2 | 4 | 2 | 1 | 2 |

*Source*: Adapted from PANI (1998).

Sinn Féin's (1996) policy on policing centred around asserting the RUC's unacceptability to nationalists and generating the momentum to ensure the force's disbandment. Although Sinn Féin spokespeople noted that some members of the RUC would obviously play a role in the force that replaced it, this was hardly an olive branch that police officers would take seriously. According to one RUC inspector:

> Sinn Féin are out of step with people . . . They talk about disbanding the RUC, yet you have community groups publishing reports calling for a police service which obviously will be based on the RUC. The RUC aren't going to be disbanded. Frankly, it's ludicrous for them to maintain that kind of position. There's a lot of people in nationalist and republican areas who have an acceptance of a police service and they would be happy to work with the RUC to get the kind of service they want, but Sinn Féin don't want to be involved in things like that, which is a pity because, their position, there's nothing to it. (Interview)

Some commentators called for the establishment of locally administered policing agencies as a means of securing widespread community support for the police and of maximizing police effectiveness against local problems (Brogden 1998; Lennon 1995; McGarry and O'Leary 1999). Calls from Sinn Féin and others for locally based policing received short shrift from the RUC, particularly in so far as it raised the possibility of members or former members of paramilitary organizations being involved in those structures. Dismissing such proposals outright, Annesley observed: 'Neither, may I say, does the RUC warm to being lectured by convicted terrorists about how policing should be conducted' (*Irish News*, 15 November 1994). Nevertheless, the proper role of the community in new policing arrangements generated significant amounts of debate. Some of this was in local settings, such as a system of police wardens that was proposed at the Ardoyne conference, but dividing the police force on the basis of either function or region featured in several policies on policing. The SDLP proposed the development of a two-tier system, with one being responsible for major crimes, security activity and international crime, and the second locally based tier dealing with minor crime and 'quality of life' issues (SDLP 1995). Sinn Féin also proposed local-level policing forces (1996). Other groups were less positive about this proposal, and some dismissed it outright (Alliance Party 1995; PUP 1995). The PANI survey did address this issue, and while Catholics were evenly divided between those who favoured the idea of regional forces and those who were opposed to it, a majority of Protestant respondents were opposed to the idea (46 per cent disagreed strongly with this proposal). In contrast to the issue of regional police forces, proposals for a two-tier model of policing attracted the support of a majority both of Protestant (57 per cent) and Catholic (67 per cent) respondents (PANI 1996: appendix 6, table 5). The RUC, however, was hostile to these suggestions of separate forces whether on the basis of function or region, with Annesley describing these proposals as 'spurious in the extreme' (*Irish News*, 15 November 1994).

The issue of community involvement in policing structures *did* feature in official debates on reform, but generally only through a greater community consultation role for PANI, with the results of this process being used to inform the local policing objectives which would then form part of the Chief Constable's annual policing plan. By abolishing the divisional tier of command, RUC subdivisional commanders would be in a position to develop policing styles – and police priorities – in line with the needs of the local community. The RUC also envisaged the further development of the system of community police liaison commit-tees, which would serve as a conduit for relating local concerns to the police. Hayes (1997) favoured an expanded role for CPLCs, as did PANI which established a steering group to coordinate developments towards this goal. Traditionally, CPLCs were widely considered little more than talking shops, and perhaps not even that (Weitzer 1995, 1992). Sinn Féin and the SDLP formally boycotted them, and the SDLP described them as 'essentially RUC public relations activities' that 'cannot by any stretch of the imagination be regarded as a basis for accountable policing' (1995, para. 32). Whatever form it took, local oversight of policing remained an important issue. Sinn Féin, for example, suggested a system of 'local police advisory committees' to ensure the 'democratic accountability' of local policing structures (1996: 13). Overall, though, proposals for regional or tiered forces were firmly rejected by the RUC and by unionist representatives:

> If a unionist knew that when they went to the city centre and they were in a car accident, that they would be meeting a Catholic officer and possibly a nationalist officer, and Catholics knew the opposite would happen in [a Protestant area], people would retreat complete-ly into their own ghettoes, people would never go into the other territory. West Belfast Catholics would not go to East Belfast, because they would say, 'Well, I might meet, I might come into contact with, I might be stopped by a unionist policeman who takes offence that his police force has been divided up into West Belfast and East Belfast.' And so the East Belfast Protestant going into West Belfast would be very indignant about the police force being divided up to, as he would see it, facilitate nationalist demands in West Belfast, and he would become embroiled [in a difficult situation] if he were to come into contact with a nationalist policeman in West

Belfast with a nationalist agenda. I mean it would be a nightmare, an absolute nightmare. (Interview with DUP councillor)

The irony is that what this interviewee saw as a potentially dangerous future situation – one social group being policed by a force composed almost entirely of members of a different group – was something that nationalists saw not in a police force of the future, but in the police force of the present.

## Conclusion

Police reform was the most contentious and emotive issue in the post-ceasefire period. Several prominent initiatives on policing were undertaken, including proposals for an independent complaints system, for a reworked tripartite relationship and for various organizational changes within the RUC. While official proposals often led the reform debate, there was a strong groundswell of public opinion in many communities over the need to have a wide-ranging debate about the future role and structure of the police in Northern Ireland. Despite this, official proposals for reform were striking for the extent to which they proposed efficiency-oriented changes to existing structures rather than more radical reforms. Few of nationalists' longstanding criticisms of policing were reflected in these proposals.

Otherwise, the official reform (or 'evolution') agenda meshed closely with contemporary trends in policing: managerialism, increasing governmental control over policing policy and a privileging of the form of accountability over the substance, through, for example, the use of performance indicators and objective-setting (Newburn 2003). It was as if the conflict had never been. While the RUC relied so heavily for its legitimation on a set of organizational memories that reflected very specific and circumscribed readings of history, the measures it proposed to enhance police effectiveness and enhance police–community relationships were striking for their ahistoricism. They were generated as if from a social and political vacuum. The memories through which the RUC had sought to legitimize itself appeared to fade away, leaving in their wake a discursive framework of managerialism whose neutrality and normalcy was apparently self-evident. Yet official preferences for the future of policing in Northern Ireland were not manifested solely in the initiatives discussed in this chapter. They also were articulated through specific visions of normal policing that dominated post-ceasefire police discourse, and which I consider in the following chapter.

# Chapter 6

# Visions of normality: peace and the reconstruction of policing

With the advent of police primacy, official government policy in Northern Ireland sought to normalize what was in effect a small-scale war. Following the ceasefires, this yielded a dilemma: given the enormous lengths to which it had gone to normalize the policing of conflict, how would it now normalize the policing of peace? The theme that the RUC was a normal force – embroiled in an abnormal context, armed and trained to a high degree, equipped with considerable powers, but essentially normal nonetheless – was often difficult to sustain during the conflict (see Chapter 4). The ceasefires gave the RUC an unparalleled opportunity to re-articulate its self-understanding as a 'normal' police force. This chapter examines the visions of normality that underpinned RUC discourse during this period.

## Out of the shadows: promoting the RUC

Soon after the announcement of the 1994 paramilitary ceasefires, a massive public relations campaign got underway in Northern Ireland. To the tune of Van Morrison's *Days like this* – and the closing lyrics from his evocative *Coney Island*, 'Wouldn't it be great if it was like this all the time' – the Northern Ireland Office (NIO) launched an extensive media campaign: 'It's time for the bright side'. On billboards everywhere, the towns of Crossgar, Arglass and Downpatrick were officially transformed into *Happy*gar, Ard*pint* and *Up*patrick. The RUC also seized this 'opportunity to highlight, as never before, the all-round work of the Force' (RUC Annual Report for 1994: 71), reflected in various crime prevention campaigns, as well as a campaign to promote a new confidential police telephone number with its accompanying caption: 'Build the Peace – Support the RUC'.

Policing during the Troubles was always characterized by a high measure of secrecy. Although some aspects of police activity were extensively promoted, other aspects were the subject of denials, fabrications and other strategies of information control (Curtis 1984; Miller 1994a, 1994b). However, as the ceasefires took hold, any reticence the RUC may have practised quickly gave way to an eagerness to grasp the opportunities for promotionalism offered by the peace process. This 'greater openness' on the part of the RUC was epitomized by a 'force information day' in March 1995 at which senior RUC officers gave presentations on the work of a variety of departments to an invited audience of over 200 community representatives. The inclusion of a short presentation on the RUC's Special Branch (which had primary responsibility for activities directed against paramilitary organizations) gives some indication of the significance of this event; it simply would have been inconceivable for this to occur at the height of the conflict. Following the ceasefires, Ronnie Flanagan, soon to become Chief Constable, also participated in live media debate on policing (for example, BBC1/Radio Ulster's *On Air* on 17 January 1995), again, a distinctive break with the past. This strategy was also reflected at ground level in the greater willingness of operational officers to appear on television at a crime scene: 'Before the ceasefires, had we had a murder out there, it was always very difficult for us to actually get a policeman to front the thing, to actually go on television. Purely and simply for security reasons, their own security . . . All that has eased greatly since the ceasefires' (RUC superintendent).

The *Inside the RUC* television series was perhaps the most significant promotional measure undertaken by the RUC after the 1994 ceasefires. Filmed in 1995 and shown on Ulster Television (UTV) in January and February 1996, the format for its eight episodes was documentary-style: the producers filmed RUC officers in the course of their duties and allowed them to talk at length about their experiences; throughout, the programme makers are neither seen nor heard. The idea had been mooted by UTV in 1994, but the RUC had then turned it down. In 1995 UTV broached the subject again, and this time the RUC gave it their support. In this respect, the series exemplified the opportunities arising from the ceasefires: 'The ceasefires that continued through 1995 created an excellent climate for the Force Information Centre to exercise a greater proactive role than was possible during 25 years of overt terrorism, and every opportunity was taken to promote the full range of RUC activities' (RUC Annual Report for 1995: 73). As one RUC press officer said, '*Inside the RUC* was a first for us, that was the first time we ever let any camera crews inside to actually film the police, talk to the police and let them talk.' Moreover, the fact that the producer was from Dublin was viewed as a bonus by the RUC: 'It lessened the fact that you'd have people saying "Here's the RUC producing a programme on themselves," you know.' The series generated considerable public interest, averaging a 53 per cent share of the Northern Irish viewing audience, and getting up to 67 per cent of the viewing audience (for the third episode). This is in contrast to the UTV average audience share of 43 per cent (data from UTV Press Office). Ironically, one of the initial difficulties facing the producers was a general reluctance among many officers to participate in the programme:

> You know, the ceasefire was very new at that time, and if you go back to the beginning of [1995], and there was still a lot of policemen who said, 'No, I wouldn't be prepared to do that.' So it was a matter through my contacts getting policemen to feel confident enough to come forward and meet [the producer] and talk to [him] and get an idea of what he wanted to do. [*Did you have to do a bit of cajoling?*] Oh yes, I had to keep them encouraged, 'This is our chance to let people see what we do and talk, so what about it? C'mon and do it.' (RUC press officer)

The series portrayed what can only be described as a positive account of post-ceasefire policing. For instance, in the 'War or Peace?' episode (filmed before the breakdown of the first IRA ceasefire, but aired on UTV on 26 February 1996 shortly after the Canary Wharf bombing), an RUC superintendent described the new policing climate: 'Almost overnight, people were openly friendly to the police who would have been a bit guarded before that. And the young officers that I expected who would need to retrain have taken very quickly to this community policing. It's exactly what they want to do.' The series is also striking for its close reflection of the tenets of official discourse discussed in Chapter 3: sacrifice, hidden community support and accountability. All three elements feature prominently in the 'XMG' episode (UTV, 15 January 1996) through the comments of the RUC inspector with responsibility for policing Crossmaglen, a republican village in south Armagh. Describing the dangerousness of the district for members of the security forces, he focused on the deaths of his colleagues and the contribution these made to securing peace:

> When one reflects over the last 25 years and what it has cost, the sacrifice the RUC, and indeed the army who are here to support us, has made. I mean in those 25 years, 56 police officers murdered in this sub-division alone, and 122 members of the security forces. That is a colossal sacrifice ... That's totally inexcusable, but if it's the price for peace, then it's the price we have to pay.

In another section of the programme, he mentioned the hidden community support that RUC officers received: 'We don't treat the community in Crossmaglen as hostile. We do receive a collective anonymous support from the majority of the population in the town. They don't want to see the terrorists here.' In a further statement, he defended the RUC's record, dismissing criticisms of impartiality: 'I certainly can't believe anyone could stand over and say that the RUC is a bigoted unionist force, I think that's rubbish.' Although the 'XMG' episode stands out for failing to show RUC officers in contact with members of the local community, the inspector still managed to present a positive image of local police–community relations. In the absence of dissenting voices, the comments of those featured in the programme carry the weight of fact and function to enhance the RUC's status and reputation. Within this discourse of impartiality, the role of the RUC is simply to maintain the (neutral) rule of law, and intervene as necessary in the internecine tribal warfare between Catholics and Protestants. Thus the inspector featured in the 'XMG' episode described his role: 'Our primary aim, our main objective, is to bring normality to this area, and we feel we're working towards that at this point in time.' Quite what the inspector means by 'normality' is unclear. Given the enormous casualties suffered by the police in Crossmaglen, this might amount to nothing more than 'an absence of violence'. But the use of this terminology also lends itself to the view that 'normality' speaks for itself, that there is one obvious, irrefutable and universally shared vision of normality that is beyond questioning, and certainly beyond politics. In the following section, I consider how idealized modes of police–community relations featured in the visions of normality articulated in RUC discourse.

## Visions of normality

Through the conflict, the RUC maintained that its heavily militarized style of policing was thrust upon it as a means of self-preservation, and was necessary to enable it to carry out its duty to protect the Northern Ireland population from violence. As one NIO publication expressed it: 'the RUC wants to be an unarmed, civilian-type police force', but 'the reality of the terrorist threat means that the force has had to be equipped with a variety of weapons to defend itself and the community' (NIO 1989: 34). The advent of the ceasefires offered the RUC 'a rare occasion when previously professed desires to pursue a more 'normal' policing role . . . could be tested in a climate of relative social calm' (Bryett 1997: 50). This was the view expressed in the RUC's *Fundamental Review of Policing* (1996: i):

For many years the conduct of a most vicious terrorist campaign forced us to operate from fortified stations; forced our officers to travel in armoured vehicles; forced them to patrol wearing flak-jackets, bearing arms and often accompanied by military colleagues. This inevitably caused barriers between us and the people we seek to serve. We long for the day when such barriers will be totally unnecessary. The period between August 1994 and February 1996 gave but a foretaste of how things could and should be. All right-thinking people of course prefer to see police patrolling and operating in the way that this period began to make possible. No-one feels more keenly the desire to engage in normal policing than the police themselves.

Throughout the RUC, freedom from the threat of targeted violence was undoubtedly the most immediate and compelling consequence of the ceasefires. In spite of the massive levels of disquiet that the debate about the future size and composition of the police force was creating, there was a palpable sense of relief among RUC officers. One RUC officer (interview) gave a telling example of this, describing the changes he made in his personal security precautions (which he did not change, even after the first IRA ceasefire was abandoned):

One of the things I religiously did was I didn't get into my car without a ten minute search. I don't carry a gun, I have no concerns about personal safety, but my inner self wouldn't allow me to sit in that car without doing a full check. I did that religiously. A ten minute job every morning. Because I knew policemen [who] had their legs blown off, and the one thing I was going to try to avoid was ending up with no legs. But one day after that ceasefire was declared, I stopped doing it and I've never done it since. There were mornings I used to get under the car and look, search – I wore old clothes – and then I'd walk away and think 'now you didn't concentrate on doing that properly, get back there'. And even [if it was] bucketing rain I'd force myself to do that religiously every morning. And one day after the ceasefire, I shocked myself. I just got into the car and I've been doing that ever since. It never crosses my mind. It's wonderful.

But even amid the pleasure that officers drew from the relatively peaceful environment in which they now policed, it was clear that the 'normal policing' role they were creating for themselves was anything but straightforward. Even Annesley's description of how he saw normal policing developing remained unclear, aside from the obvious desire to see an end to violence:

I would love to see a situation that young men and women in a police canteen, maybe ten years into the next century, and somebody might turn around and say 'When were these Troubles?' and the others would look around and say 'I can't remember.' ('War or Peace?' UTV, 26 February 1996)

The suggestion that 15 years from when Annesley made this statement, the Troubles would no longer be remembered seems somewhat far-fetched. This was not merely a feature of Annesley's imagination, though; several other RUC officers made similar statements, all of which offered a view of the ceasefires and of the new normality that proved difficult to situate in the political and material conditions of the time. Consider the following statements:

The summer of the IRA ceasefire, the weather was spectacular, and I think that did more to make people appreciate the value of peace than anything else. I think that just came at a great time. It was almost divine intervention, and I think people forgot about politics, and about the war. Obviously victims' wives and families couldn't, but [for] the rest of us it was wonderful. I think peace is now so precious to us all, we want it, and I think it will come. (Superintendent)

Now we operate under [the Police and Criminal Evidence Act], there has to be reasonable suspicion for someone to be stopped and searched . . . And for the public now there are no windows coming in, no 'wains' screaming, no bullets cracking outside. And we can now work towards providing the kind of service that people want. The people of West Belfast have seen the holy land of normality, after 25 years in the desert, and now they're half way across the river Jordan. There is a promised land of milk and honey and jobs out there, and they have seen it. (Chief inspector)

We all have to adapt. It'll be hard, I've never policed in peace, but we all have to learn to change and adapt with the times. And I hope it lasts. Tomorrow has come for us, peace is here . . . it's just brilliant. (Constable, *War or Peace?* UTV, 26 February 1996)

While the above quotations undoubtedly reflected a sheer human reaction to what appeared to be the end of the conflict, they also revealed a predicament for RUC officers. Policing in Northern Ireland bore all the hallmarks of the violent conflict there; normal policing, in the sense of everyday routine, was a paramilitarized form of policing. Yet the RUC's official discourse explicitly functioned to minimize the conflict's significance. Much as the above quotes expressed an overt relief, they also foreshadowed a problematic arising from the changing political (and policing) circumstances. Nowhere was 'normal policing' situated in terms of a concrete human activity: it was from another dimension (divine intervention), another time (tomorrow) or another place (the 'promised land'); it was anywhere but the here and now. In that sense, peace generated a crisis for the RUC, raising the prospect of massive changes to the force while also posing a more basic question over its role in the mode of policing that would develop in Northern Ireland. Given the longevity of the RUC's role in countering paramilitary violence, its status as a key marker in entire communities' relationships with the state, and its difficult if not hostile relationship with a significant proportion of the population, what visions of normality would be conceived, articulated and mobilized to secure a role for itself in the future and inscribe itself within particular configurations of Northern Ireland's history?

The remainder of this chapter discusses three particular visions of normality evident in the RUC's depictions of its role and relationship with the community. These refer to: first, a golden age prior to the outbreak of conflict; second, Northern Ireland's inherently law-abiding character; and third, the application of a managerialist framework to policing in Northern Ireland, envisaging the police as professional providers of a neutral service delivered through partnerships forged with the community. While these depictions of normal policing were articulated throughout the conflict in various ways, they gained a heightened prominence in the post-ceasefire period.

### Policing past perfect: normality as policing regained

Constructions of pre-Troubles policing featured heavily in official debates on policing following the 1994 ceasefires. Many commentators stated that the solution to the policing question lay in the natural equilibrium that would develop once the pressures of the security situation were lifted. The PANI chairperson suggested that the ceasefires provided an opportunity 'once again to rekindle the vision of the new policing order first outlined by Lord Hunt in his 1969 report on policing here, but so violently smothered at birth by the onset of terrorism' (PANI Annual Report for 1994/95: 8). For most RUC officers, though, the vision of normality most often articulated was not the set of reforms proposed by Hunt. Instead normality comprised the policing practices that actually preceded the Hunt Report, and which Hunt viewed in such great need of reform. In these instances, normality was nothing other than a return to the golden age of the pre-Troubles era. As one officer put it: 'Now we're released from security arrangements we can try returning to the situation prior to '68, '69, and get closely involved with the community, get involved, provide a service' (RUC chief inspector). In a similar vein, the chairperson of PANI's community relations committee highlighted the opportunity that the ceasefires presented 'to re-establish the intimate levels of community policing which once flourished throughout Northern Ireland' (PANI 1994/95 Annual Report: 15).

One RUC superintendent (interview) offered a clear comparison of the normal policing that existed pre-1968. This was 'good' and 'normal' policing, administered and delivered from a bicycle, and illustrative of the non-contentiousness of pre-Troubles policing:

> When I joined, the experience was very good. Things were normal in '65, in actual fact in '66, '67, we weren't even carrying guns in those days . . . I was posted to Tyrone, I didn't even know the place I was going to, I had to have a look at the map, and they set me on a bus and away I went from Enniskillen [the RUC training depot]. And I was there two years. I must say it was very good. We cycled about, normal like, probably the way the Guards have done for years down south.

He continued by depicting the subsequent outbreak of widespread violence in the late 1960s as the death knell of this normality, and also the catalyst towards the 'abnormal policing' required to deal with that violence:

> It was a pity, you know, a young fella coming from a normal society, [doing] normal policing in [Tyrone], to suddenly seeing all that being lost, and steadily going down the drain during the '70s, the terrible bombing campaigns, the amount of people being killed . . .

The absence of political conflict was a recurrent feature of this vision of normality. Depictions of policing were instead dominated by mundane police work, by the internal relations of the RUC rather than external relations with the community. In this context, errant cyclists were often the most pressing problems facing the police. The former Chief Constable Sir John Hermon (1997: 15) noted that his first RUC patrol – a cycle patrol – involved a 'hot pursuit' of a man on an unlighted bicycle. He also recounted how life within the RUC was covered by an enormous number of regulations, their impact softened only by the 'common sense and humanity' which characterized their implementation (p. 15). In a similar vein, one RUC constable featured in the *Inside the RUC* episode 'The Middle Men' (UTV, 19 February 1996) discussed his experiences of policing in the village of Castlederg prior to the Troubles:

> I came in one night at twelve [midnight] and the sergeant asked me how many cases I had. And I told him there'd been nobody about,

dead of winter, didn't get any cases that night. Sent me out again, told me I couldn't get back in until I got a case. So I wandered down the village again, not a sinner about. Came back in at one. Asked me again, sent me out again when he found the answer was nil. And thank god some fella was going home on a bicycle, and he had no light on the back of his bike, and god help me I had to book him to get in to my bed. So I came in, put the 'no tail light' in the book. I'm not sure what the fine was, I'm sure it wasn't much more than two shillings in those days. That's what you had to do.

In this confessional tale the mundaneness of policing activity and the petty discipline that characterized relations between constables and their supervisors form the backdrop for a broader characterization of consensual policing arrangements in the area. As this officer went on to note: 'It's a troubled area now, but in those days it was very agriculturally minded. Very, very friendly town, very pro-police town.'

The Police Museum publication *Arresting Memories* (Sinclair and Scully 1982) offers a further example of pre-Troubles policing with a 'delightful' cartoon entitled 'I remember . . .!' (plate 105). This image depicts an elderly former RUC member recounting 'some earlier memories' of life in the RUC to a 'very young constable'. These are memories of: 'short haircuts, barrack regulations, station lamps, pumping water, anti-smuggling patrols, trestle tables and hard beds, not to mention the fair day duties, the early morning "rising patrols" and the all powerful barrack cook.' The text for the cartoon claims that 'Many readers will be able to share his memories'; in other words, they are not the atypical experiences of one particular officer, but instead resonate with an entire generation of RUC officers and form part of the RUC's collective memory. According to this cartoon, policing boiled down to the internal workings of the police organization, the petty discipline and harsh living conditions which doubtless were a rude awakening for a great many young recruits. No hint of political conflict appears. Even the young constable's conception of policing is abstracted from the Northern Ireland conflict: his daydreams about 'the next century of policing' amount to futuristic 'cosmocops' flying in a space-age aircraft. The border with the Irish Republic is featured in the cartoon, but only in relation to cattle smuggling and certainly not as a contested entity. In a later photograph in the *Arresting Memories* collection, the border re-appears (again in relation to cattle smuggling), in the guise of 'a land boundary with a variation in food prices on either side' (1982: 68). Throughout these characterizations, the public is largely absent: the only non-police characters in the 'I Remember . . .' cartoon are the physically imposing female 'barrack cook' and the smuggler, and the only hint of conflict in these stories involves the apprehension of errant cyclists.

Instead, the social milieu of policing is populated with nothing more contentious than abrasive superiors and a great many regulations. Such characterizations of pre-Troubles policing offer an implicit non-sequitur: as political conflict is not mentioned, there must have been none.

### Normal all along? Policing the 'peaceful province'

Related to this notion of a golden age of policing in the pre-Troubles era is the assertion that policing in Northern Ireland was normal all along. This vision of normality was a staple element of RUC discourse throughout the conflict and also during the post-ceasefire period. It focuses attention not on the abnormalities arising from the conflict but on the ever-present normality that always existed behind the news headlines of violence and conflict. If Northern Ireland is atypical, it is through an excess of calm rather than turmoil, an approach that McEvoy, Gormally and Mika (2002: 185–6) call the 'surprisingly low levels of crime despite the Troubles thesis':

> Whilst terrorism and its effects pervade life in Northern Ireland, it is important to emphasize that even when one counts terrorism into the statistics, the crime rate here is lower than any other police force area in England and Wales. Moreover, our detection rate compares very favourably with the mainland. (RUC, 1992a: 5)[1]

The overall tranquillity of the region is enhanced by the fact that, as the PANI chairman noted: 'Community strife is limited to relatively small areas of Northern Ireland. In the main it is a beautiful country in which many people born elsewhere choose to make their homes and set up business' (PANI 1988: 2; see also NIO 1989). Even former Chief Constable Annesley (1992: 287) was moved to observe that 'Northern Ireland has some of the warmest people and some of the finest scenery imaginable.'

The mention of Northern Ireland's relatively low crime and victimization rates and high detection rates extended beyond a description of statistical reality. It was actively used to attribute specific characteristics to the majority of the population. The putative 'law-abiding' nature of the population features prominently here. For example, the NIO referred to Northern Ireland as 'the most law-abiding part of the United Kingdom' (NIO 1989: 37). Former Chief Constable Hermon also described the population of Northern Ireland as 'overwhelmingly decent, warm-hearted, essentially law-abiding people' (quoted in PANI 1988: 2). In a noteworthy instance, these traditional values were credited with functioning as a major impediment to the widespread use of illegal drugs. According to the House of Commons Northern Ireland Affairs

Committee, in its 1997 report on drug use in Northern Ireland, the 'strong social and family ties that exist within all communities in Northern Ireland' had prevented illegal drug use from reaching the levels evident in other countries (RUC press release, 14 February 1997). This assertion that Northern Ireland is, contrary to media stereotypes, an essentially benign location, peopled by warm-hearted and law-abiding 'folk', is telling. It implicates the RUC in an organic relationship with the community (see PANI 1988: 2); moreover, it privileges social consensus to the exclusion of any hint of conflict. The 'folk' envisaged here are far removed from any notion of a politicized citizenry.

These various enunciations on the theme that Northern Ireland is atypical not because of its violence but because of its tranquillity, all point to such indicators as crime rates and clearance/detection rates as a measure of the pastoral calm of its social landscape. Moreover, these factors also highlight the fact that, even at the height of the conflict, the RUC was doing exactly what a normal police force would be doing: preventing and investigating crime. The police bicycle patrol that featured so prominently in the constructions of a pre-Troubles idyll continued its journey as an ideological vehicle in the assertions that the RUC engaged in normal policing all along. In one example of this, beside a photograph showing two RUC officers on bicycle patrol giving directions to another cyclist, an NIO publication highlighted how police officers were 'walking beats in country villages, patrolling shopping areas, working with local schools and trying to instil a new sense of road safety in the population' (NIO 1989: 37; see also Miller 1994b). Similarly, in *Arresting Memories* (Sinclair and Scully 1982), one picture with the caption of 'Progress without change' (plate 103) epitomized the continuity and seamless moral authority that bicycle patrols symbolize. This mode of patrol allows police officers the opportunity to engage in leisurely conversation with members of the community, but also creates the opportunity, as the photo suggests, for the officer to be engaged *by* members of the public in conversation. In this untroubled social landscape, the officer on cycle patrol is:

being engaged in conversation by a couple of young cyclists. The common denominator is the bicycle and no doubt the conversation centres on the problems of modern day cyclists. Police in some areas have recently rediscovered the bicycle as a mode of transport and enjoy the opportunity of more leisurely patrols with time to converse with passers by. The public for their part feel that they have rediscovered the policeman and both are happy in this new relationship.

Other examples of this view offer a more qualified view of police normality during the conflict. These suggest that the true measure of

RUC officers was evident in the fact that although the situation around them was dangerous and difficult, the 'abnormal' policing that this forced upon them never supplanted the authentic crime-prevention policing that officers performed. The theme that critics of the RUC focused on security-related policing, while failing to acknowledge the 'normal' policing carried out by the RUC, is a further thread to this broad argument. Some examples of this trend entirely eclipsed the fact that there was a conflict to begin with. For instance, the PFNI's banner for its 1997 conference read '75 years of Putting People First'. From this perspective, one of the true measures of RUC professionalism was that even at the height of the Troubles, with all of the difficulties that entailed, officers continued to perform normal policing, enabling them to claim that by doing so they remained a 'normal' police force. As Ronnie Flanagan noted during a radio interview:

> *Do you think you'll ever come to the point where you will be able to be the Dixon of Dock Green so to speak?*
> In many areas and in many circumstances we are the Dixon of Dock Green. It's interesting you know that people try and portray [a need for] massive change, but if you look at Woodbourne and Andersonstown Sub-Division [in West Belfast] there were 20,000 contacts between the community there and their local police last year. Now that was in an era when violence was at its height. So I think that represents a tremendous dialogue between the police and the community. So this isn't something that has suddenly come about; it's something of course that we can now really foster and build upon. But we've always had the closest contact with the community right across the Province, and that's something we want to see continually develop. (RTÉ interview, 9 March 1995: 18–19)[2]

Similarly, after describing the increasing violence during the early 1970s, one RUC superintendent (interview) complained at the lack of acknowledgement given to the RUC's service role, stressing that this role was never wholly supplanted by the security situation:

> I suppose as time went on you just got hardened up to it, and you did your best to deliver the service. I think that's the big thing that galls me sometimes when we're criticized, that all the RUC are this, this or this. I think that the RUC over 25 years kept a reasonable degree of normality and delivered a policing service in extreme circumstances that probably very few police forces throughout the world has ever had to do. I think this is the positive side, that we did still deliver a policing service, we still dealt with traffic accidents, investigated burglaries, delivered the whole policing

service to the backdrop of terrorism and being killed in doing that. As I said, we didn't always get it right, we made mistakes along the way. But I like to think that my career was one of commitment and service to the people of Northern Ireland, regardless of who or what they were.

This vision of normality amounted to a celebration of the 'unsung' activities of the RUC. It stressed that the RUC's focus remained on being a normal police force in a normal community doing normal policing, and never wavered from that by succumbing to the pressures of the conflict. The consequence of this approach was to minimise the significance of the conflict and the 'distortions' it generated for the RUC. Clearly, if the RUC was normal all along, there could be little need to reform it.

### Policing in partnership: normal policing as managerialism

The conceptions of normal policing described in the previous two sections have, whether implicitly or explicitly, a historical dimension to them. They flesh out a model of policing that has at its core a very traditional conception of community. They hark back to a mythical past and invite the idealized police–community relations contained therein to be accepted as the model for – and the reality of – the present day. In the aftermath of the ceasefires, however, a more prospective vision of policing was articulated. Drawing heavily on the notion of policing as 'service provision', this model of normal policing offered the language and concepts of managerialism as the primary means of mediating public expectations of the police.

The major thrust of managerialism within the RUC emerged with the publication of the RUC's *Professional Policing Ethics* in 1988, the RUC's *Strategic Statements* during the 1990s, the RUC's *Statement of Purpose and Values* in 1992, and the *RUC Charter* in 1993. Hermon (1997) also charts how his tenure as Chief Constable was increasingly affected by the imposition of financial constraints on the RUC as central government sought to curb public expenditure. The ceasefires greatly raised the profile of this approach. The RUC's *Fundamental Review of Policing* was the culmination of a major examination of how a permanent peace in Northern Ireland would affect the role, structure and style of policing. The vision of policing offered in that document is entirely consistent with the principles and ethos of managerialism: 'It concentrated on first principles of policing, recognizing that what really matters is the quality of the service that is delivered and how that matches community needs and expectations' (1996: i). In another example, in October 1995, a Service Quality Development Branch was set up for the purpose of 'taking a structured approach to providing a better service' (RUC Annual Report for 1995: 73):

The RUC is fully conscious of the need to satisfy ever changing public and government demands for a policing service which is effective and provides real value for money. This means continually improving both what we do and how we do it. Through the Service Quality Development Branch we are developing a strategy for continuous improvement, based upon the provision of proven business tools and techniques, to support individuals and teams striving to deliver ever more efficient and effective services. Our ultimate aim is to foster a culture dedicated to the pursuit of policing excellence. (RUC Annual Report for 1996: 59)

Managerialism was not confined to statements from RUC headquarters or to its official publications; it was also evident in the comments of operational policing commanders. In the context of discussing how policing might change in the event of a permanent peace, one officer noted that:

In four or five years I would think the RUC will be a totally different organization. We'll be a policing service, the war machine will have been dismantled. The priority will be to meet local people, all over the place, find out what they want. And that's actually what's happening at the minute. (RUC superintendent)

Another officer emphasized that the ethos of service provision would increasingly come to the fore as peace became more solid. Moreover, he identified the public credit that the RUC would get for this as a major bulwark to the peace process, suggesting that a high-quality policing service would undermine the support the IRA received:

[We can] get closely involved with the community, get involved, provide a service. Not just law enforcement, but getting involved with community service. We can get more involved in supporting the victim. I think maybe we'll surprise people with the quality of service we can provide. I think it will be harder for the IRA to go back to a conflict situation when people have seen the kind of service we can deliver. (RUC chief inspector)

### From security to service delivery: normal policing in action

This shift to normal policing as manifested in managerialism and service delivery formulae was exemplified by the RUC's emphasis on 'policing in partnership' in the post-ceasefire period. While on the one hand this related to new and improved relationships between the RUC and sections of the community, it also referred to the RUC working hand in hand with the community to address issues of common concern. By focusing on 'normal' problems, the RUC emphasized what would be seen as meaningful yet non-contentious activities, particularly in relation to crime prevention. Crime prevention initiatives also received greater amounts of media attention than in the past. Under the title of 'Crimecall', a crime appeals programme was relaunched on UTV, while a 'Crimestoppers' column in the *Sunday Life* newspaper was supplemented by a 'Crimebeat' column in the *News Letter* newspaper (RUC Annual Report for 1995: 73). The Police Federation also demanded that attention be focused on ordinary crime. Even in the first *Police Beat* editorial following the IRA ceasefire of August 1994, there was a focus on the need for 'ordinary' policing. Of its three paragraphs, one called for the ceasefire to be made permanent, one focused on the memory of RUC officers and others who died in 'the past barbarous twenty-five years', and one described the 'policing job to be done throughout Northern Ireland. Rackets, fraud and ordinary crime have still to be tackled; the road traffic rate has leapt during the course of this year and must be a priority for reduction' (*Police Beat*, September 1994: 4).

Traffic policing would indeed be a major focus for the RUC as it set about reconstructing itself as a normal police force engaged in partnership with the community and tackling normal and non-contentious crime. Placing a heavy emphasis on the huge number of road deaths in Northern Ireland was, ironically, a familiar aspect of official attempts to assert normality. No Chief Constable's Annual Report was complete without mention of the 'carnage' on the roads, or the fact that road deaths far outnumbered those arising from the conflict. It is clear, however, that while this information serves on the one hand to maximize the severity of road deaths, it also functions to minimize the severity of the conflict.[3] Thus, after reassuring the reader that the crime rate in Northern Ireland was significantly lower than in many other jurisdictions, one NIO publication reassured the reader still further: 'More people have died in road traffic accidents than in the Troubles. Statistically, an Ulster citizen is twice as likely to be killed on the roads as he is at the hands of the terrorist' (1989: 36).

After the ceasefires, the significance of traffic policing increased further, and became a central measure of normality. In a *Police Beat* editorial entitled 'Resuming Normal Service' that appeared shortly after the declaration of the loyalist ceasefire, the PFNI called for police attention to swing towards the problem of road traffic deaths: 'There are still a number of major battles to be fought and won, none more pressing than the almost daily carnage on our roads' (*Police Beat*, November/ December 1994: 7). The RUC's *Roadsafe* campaign, launched in March 1995, was 'the biggest road safety campaign to be mounted by the force, aimed at reducing the number of deaths and injuries on the roads' (RUC

Annual Report for 1995: 73). It reflected force rhetoric that road traffic should be an immediate source of police energies, and was facilitated by the release of personnel from security-related duties (p. 45). As with other normal policing ventures, the RUC 'availed of every opportunity to publicize the commitment to road safety' (RUC Annual Report for 1996: 61). For one RUC chief inspector, this translated to sound policing, as evidenced by the outcome:

> One of the things we've been doing is working on traffic matters. People think we're hammering the public with the numbers of people in court. But people are driving more slowly now, and the fact of the matter is that more people have been killed by cars than in the conflict. (Interview)

While road traffic matters were a prime focus for the RUC's newly released resources, the issue of drugs quickly emerged as an even more prominent dimension of normal policing (Hollywood 1997). At the start of the 1990s, the Chief Constable stated that: 'there is not a serious drugs problem in Northern Ireland' (RUC Annual Report for 1990: 10). In the immediate aftermath of the ceasefire, however, illegal drugs came to epitomize the RUC's engagement in normal policing activities. Throughout the 1990s there was a steady and often dramatic increase in the amount of drugs seized and the number of drug-related arrests, but this was mostly in relation to 'soft' or recreational drugs. Concerning heroin and cocaine, year after year the Chief Constable noted that 'the abuse of "hard" drugs is not widespread' (RUC Annual Report for 1991: 35). Even after the ceasefires, the Chief Constable observed that: 'Seizures of opiates and cocaine are down on previous years and are minuscule in comparison to the rest of the United Kingdom' (RUC Annual Report for 1995: 32).

As the peace process developed the RUC substantially increased its involvement in the policing of the illegal drugs market, and its actions 'against the growing drugs menace' (RUC Annual Report for 1995: 33–4) assumed far greater prominence. Some of this rhetoric verged on the hysterical:

> This community faces an evil just as deadly and insidious as terrorism. The menace of drugs mirrors terrorism. It grows from small beginnings, thrives on initial official complacency and in the end we are all targets. Drugs, like terrorists, do not discriminate in their victims ... the fear is now of drugs corrupting people's lives and ultimately destroying families just as surely as contamination by terrorism. (Les Rodgers, speech to the 1996 PFNI Annual Conference)

The RUC's rhetorical commitment to countering illegal drug use was matched by significant increases in the size and profile of the Drugs Squad. The chief inspector in charge of the unit was promoted to superintendent, the Drugs Squad was increased from 38 to 52 officers (a recommendation already made by HMIC (1995: 30)), the number of regional offices expanded threefold and a drugs liaison officer was appointed in every sub-divisional area throughout Northern Ireland, effectively adding over 100 further officers to the policing of illegal drugs. This commitment to tackling drugs was also given organizational backing through the RUC's Strategy Statements. While the RUC's *Strategic Statement for 1992–1995* noted that 'drug abuse is not a major problem, with no evidence of the widespread use of highly addictive drugs' (RUC 1992a: 5), the *Strategic Statement for 1997–2000* identified drugs as 'an important priority' (RUC 1997: 13).

In terms of the RUC's self-portrayal as a service- rather than security-oriented organization, the emphasis attached to road traffic safety and illegal drugs met with a very positive response, certainly at an organizational level. In 1996, both units became 'the first police departments of their kind in the UK to be awarded the Charter Mark for outstanding service to the public' (RUC press release, 2 December 1996). As the Chief Constable noted: 'Such recognition in our special circumstances is, I feel, particularly meritorious' (RUC Annual Report for 1996: 8). Moreover, the Northern Ireland Affairs Select Committee, in its report on illicit drug use in Northern Ireland, reported that Northern Ireland was 'a success story in preventing drug abuse from reaching the same proportions as elsewhere' (RUC Press Release, 2 December 1996). Viewed in this light, the RUC's policing of illegal drugs would be seen as one major step towards demonstrating the effectiveness of the new productive relationships that could be forged between the police and the public as normal policing developed in Northern Ireland.

## Conclusion

The relaxed security situation that followed the ceasefires served as a window of opportunity for the RUC to shift from a security-oriented mode of policing to a more civic and service-oriented one. Claiming that the distortions the conflict had forced upon their role were now removed, RUC officers at last seemed to have an opportunity to perform the normal policing that for so long they had envied in other jurisdictions and expressed a desire to perform in their own. However, the visions of normality articulated here shared in common a deeply depoliticized expression of social relations. This was particularly evident in the greater emphasis placed on managerialism as the force hoped to shrug off the effects of the conflict and establish itself firmly in the mode of service deliverer, operating in partnership with the community and offering technical solutions to meet the needs of customers. However, this view runs counter to the ways in which policing was implicated in the overt politicization of the social landscape in Northern Ireland. Not only were the identities of communities established and reinforced through the relationship they had with the police, but so too at a rhetorical level the police implicitly politicized the public sphere in Northern Ireland by establishing itself as an impartial umpire 'holding the ring' (Mulcahy and Ellison 2001) between two irredeemably politicized antagonists, nationalists and unionists. Its greater professionalism was always juxtaposed against the embedded political character of the 'immature communities' it policed (*Police Beat*, July 2004).

The three visions of normality discussed here dominated post-ceasefire RUC rhetoric. Just as a major debate on police reform was unfolding across Northern Ireland, these models of policing and police–community relations offered the RUC a means of refuting the need for reform by denying the existence of any conflict over policing to begin with, certainly none that would not be resolved once the distorting influence of paramilitary violence was removed. The experience of policing in many communities, however, diverged sharply from the RUC's own recollections of past idylls, or of a mode of normal policing that persisted throughout the conflict. In the next chapter, I examine how communities which traditionally had a conflictual relationship with the force would articulate their own memories of policing and seek to realize their persistent demands for reform.

## Notes

1 The RUC's clearance rate for recorded crimes peaked in 1988 at 45.1 per cent, before dropping in the following years to the mid 30s. Throughout the conflict, its clearance rates usually were higher than rates in Britain, although they dropped significantly following the restructuring associated with the 1999 Patten Report (see Chapter 9).
2 There was probably considerable variation in police–public contact from station to station, and much of a station's day-to-day business may have been conducted by telephone rather than through face-to-face visits. Nevertheless, in some cases the number of public visitors to police premises was extremely low. For instance, the local police commander for Rosemount PSNI station in Derry noted that '12 people had visited the station between October 2003 and October 2004' (*Irish Times*, 2 December 2004).
3 This strategy of 'favourable comparison' is used across a range of contexts to downplay the significance of particular events. One Fox News commentator provided the following (inaccurate) analysis in 2003 in relation to the war in

Iraq: 'Two hundred and seventy-seven U.S. soldiers have now died in Iraq, which means that, statistically speaking, U.S. soldiers have less of a chance of dying from all causes in Iraq than citizens have of being murdered in California . . .' (http://www.foxnews.com/story/0,2933,95850,00.html).

# Chapter 7

# Resistance narratives: from lollipop protests to Drumcree

During the peace process, divergent histories of policing in Northern Ireland collided head on. The Chief Constable's call for the debate about future policing arrangements to be 'constructive' and free from 'rancour and recrimination' (RUC Annual Report for 1995: 15) was sharply at odds with all-too-evident bitterness of the debate that materialized. Many nationalists were keen to engage with the RUC at various levels, and viewed the ceasefire period as a long-awaited opportunity to do so. However, even among those who were keen to develop better relations with the RUC, most still favoured reforms, ones that extended far beyond the official proposals on policing. The explanation for such widespread demands for reform lies, partly at least, in the fusing of past and present in nationalist understandings of policing. This chapter builds on the discussion of nationalists' attitudes towards and experiences of policing contained in Chapter 4, by exploring a series of resistance narratives that articulated unofficial or popular memories of policing. These representations of policing highlighted both major 'signal' events as well as more mundane 'everyday' policing issues, and provided a cognitive and affective basis on which criticism of the force was based, and through which demands for reform were articulated and mobilized. The chapter begins with a discussion of the RUC's post-ceasefire efforts to promote its crime prevention and community relations activities, and of the protests this gave rise to. I argue that such protests can best be understood through the linking of minor incidents to major events and, significantly for our purposes here, the past to the present.

## Lollipop protests: Community Affairs policing and the 'charm offensive'

In the aftermath of the 1994 paramilitary ceasefires in Northern Ireland, the RUC's top priority changed from addressing the threat of paramilitary violence to improving police–community relations. An RUC superintendent described the importance attached to this: 'It was the number one issue, the key issue. It was top of the agenda. If you wanted money for community relations activities, you got it. There was nothing that was more important than working on community relations' (interview). During the autumn of 1994 and the spring of 1995, the RUC sought to maximize the opportunities provided by the ceasefires in terms of engaging in a 'normal policing' role. This included distributing crime prevention literature outside supermarkets and holding crime prevention 'information evenings' and other similar activities. The speed and energy with which these measures were implemented was the subject of much comment and, to many observers, the RUC's exuberance in this regard seemed somewhat excessive. According to one NIO official: 'In the early days of the ceasefires, I think they went a little over the top. They were smiling at people they'd arrested the previous day, saying "Have a nice day, missing you already" [laughs]' (interview). A spokesperson for the Catholic education system described it as the police 'blowing their bugle a bit' (interview). Other observers had a more critical view of these activities. Republicans in particular characterized the post-ceasefire community affairs policing initiatives as part of a 'charm offensive', the 'velvet glove' that disguised the RUC's underlying coercive potential. This drama of legitimacy and protest was enacted in a variety of apparently benign policing contexts and in the protests that accompanied them. One of the first events to spark controversy was an RUC crime prevention stand erected outside a supermarket in West Belfast. Sinn Féin claimed this was 'provocative' and a 'stunt', and picketed the event (*Andersonstown News*, 24 September 1994). In another incident, a protest was held when a local priest in the republican Short Strand area of Belfast invited RUC officers to present an 'information evening' on 'crime prevention' measures (*Andersonstown News*, 29 October 1994; *An Phoblacht/Republican News*, 3 November 1994). The most contentious aspects of this debate involved Catholic schools' participation in RUC Community Affairs policing schemes.

Following the 1994 ceasefires, some Catholic schools that previously had declined to cooperate with the RUC now allowed its officers to provide instruction to their pupils. It seems clear, though, that there was no sudden revolution in police contact with schools, and that the increase in school participation in the RUC's programme was probably of a limited order. The major change in these activities was their profile: some schools participated at a higher level, while the secrecy that hitherto had characterized their operation was often dispensed with. In 1992 the RUC was involved in 88 per cent of all schools, rising to 91 per cent the following year, and remaining at that level for 1994 and 1995 (RUC Annual Report for 1994; interview with RUC CA sergeant). It is difficult to measure, however, what exactly is meant by a school's 'participation' in such activities. The one community affairs officer I asked about this was unwilling to clarify precisely what these terms meant, and it appears to cover vastly different levels of involvement, ranging from, as a minimum perhaps, one visit by a plainclothes officer to meet with school staff, to the other extreme in which the pupils participate in police-sponsored school quizzes, ramble schemes and other events, and receive instruction from RUC officers on a range of crime prevention and safety issues.

Whatever the precise level of police contact with Catholic schools, it generated considerable controversy. Protests had been held on various occasions in the months following the ceasefires, but it was in the spring of 1995 that allegations of a charm offensive directed at RUC involvement in Catholic schools gained prominence. That January, an *Andersonstown News* (21 January 1995) story headlined 'RUC Charm Offensive' described visits by RUC officers to various Catholic schools in West Belfast to make presentations on drug use and 'stranger danger'. As other instances of RUC school presentations emerged, Sinn Féin councillor Alex Maskey complained to the Catholic hierarchy involved in school governance, noting that 'Nationalist parents will not allow this force to be paraded through our schools as a normal or acceptable police force' (*Andersonstown News*, 4 February 1995). Terminology of invasiveness was a striking feature of republican criticisms of RUC community affairs' activities. One community worker said the RUC was 'breaking its back it was bending over backwards so far' to become involved in nationalist communities (interview); others spoke of the RUC trying to 'get into' communities. Sinn Féin claimed that the RUC 'has sought to exploit community needs by, for example, *imposing themselves* on schools to deliver "talks" on issues such as [stranger danger and road safety] which are already competently dealt with by less controversial and unacceptable agencies' (1996a: para. 4.2; emphasis added). Some schools were also picketed in February 1995, and several announced that they would pull out of future contacts with the RUC (*Andersonstown News*, 11 and 25 February 1995).

Police officers stressed that this community relations activity 'was not something that was concocted after the ceasefires' (RUC constable). One superintendent reiterated this point: 'The RUC were doing that during the war, it's not just stuff that started with the ceasefires. It wasn't something we started since August 1994, we were always in most schools, or we tried to be in most schools.' While RUC officers highlighted the enthusiasm with which they embraced a civil policing role, they unfailingly described republican protests with a sense of dismay. Officers argued that republicans distorted the benign nature of these policing activities, being so fixated with criticism of the RUC that they blindly placed the children in their own communities at risk by preventing the police from delivering 'road safety' lessons and similar programmes. Road traffic safety was viewed within the RUC as a major means of asserting its commitment to normal policing, and it viewed the Charter Mark awarded to the Traffic Branch in 1996 as evidence of its expertise in this respect (see Chapter 6). It was somewhat ironic therefore that while road safety issues were used as a measure of the RUC's commitment to 'normal policing', these issues also figured prominently in republican protests about post-ceasefire policing activities. Republican protests surrounding the use of police officers as substitutes for absent school traffic wardens – known as 'lollipop' men and women – encapsulated many of the schisms regarding the nature of policing in Northern Ireland. From the perspective of RUC officers, such protests confirmed their view that they were engaged in the provision of a public good, while republicans were merely engaged in its disruption. One Community Affairs inspector described a lollipop protest with incredulity:

> There was one case of a school crossing warden who didn't show up one day and the school called us and asked if we could send someone along to help the kids cross the road. So we provided a stand-in just to help out, and Sinn Féin picketed, *just because we were helping school-children cross the road*! (Interview, original emphasis)

Shaking his head in amazement, another inspector described his shock at these events: 'I mean at the end of the day [if] a car goes down the road and knocks a child down, the car doesn't say: "That's a Roman Catholic child, I will knock that child down; that's a Protestant child, I will not knock that child down" ' (interview).

Such incidents were also viewed within the broad unionist community as symptomatic of republican tenacity, fixated upon criticizing the RUC while oblivious to the benefits arising from the service it provided. One DUP councillor noted the amazement that such protests generated among his constituents:

> After the ceasefire, a Catholic school in the city centre had their lollipop man off sick and they brought in a policeman, and Sinn Féin

picketed this guy, and they had a picket up to say that this was part of the charm offensive, this was the police trying to ingratiate itself into the nationalist community. Now thankfully, most of the Catholic parents didn't look at it like that, and thanked the police for doing it, and the reality of it is if the police hadn't done it, there could have been a child killed because the police didn't do what they'd always offered to do. There was some intransigence in certain sections of the community [that] didn't allow [the school] to take it up, but because of the ceasefire the principal thought we could take advantage of this now. And when he did it, Sinn Féin objected and complained. That was looked at in our community as ludicrous, and yet the Sinn Féiners described that as part of the charm offensive. I think that sums it up. It was some time after the ceasefire, and I remember thinking surely enough time has elapsed now for people, if they ever had any resentment, to say 'Well, this guy's coming and he's seeing our children across the road. What on earth could we have by way of objection to this?'

Among nationalists also, responses to these protests were varied. Some remained sceptical that it was anything other than an RUC public relations exercise, while others noted their support for such policing initiatives. As one young mother from a nationalist area stated: 'I thought it was great, cos you couldn't actually get in to school, I was glad to see them. If I had been there I would have argued with them [the protesters]' (Quoted in Brewer et al. 1997: 154).

The protests also materially interfered with the RUC's efforts to consolidate its role. As one Community Affairs inspector noted: 'we had to back off' (interview). A spokesperson for the Catholic school system met with a senior RUC officer 'and we came to an agreement that the RUC would be a bit more subtle in some cases and in others that they would scale down their activities' (interview). In that sense, republican protests were consistent with what the police viewed as a historical pattern of intimidation to prevent people in nationalist areas developing links with the RUC and thus gaining an appreciation of their commitment to impartial and professional policing (Ryder 2000: 494). As one officer noted: 'Today we called into an old folks home, and we were just chatting with the people there. And as we were leaving one of the people working there said that as soon as we left someone would be rapping on the door asking us what the RUC was doing here' (interview). The Chief Constable also criticized the 'odious practice' of 'pressurising local people in some areas not to engage in police/public consultation' (RUC Annual Report for 1995: 14).

In addition to focusing on intimidation, RUC officers frequently characterized their critics as an impossible audience, whose demands were so excessive that they were incapable of satisfaction from even the most innovative or progressive reforms. This was particularly evident in relation to RUC responses to proposed changes in the police complaints system. In an address to the 1993 PFNI Annual Conference, a speaker cautioned against changing the police complaints system if the sole purpose in doing so was to gain the confidence of the RUC's critics, on the basis that 'that kind of aggrieved public has an insatiable appetite for police humiliation' (*Police Beat*, June 1993: 3). In responding to the 1997 Hayes report, PFNI Chairman Les Rodgers also cautioned against introducing changes 'to please those people who, in practice, are incapable of being satisfied by any investigation no matter how thorough' (speech to the 1997 PFNI Annual Conference). This view extended to a general characterization of republicans as 'anti-RUC' (RUC superintendent) and as 'people who will never change their minds, and Sinn Féin will never accept the RUC. That's just the way they are' (RUC Community Affairs inspector). These explanations – irrationality, intimidation and insatiability – as the dynamic behind much of the reform debate shared a common sub-text. They each implied that there was little need for reform because there was little wrong to begin with. Moreover, this rendered the measures advanced by reform proponents liable to being dismissed out of hand given the dubious motivations attributed to them. This view of republicans and RUC critics as an impossible audience was also reflected in broader circles. As I began an interview with a UUP councillor and prominent member of the Orange Order by explaining that my research concerned 'police–community relations', he asked: 'Do you not think police-community relations is a thing of the mind?' [*You mean some people just decide they won't support the RUC?*] Exactly!'

## Resistance narratives and oppositional discourse

The depiction of police–community relations as 'a thing of the mind' reduces the complexity of these viewpoints to a stereotypical amalgam. Falling back on allegations of irrationality and innate belligerence as explanations for resistance towards the RUC equates the RUC's official discourse with proven fact, and oppositional discourse with unfounded and vexatious allegations. Moreover, to depict criticism of the RUC as inherently unfounded directly challenges the memories of policing around which oppositional discourses are constructed. Importantly, it erases the role that experience – whether based on memories formed from first-hand or mediated through other avenues – plays in moulding and sustaining criticism of the RUC. Oppositional narratives of policing, however, rely heavily on experiential claims to bolster the 'story' of policing contained therein. In the remainder of this chapter, I outline the nature of this oppositional discourse by charting its narrative form in relation to accounts of 'signal' events and everyday policing. Such accounts provide an ontological basis for resistance that taps into and becomes a means of articulating 'popular memories' of policing. These narratives are 'popular' in that they circulate widely and reach a wide audience, and also in so far as they are unofficial in character and relate to constructions of experience that usually are either not recognized within or are actively 'disallowed' by the RUC's official discourse. Resistance narratives that challenge state orthodoxies are often a feature of political transitions (Teitel 2000), and their prominence in these contexts may reflect a redrawing of power relations (Scott 1990).

## Signal events

'Signal events' are a fundamental part of oppositional memory on the RUC. While Innes (2004) uses this term to describe high-profile crimes or other events which lead communities to demand a greater police response, here I use it in reference to a specific set of allegations of police misconduct. These are the major controversies and scandals surrounding the RUC that 'everyone knows about' irrespective of whether or not they were personally present, or for that matter whether the precise nature of these 'events' has even been established (a point to which I return below). These 'watershed' events (Pickering 2002: 67) are key markers in individuals' biographies and they become the fulcra around which experiences of and attitudes towards the security forces come to be understood, structured and articulated. The widespread knowledge of these events is also a means by which individual memory becomes community memory, and vice versa (Matassa 1999). Their symbolism extends far beyond the immediate ramifications of the event. Recounted as part of a broader historical pattern, they provide the parameters within which the significance of everyday events is established.

Narratives about signal events generally have three common strands. First, they are historically grounded in that they generally refer to specific historical events or to a specific temporal point of origin involving allegations or substantiated claims of police misconduct, which are in turn used to explain the development of hostility towards the RUC. Second, they are expressed as part of a litany of what probably remain the major scandals (or unresolved questions) surrounding security force activities in Northern Ireland. Third, these various events are seen as interconnected. The significance of each, therefore, is magnified to the extent that it resonates with other signal events and is recited as part of a larger whole, itself a lens through which to read off the definitive history of policing in Northern Ireland.

*Origins*

A key feature of many oppositional narratives is that their account of policing has a historical origin that serves as the starting point for the subsequent unfolding sequence of events. This contributes to its familiar narrative structure, with the point of origin serving as 'the beginning' of the account. Importantly, this point of origin embeds it within a particular historical context. As such, narratives are not articulated in terms of obscure referents, but instead are structured around events to which people have ready cognitive and cultural access. This may be because the narrators either saw or experienced the events directly, or because older generations or others have related it to them. Certainly the events they speak of have been extensively covered in the media, but individuals are not solely reliant on such conventional sources as many of the key moments to which they refer date from the late 1960s, and so are within easy recollection of individuals present at that time, and have become incorporated into community folklore (Ardoyne Commemoration Project 2002; De Baróid 1999; Matassa 1999).

Probably the clearest example of this is the identification of 1969 as the point when a 'fateful split' (Scarman 1972: 15) developed between Catholics and the RUC. This view was evident in the words of one republican man who stated: 'What brought the whole thing to a head was the civil rights movement in 1969, when the Stormont regime used the police to destroy the nationalist demands for civil rights ...' The designation of 1969 as a crisis point establishes it as the first in a series of events that highlight and, in turn, extend the divisions between the RUC and nationalists, such that it sets the tone for subsequent events and remains the ultimate reference point against which attitudes towards the RUC are framed and assessed:

> If you look at '69, the attitude towards the civil rights marchers, when they were attacked and the RUC stood by and let it happen, and in Derry you had worse again, they just went in and batoned people to death. And then you go back to the Falls [Road], and it was the RUC shot the first people ... just indiscriminate shooting all over ... It's just an ongoing ... I can't tell you any good things about the RUC.

The identification of one set of events – in this case, the policing of the civil rights movement – as *the* turning point in relations between the RUC and the broad Catholic community situates narratives about this topic in terms of a specific time and place. It structures them in a linear storytelling format with this period becoming the point of departure for oppositional readings of policing in Northern Ireland.

*Litany*

The second feature of signal event narratives is that the events to which they refer are part and parcel of the Northern Irish political and historical landscape. The individuals associated with these events have become household names – for example, John Stalker (appointed to conduct an investigation into events surrounding several controversial killings by the security forces, and removed from the investigation in equally controversial circumstances), John Stevens (appointed to investigate allegations of collusion), Samuel Devenny (who died several months after being beaten by RUC officers and from which no prosecutions resulted), Nora McCabe (killed by a plastic bullet fired by an RUC officer in disputed circumstances), Pat Finucane (a lawyer shot dead by loyalists amid allegations of collusion between RUC officers and loyalists). Signal events (or their locations) share a similar 'common knowledge' quality – 'shoot-to-kill', collusion, Castlereagh (an RUC barracks used to interrogate paramilitary suspects), the civil rights movement, Burntollet Bridge and so on. Their significance is reflected in the fact that, in an everyday sense at least, one does not know the history of Northern Ireland until one has learnt about these events.

In support of this point, when an earlier version of this chapter was presented as a seminar in Northern Ireland, a member of the audience wondered whether Nora McCabe was, in fact, still alive, having been blinded rather than killed by the plastic bullet. Other audience members corrected him, pointing out that he was confusing Emma Groves (who *had* been blinded by a plastic bullet) with Nora McCabe. This illustrates both the manner in which such narratives are 'learnt', and the fact that while individuals may confuse specific events, they nevertheless retain a sense of the tone of the overall litany of events. The litany format binds individual events into a larger whole comprising 'more of the same': the narrative format is the conveyer belt along which each event is dispatched until all are cumulatively assembled together to reach the 'complete' understanding of policing in Northern Ireland offered by this oppositional discourse.

*Connections*

The third feature of the 'signal events' narratives – and one that follows on from the previous point – is that the events mentioned in such a litany format are not viewed as discrete or isolated incidents, but rather as part of an interconnected whole. By being seen as part of a larger historical process, their significance is not merely in the immediate ramifications of the event itself, but also in the manner in which it is linked to and sequenced with other events. Thus concerns over police accountability are expressed in terms of the Stalker affair and the killing of Nora McCabe. Each specific event highlights a larger point:

Anything that has happened, if you go back to Stalker, if you go back to any investigation, it's all investigated within the RUC, and there's no people held accountable ... There's nobody made accountable for ... if you take Nora McCabe,[1] who was killed by a plastic bullet on the Falls Road ... the local inspector who was promoted ... He said there was a riot going on in the area, and there was no riot. That's not just the ordinary constable on the ground ... it's their chiefs and their inspectors and others. So again, where can you get the trust, or where can you build on the trust?

In the following narrative, events in 1969 provide the basis for an account that includes each element of signal events narratives outlined above. It begins by describing the negative impact of police behaviour towards civil rights protesters at that time:

... that began the alienation, a real bitter alienation, of nationalists and the RUC. And that was accentuated by the riots on the Falls in 1969, loyalist mobs invaded the Falls and were pushed back, and the RUC came and machine-gunned 4 or 5 people to death. They literally led the campaign in, and that break was, I would think, it was irreconcilable. There are too many lingering memories of what took place in '69 for the present RUC in its structure to remain ... [When the RUC resumed control of security in the mid–70s] that antagonism with all that whole baggage that the RUC were carrying from past legacies was brought with it: Castlereagh, interrogation centres, shoot-to-kill, a whole raft of really serious problems.

These 'past legacies' placed together as a 'whole raft of really serious problems' illustrate the cumulative impact arising from the constitution of these events as elements of an interconnected whole rather than as a set of discrete independent events. Each contributes 'added value' to the others. Below I illustrate the means by which this litany can be mobilized to explain more recent events (in this case events surrounding an Orange Order parade at Drumcree in 1996), but first I consider narratives relating to everyday policing.

## Everyday policing

The second dimension of local memory to be examined comprises a set of events that, when compared to the signal events discussed above, are more mundane – not in their impact, but in the specifically local character of their reputation and their associated ripple effects. These narratives are not necessarily reported in the national media or exhaustively described in history books, but they become part of community understandings nevertheless. They become accepted as part of a locally contingent reality: as the way that things happen, have happened or – importantly – may happen, in a given locality. Three features characterize these accounts of everyday policing. First, there is a specifically local quality attached to these events. Second, they reflect the prevalence of negative experiences of policing. Third, the unusual character of some everyday policing narratives lends a plausibility to what would otherwise be viewed as impossible and hence dismissed as fantasy, leading to the routinization of the unprecedented.

## Local

The first dimension of 'everyday policing' narratives is that the events they describe are considered specifically or, at least, primarily as 'local' events, being generally situated within a precise geographical boundary and of direct relevance only to the residents of that area or those who are otherwise familiar with it. As such, they become part of a specifically local consciousness. For residents in these areas, these events either happened to them first-hand, to someone they know or in a place they know well and perhaps regularly frequent. These events may come to be associated with precise locations (as McVeigh 1994 suggests happened in relation to 'sites of harassment'). The immediate quality of such an event implies that while it may have happened to another individual, it could nevertheless have happened to anyone else in that area, oneself included. If one's very presence in a particular area, or one's status as a member of a specific community (such as a resident in a largely republican area), leaves one liable to be harassed, then the experience of the individual and the community are seen as intertwined (McVeigh 1994; Matassa 1999: 189–90). One interviewee in West Belfast suggested that experiences of routine police misconduct formed part of the taken-for-granted lore of many communities. Whether experienced at first- or second-hand, harassment was considered a persistent reflection of RUC attitudes towards the community, and thus implicated in negative community attitudes towards the RUC:

> Basically, people form their opinions of the RUC through experience. Communities here are closely knit ... You don't have to be beaten up by the RUC yourself to have a negative opinion of them. And in closely knit communities, the harassment of one becomes the intimidation of the community. And the community experience is widespread enough for most people to have serious concerns about them. (Youth worker)

Much of the everyday occurrences and experiences of policing involve allegations of harassment by RUC officers, particularly of young people. This is not solely a feature of republican and nationalist areas, as research suggests high levels of hostility towards the RUC among Protestant youth also (Ellison 2001; Weitzer 1995). Youth workers suggested that police harassment was simply 'a part of life here' (McVeigh 1994):

> I'm just an ordinary tenant. Maybe I sound very political, but I've been working with young people here over the years, and a lot of young people have been bullied by the RUC, they've been accused by the RUC, they've been used, literally used, by the RUC to become informers. I worked with a group of young offenders there for the last 12 years, and anytime we were going on a weekend trip, a day trip, the Edinburgh Awards schemes, they literally *knew*, they stopped us at Lisburn, pulled all the canoes apart, took us apart, knew us all by name, before we got there, and when we got to the border checkpoint, we knew they would pull us in again, and we were sort of complaining, and they said this is just a spot check . . . So how do you get these young people who have been used, abused and bullied by them to accept them? I dunno. (Youth worker)

A consequence of this immediate, local quality is that residents in an area generally learn about such events either through first-hand experience or from someone else in the locality. The fact that this knowledge is likely to be relayed through local and trusted sources – such as networks of family, friends and/or neighbours – means that accounts of these events become accepted as truth. The significance of such narratives rests not with their proven veracity, but with their accepted veracity. The trust that is invested in these accounts is pointedly contrasted with the deception that is attributed to official accounts of these events.

## Prevalence

One of the crucial aspects of 'everyday policing' is quite simply the prevalence of negative experiences of the security forces. This arises partly through the immense scale of security force activity in Northern Ireland, particularly during the 1970s and 1980s when army involvement in security operations was much more readily apparent and abrasive contact between nationalists and the security forces was routine (Burton 1978; Ó Dochartaigh 2005; Sluka 1989; Taylor 2001). As discussed in Chapter 4, nationalists' experiences of security policing, house-searches, questioning and harassment came to be seen as part of an accepted reality. The ready availability of examples of perceived misconduct endowed them with the quality of common, everyday events. This prevalence ensured that while they were routine in terms of frequency, they were enormously significant in terms of impact. Denis Faul, a Catholic cleric who in the post-ceasefire period was frequently depicted as a voice of moderation (Mulcahy and Ellison 2001: 391–2), noted the prevalence of victimization among nationalists:

The majority of nationalists would say things are okay, they're not the impartial police force we want, but they're okay in non-political matters . . . Too many skeletons in the cupboard . . . No RUC man served a day in jail since 1968 for killing people or torturing people, thousands of people. Not one of them served a day in jail . . . You have a major problem there, that's a big problem with acceptance. [*Is the past the major block when it comes to accepting the RUC?*] It would be. Nearly every Catholic family in Northern Ireland has suffered at the hands of the RUC, certainly two-thirds of them have. Especially poor people, Ormeau Road, Ardoyne, poor villages, they hold them up on the road for four hours, they search them, they insult them, sectarian names, and if you say a word then you're arrested and charged with obstruction. That's still going on, all that kind of carry on. Say a word and you're charged with obstruction and assault. They perjure them into jail. It's at a small level at the moment compared to what it used to be. And all the men who put down false evidence, and torturing, and the supergrasses,[2] thousands in jail. (Interview)

## Routinization of the unprecedented

The third dimension of these narratives amounts to the 'routinization of the unprecedented'. This involves experiences that are in some respects so unexpected and bizarre – even fantastical – that they usher in new parameters for what constitutes 'normality'. In this way uncommon, and perhaps hitherto implausible, events become the template for interpreting and anticipating police activity. Some accounts elaborating this point relate to incidents that can only be described as surreal, and often involve allegations surrounding surveillance operations conducted by various branches of the security forces (see, for example, Faligot 1983; Taylor 2001). In one instance, Murray (1990: 207) describes the discovery of one military observation post in the yard of the home of relatives of Paul Duffy, an IRA member shot dead by SAS officers a year earlier:

They concealed themselves under a large old van which the Forbes used for growing mushrooms. The wheels had been removed and it made a handy shed. The SAS were discovered by accident. A scrapman called at the house and when Gerry went searching for scraps of iron on the yard his eye fell on a man's finger with a ring on it when he looked under the van. He raised the alarm. A crowd gathered. The family rang the RUC and the local priest. The people gathered round the van, then called on those concealed to come out. It seemed hardly possible but three men with blackened faces emerged from under the van. They reversed on foot into a nearby field away from the people until they reached a helicopter which they must have called for by radio.

Another incident occurred in West Belfast in December 1994. As a man walked along the waste ground at the end of the street in which he lived, he noticed an object in the ditch. He approached it and saw that it was some form of electronic device. A light on it started to flash. He called his neighbours and some of them gathered around it. Minutes later, a convoy of RUC and army Land-Rovers arrived. They sealed off the street, ordered residents back into their houses, removed the equipment, and left. Seeking more information, an *Andersonstown News* reporter contacted the RUC, but could only report that: 'This week the RUC said they had no knowledge of any such incident' (*Andersonstown News*, 10 December 1994: 20). In this event no one died, no one was injured, no one was imprisoned. In terms of such criteria it was, literally, a non-event. Moreover, it is certainly possible that no conspiracy to beguile the public was involved here – the officer may simply have just started work, or may not have been fully briefed (Special Branch operations were often conducted without the knowledge of the local police). What is significant here, though, is less the official account of the event – the various possibilities which might explain the officer's lack of knowledge of the event are conspicuous by their absence – than the locally prescribed one. Within an oppositional discourse on the RUC, which constitutes the locally understood frame of reference among nationalists and republicans in the area, what the story describes needs no further elaboration as it is clear how policing operates: furtively, deceitfully and with an underlying menace. The significance of this minor event materializes only within a historical framework in which the coercive potential of the state is embodied in such seemingly frivolous – albeit bizarre – accounts. Ironically, one hugely significant consequence of the routinization of the unprecedented is that it helps bolster the credibility of claims about a whole array of other more mundane events. After all, if one's boundaries of reality had already been stretched to include the surveillance practices described above, it was hardly extending them further to believe that police harassment was a routine event.

## The coherence and salience of resistance narratives

While these various narratives may be discussed as discrete issues for analytical purposes, their full significance arises from their consolidation within a broader, more cohesive framework. In so far as they express a unified history of experience, the resonance of each set of narratives extends beyond the immediate events to which they refer. Their impact is in the manner in which they enable connections to be made between major and minor events, national and local ones, and, crucially, between the past and the present. Such processes were also evident in relation to the issue of road safety, discussed earlier in terms of the lollipop protests. The historical emphasis that the RUC had placed on the high rate of traffic accidents and fatalities in Northern Ireland served to highlight the view that it was a normal society confronted with the normal dangers of modern living (of which traffic accidents have become emblematic; see Garland 1996), and thus requiring the same normal policing as found in other normal societies. In that sense, traffic policing and road safety had become an icon of normalcy within the force (see Chapter 6). While RUC officers explained their lollipop policing duties in terms of the self evidently benign nature of that discrete act, republican critics did just the opposite, trying to embed these events within a broader horizon of understanding. One instance of this occurred at an anti-RUC rally held in the largely nationalist village of Pomeroy in March 1995 (*An Phoblacht/Republican News*, 9 March 1995: 16). The protest included the staging of a short satirical drama whose cast included RUC constables 'Collusion', 'Shoot-to-Kill', 'Token Taig' (a derogatory term for Catholics) and 'Ever So Nice'. Constable 'Ever So Nice' was pictured holding a 'Children Crossing' lollipop sign, and his role in the drama was to help nationalist children cross the road as he simultaneously held them by the throat. In that context, the lollipop incidents that provoked such dismay among RUC officers were explicitly linked to broader questions about scandals implicating the RUC in collusion with loyalist paramilitaries and unlawful killings of paramilitary suspects. Standing in for absent lollipop men and women would always be vulnerable to such challenges while events like these remained unresolved.

### Familiar troubles: Drumcree as signal event[3]

During the 1995 marching season, the RUC became embroiled in a lengthy series of confrontations arising from loyalist parades passing through predominantly nationalist areas. Allegations of serious RUC misconduct during these events elevated concerns over public order policing to the fore (Pat Finucane Centre 1995). The ending of the IRA's ceasefire in February 1996 effectively forced a return to the security measures that had formerly characterized the RUC, but by then the damage done by the controversies associated with the 1995 marching season was considerable. Far worse was to follow during the 1996 marching season.

On 7 July 1996 the RUC blocked an Orange Order parade going from Drumcree church in Portadown down the predominantly nationalist Garvaghy Road. Several thousand marchers engaged in a stand-off with the security forces. As the numbers of marchers continued to swell, disorder spread through other parts of Northern Ireland. A Catholic taxi-driver in Portadown was killed by the Loyalist Volunteer Force (a loyalist paramilitary organization opposed to the peace process); road-blocks were set up throughout Northern Ireland, blocking the international airport, Larne port and many of the major thoroughfares. On 11 July, facing the prospect of many more loyalist protesters joining the stand-off as the weekend approached, and with no resolution in sight, the Chief Constable reversed his earlier decision to block the parade, effectively capitulating to the threat of force posed by the loyalist protesters. The RUC moved into the Garvaghy Road area and forcibly removed nationalist protesters blocking the road. On another highly contentious parade route, the RUC imposed what amounted to a 24-hour blockade of residents in the nationalist Lower Ormeau to allow an Orange Order parade to march through the area into Belfast city centre.

During the Drumcree stand-off, RUC officers were subjected to severe abuse by loyalists. This included the names and addresses of specific officers being broadcast over a public address system, and intimidation of officers' families (the Police Federation of Northern Ireland reported that 42 officers' families had been forced to move house due to intimidation). However, the violent manner in which nationalist pro-testers were cleared from the Garvaghy Road was in stark contrast to the relatively restrained manner in which RUC officers had dealt with many loyalist roadblocks, barricades and demonstrations. Many nationalist areas were effectively cut off for a time by these roadblocks, yet in the vast majority of cases the RUC failed to intervene, even in cases where the number of protesters was minimal. Nationalists throughout Northern Ireland (and many unionists also) were appalled and outraged by the RUC's reversal of its earlier decision at Drumcree, and by the enormous disparity in treatment of both communities. Widespread violence in nationalist areas throughout Northern Ireland erupted immediately, at a level not seen in Northern Ireland for years. A republican protester was killed in Derry after being run over by an army vehicle. In the week prior to 14 July, the RUC and Army fired 6,002 plastic baton rounds (the highest number fired since the 1981 hunger strike), 662 of them at loyalists during the Drumcree stand-off, and 5,340 during the subsequent nationalist protests. The Chief Constable explained the disparity in the numbers fired by claiming that officers were merely responding to the respective number of petrol bombs and other missiles thrown at them: nationalists threw far more petrol bombs at the RUC, so the RUC fired more plastic bullets at them. This logic breaks down when one considers that the RUC appeared perfectly willing to 'take on' (Ó Dochartaigh 1997: 317) nationalists but blatantly shied away from engaging in similar confrontation with loyalists (although some unionist commentators complained that the RUC had used excessive force towards the Orange protesters at Drumcree; see Lucy 1996). Had the RUC proved willing to confront loyalists over the four and a half days of protest preceding the Drumcree turnaround with the same vigour with which it had confronted nationalist protests over the years – and the same forcefulness with which it cleared nationalist protesters from the road – the RUC's claims of impartial treatment of each community might carry more credence. They certainly seem at odds with Chief Constable Annesley's statement some years previously:

If someone puts up a barricade across the road, we drive an army vehicle through it and we would take the ground. We would take it from the air, we would take it from the sides, but we would take it. We could not give an inch, because if you give an inch, they will take a mile. (*Police*, November 1991: 26)

The impact of Drumcree was profound. Not only did it implicate the RUC in familiar troubles and controversies surrounding public order, excessive force and use of plastic bullets, but it re-immersed it in debates on its respective relationships with the communities in Northern Ireland, specifically debates about partiality and impartiality that the RUC had striven hard to put behind it. In no uncertain terms, it raised the spectre of a police force that, after more than two decades of professionalization, and long after it had vocally declared its impartiality specifically through its willingness to confront loyalist protests against the 1985 Anglo-Irish Agreement, still proved unable to treat both communities equally. In terms of its community affairs policing, Drumcree was a massive setback. The Mediation Network withdrew from the RUC's Community Awareness Training Programme given to new recruits, claiming that senior officers had breached assurances with local residents after the 1995 march that no further marches would be allowed down the Garavaghy Road without the consent of the residents. Within the educational sector, there was a similar acknowledgement that the landscape of police–community relations had been badly shaken by these events: 'Drumcree led to a hardness in people,' one educator said, 'it was a watershed of sorts':

After Drumcree there was just a reaction, just a feeling people had. It wasn't orchestrated, it was a gut reaction, a feeling. Before Drumcree, Sinn Féin were orchestrating a lot of the protests against the RUC being involved in school activities, but after Drumcree, a lot of people just turned away from the RUC. I don't know that that is irreversible, but it was quite a change from the way things were prior to the Summer. Schools were afraid to involve the RUC because of the fear of causing some reaction. Certainly some people's views changed after Drumcree. We found that school boards of governors looked much more carefully at bringing the police in. Some of them pulled out, some of them said 'The time's not right', but usually that euphemism was them just being diplomatic, a more polite way of saying 'No, not after Drumcree.'

Drumcree also undermined the massive efforts towards the consolidation of a civil policing role that had characterized the RUC's post-ceasefire activities. While the ending of the IRA ceasefire in February 1996 and the restoration of security measures in response to this was a major setback to the development of police–community relations, officers' comments specifically highlighted the impact of Drumcree:

I think we were going from strength to strength. I think what happened was you had the Sinn Féin element with good propaganda, and Drumcree then was handed to them on a plate, and really things deteriorated from there. Sadly, I would have to admit that maybe some would say that 'Superintendent, you're being a bit naive, it was all a bit superficial anyway.' Okay, I'll maybe accept a bit of that, but you've got to start somewhere. (RUC superintendent)

Although the official description of Drumcree was that it was 'a setback for the rule of law' (RUC Annual Report for 1996: 7), the Chief Constable sought to extricate some benefit from the potentially devastating consequences of those events:

The events of 1996 showed clearly the depth of bigotry and sectarianism which, sadly, still besest us here. People who witnessed the horror on our streets and the naked danger of our situation should perhaps ask themselves, 'Where would we have been, where would we be now, without the Royal Ulster Constabulary?' (RUC Annual Report for 1996: 7)

To nationalists and republicans, the key lesson to be learnt from these events was neither the persistence of sectarianism nor the deliverance from anarchy that the RUC provided: quite the opposite. The history lesson it provided was that policing had not been resolved despite the RUC's extensive programme of professionalization, and that no matter what difficulties were posed by unionists and loyalists, the RUC's 'symbolic assailant' (Skolnick 1993) was to be found within the national-ist community. The RUC's decision was forced upon it by the imminent threat of sufficiently large numbers of Orange protesters that it would be impossible to stop by any means other than live fire. However, this merely reinforced the nationalist view that, through sheer weight of numbers, unionists could overturn police policy. In effect, Drumcree 'provided *revision classes* on lessons which had been learnt in 1968 and 1969 but which had been obscured by the shooting war of twenty-five years': that the RUC had 'utterly different relationships' with nationalists and unionists, and that police actions could be a catalyst for conflict (Ó Dochartaigh 1997: 316; emphasis added).

The U-turn at Drumcree was viewed within the RUC as one bad decision forced upon it, as a necessary step to prevent greater bloodshed (although many RUC officers were opposed to the initial decision to block the parade). Among nationalists and republicans, however, it meshed with a larger mosaic of experience. It epitomized what many republicans had claimed all along, and what many nationalists hoped had been consigned to history. 'Drumcree' became shorthand for a whole raft of other events, and for the frequent claim that policing in 1996 still resembled policing in 1969. Few things could have so acutely represented the difficulties surrounding policing in Northern Ireland, and been so damaging to relations between the RUC and nationalists.

## Conclusion

The protests against community affairs policing during the ceasefires seem absurd when placed within the framework of the RUC's official discourse. However, when understood in terms of the resistance narratives discussed above, such apparently benign practices as instruct-ing school children in road safety assume a broader significance. Among republican and nationalist adherents to this oppositional discourse, such events represent the contemporary embodiment of history, as each current event, minor or not, contains traces of past scandals and oppression. What is remembered is precisely what is so absent from official discourse. Nationalist criticism of the RUC was often articulated in relation to such relatively unnoticed events as harassment, which failed to find an audience in other communities,[4] or in the national media. Among nationalists and republicans, however, these concerns became a means of situating the RUC within an everyday frame of understanding. The scandals surrounding collusion and other events were merely extreme manifestations of the accepted reality of policing; they were everyday occurrences writ large.

## Notes

1 In 1981 Nora McCabe died after being struck by a plastic bullet. RUC officers in the area claimed that plastic bullets had been fired as Police Land-Rovers came under attack from a group of 70–80 rioting youths, and categorically denied that any bullets had been fired into Linden Street, where McCabe had been struck. However, television footage of the incident showed a bullet being fired from a Land-Rover which had stopped at the entrance to Linden Street. There was no riot in progress. Chief Superintendent Crutchley, who at the time was the RUC officer in charge of West Belfast, was in command of the Land-Rover from which the plastic bullet was fired. No officers were prosecuted or disciplined as a result of this incident. Nora McCabe's husband bought a civil action against the RUC which paid him 'substantial damages' in an out-of-court settlement. Crutchley was later promoted to Assistant Chief Constable (Jennings 1990b: 136–8; see also www.relativesforjustice.com/victims/nora_mccabe.htm).

2 'Supergrasses', or 'converted terrorists' as they were officially known, were paramilitaries on whose evidence the RUC relied – largely in the early 1980s – to charge large numbers of people with paramilitary-related offences. The practice was subsequently discontinued due to concerns over the reliability of the evidence involved, particularly following a number of supergrass-based convictions being overturned (Greer 1994).

3 For further discussion of events at Drumcree, see Baxter (2001), CAJ (1996) and Ryder and Kearney (2002).

4 One minor, but emblematic, example of this occurred in 1996 when, during a BBC radio interview, the then Irish President Mary Robinson observed that:

> One of the most awful things in those 25 years was people began to talk about an acceptable level of political violence; an acceptable level of terrorism and killing; an acceptable level of young people being constantly stopped because they came from Catholic backgrounds, put up against the side of a police car, searched, undermined in themselves simply because of their religion and their background and where they lived.

Robinson's comments drew a hostile reaction. Ken Maginnis MP, security spokesperson for the UUP, said that this allowed 'her prejudice to show through' in a way that 'offends' those who have suffered from the violence of republican paramilitaries. A PFNI spokesperson stated that 'the police acted impartially at all times' (*Sunday Times*, 9 June 1996).

# Part IV
# Police reform and conflict resolution

# Chapter 8

# A New Beginning? The Patten Report on policing in Northern Ireland

The Report of the Independent Commission on Policing, known generally as the Patten Report, formed a key component of the Northern Ireland peace process. Established under the terms of the 1998 Belfast Agreement, the Commission sought to provide a template that would resolve the policing question in Northern Ireland. Given the significance of the report, this chapter provides a detailed analysis of its context, content and reception. I begin by considering its origins in the context of the 1998 Belfast Agreement. I then examine the report's orientation and key recommendations, in particular its concern with human rights issues and with establishing mechanisms to optimize 'policing with the community'. Finally, I consider the reception of the report and provide an assessment of its overall approach.

## The Independent Commission on Policing

The paramilitary ceasefires of 1994 emerged from political developments and negotiations which could be traced back, in particular, to dialogue between John Hume (former SDLP leader) and Gerry Adams (Sinn Féin president) in the late 1980s, with other strands of this process including communication between the IRA and the British government. The 1993 Downing Street Declaration outlined key dimensions of the British and Irish governments' positions on a settlement, while the paramilitary ceasefires of the following year provided the context within which negotiations were held. While the public mood following the ceasefires was often euphoric, the uncertainty of the process brought with it considerable potential for conflict. Stalled political negotiations, an impasse over decommissioning, the persistence of paramilitary punishments, the ending of the IRA's ceasefire in February 1996 (it was renewed in July 1997), ongoing disputes over loyalist parades and a failure to resolve the issue of policing in particular, all ensured that the fragile and complex peace process was fraught to its core. Nevertheless, negotiations continued, and in 1998 these culminated in the 1998 Belfast Agreement, known generally as the Good Friday Agreement (GFA).

This agreement was proposed as a comprehensive settlement to the Northern Ireland conflict. It involved the establishment of a power-sharing executive and north-south institutions, and constitutional changes to reflect the principles of the agreement. The GFA also institutionalized the principles of 'consent' – that no constitutional changes to the status of Northern Ireland could occur without the consent of its population – and of 'parity of esteem' – requiring that the identities of unionism and nationalism would be equally recognized in the creation of institutions which could command the support of all sections of society.[1] The agreement was ratified by simultaneous referenda held in the North and South of Ireland, being carried by 94 per cent of the electorate in the Irish Republic and by 71 per cent in Northern Ireland. In Northern Ireland, however, there were considerable differences in levels of support for the agreement among unionists and nationalists. Whereas polls indicated that nationalists overwhelmingly supported the agreement, only a slim majority of unionists voted in favour of it. The fact that such a sizeable proportion of unionists opposed the agreement would continue to haunt its implementation.[2]

Despite the far-reaching nature of the 1998 Belfast Agreement, the negotiations were unable to yield agreement on policing, and instead an Independent Commission on Policing (ICP) was established to bring forward proposals for future policing arrangements. The commission's specific mandate was to make recommendations with a view to ensuring that 'Northern Ireland has a police service that can enjoy widespread support from, and is seen as an integral part of, the community as a whole' (ICP 1999: 123). This decision to refer the matter to an external body would have serious implications for the subsequent reception of the report, as the political parties in Northern Ireland had no necessary investment in it. These difficulties were compounded by the fact that the DUP, which in 2003 overtook the UUP as the largest unionist party, had refused to participate in the negotiations that yielded the agreement. As such, the ICP – however compelling its findings might be – was both potential resolution to *and* symptom of the difficulties involved.

While the establishment of the ICP relieved the GFA negotiators from assuming direct responsibility for the policing measures that would emerge, the prospect of a wide-ranging commission on policing was itself controversial (McGarry 2004), and it caused considerable alarm in some quarters. Shortly after the Belfast Agreement was reached, the staunchly pro-unionist newspaper the *Daily Telegraph* published an interview with the RUC Chief Constable, Ronnie Flanagan (22 April 1998). Carrying a front-page headline, 'Don't weaken us, says RUC chief', the interview amounted to 'an impassioned plea for his force to be preserved'. Flanagan said that he was 'confident that the independent commission into the RUC's future would conclude that it was the finest police force in the world'. In addition to this interview, the *Daily Telegraph*'s other coverage of the RUC in that issue included a double page spread describing 'the human cost of the RUC's fight against terror'. This listed every RUC officer killed during the conflict, with accompanying photos of almost all of them, as well as an interview with the widow of one RUC officer killed by the IRA. Such were the flesh and blood issues with which the commission was confronted as it deliberated.

Chaired by Chris Patten (an experienced political figure who had served as Minister of State for Northern Ireland, Chairperson of the Conservative Party and, most recently, as the last British Governor of Hong Kong, overseeing the transfer of power from Britain to China), the membership of the commission comprised individuals drawn from Northern Ireland and elsewhere, and with expertise in policing and criminal justice as well as with public sector management generally. The local representatives were: Maurice Hayes (former ombudsman for Northern Ireland, and author of the 1997 Hayes Report on police complaints) and Peter Smith, a senior barrister. The other members were: Clifford Shearing, an academic specializing in policing, transitional justice and governance; Gerald Lynch, president of John Jay College of Criminal Justice in New York; Kathleen O'Toole, previously director of Public Safety for Massachusetts; Sir John Smith, a former deputy commissioner of the London Metropolitan Police and a former Inspector of Constabulary; and Lucy Woods, former Chief Executive for British Telecom in Northern Ireland.

Following its establishment in June 1998, the commission embarked on an extensive consultation process. On the issue of policing, Northern Ireland had not yet reached the point of consultation-fatigue. Scores of organizations wrote new policy documents or updated existing ones, yielding a 'breadth of political engagement' in policing that 'was previously unheard of' (Beirne 2001: 315). The ICP commissioned surveys of public opinion, held focus groups, met privately with individuals and groups, invited written submissions from the public (of which they received 2,500) and visited a number of other jurisdictions to assess policing arrangements there. A series of public meetings were also held which attracted 10,000 people in total and at which approximately 1,000 people spoke. The tone of the public meetings was often highly charged and deeply emotional. As the report noted: 'During the course of our public meetings, the Commission heard many harrowing stories from individuals about their experiences of violence in the last 30 years. We were not established as a truth and reconciliation commission, yet we found ourselves inevitably hearing the sort of stories that such a commission would be told' (Patten 1999a: 9). In late September 1999, giving evidence to the US House of Representatives Subcommittee on International Operations and Human Rights, Patten described the context in which some meetings were held:

> I can remember a meeting in a little village cinema in Kilkeel, a fishing village in the shadow of the Mournes. Protestant fishing fleet, Catholic farmers in the hinterland. We had a noisy and quite a good meeting. At the end of it, I made the sort of speech that we all can make terribly well as politicians about reconciliation and healing and hope. At the end of it, after I had finished, to my consternation I saw a little lady at the back of the cinema getting up to say something. I sat down rather nervously. She said, 'Well, Mr Patten, I have heard what you say about reconciliation and I voted yes in the referendum campaign, but I hope you will realize how much more difficult that is for us here than it is for you, coming from London. That man there murdered my son,' and it was true. On both sides of the community, that is the reality in Northern Ireland. Two stories, two sets of pain, two sets of anguish.
>
> We had an evening which began on the Garvaghy Road. I remember Robert Hamill's sister talking to us about his murder, and the meeting was chaired with considerable integrity and skill, difficult meeting by Rosemary Nelson. We then went down the road to Craigavon, and we had four police widows, one after another, telling us their stories, ending with Mrs Graham whose husband had the back of his head shot off, a community policeman, in 1997. Mrs Graham finished her remarks by saying, 'You know, my husband wasn't a Catholic, but he didn't regard himself as a Protestant. He tried to behave like a Christian.' I have to say that I went back from those two meetings that night and had the largest drink I have ever had in my life. (Patten 1999b)

Another commission member described a meeting at which an elderly man outlined the circumstances in which his son was shot dead, including a graphic account of the blood splattered across the room and other consequences of the shooting. Yet after the meeting, when the commission member approached him to express his condolences, 'all he would talk about was sports'. It was, the commission member recalled, as if the consultations were 'cathartic', providing an outlet for grief and rage that was previously unarticulated or had no suitable avenue for expression. Such raw encounters over such consequential matters were inevitably draining to witness and subsequently draw recommendations from, although they did 'encapsulate' for the commission 'the importance of the work [they] were asked to do (ICP 1999: 9). Small wonder that Patten (1999c), when launching the report, remarked that 'This is the most difficult and gruelling job I have ever done'.

## The Patten Report: approach and key recommendations

The title of the Patten Report – *A New Beginning* – highlighted the scope of the Commission's inquiry. In seeking to establish a framework that would resolve the policing question in Northern Ireland, Patten and his colleagues highlighted the manner in which difficulties surrounding policing were intrinsically linked with issues of state. As they put it:

> Policing has been contentious, victim and participant in past tragedies, precisely because the polity has been so contentious. The consent required right across the community in any liberal democracy for effective policing has been absent. In contested space, the role of those charged with keeping the peace has been contested . . . they have been identified by one section of the population not primarily as upholders of the law but as defenders of the state, and the nature of the state itself has remained the central issue of political argument . . . In one political language they are the custodians of nationhood. In its rhetorical opposite they are the symbols of oppression. Policing therefore goes right to the heart of the sense of security and identity of both communities . . . (Patten 1999a: 2)

In identifying structures which could attract the support of all sections of the public, the commission posed five tests that any new arrangements should satisfy: whether it would 'promote effective and efficient policing'; deliver 'fair and impartial policing, free from partisan control'; 'provide for accountability, both to the law and to the community'; 'make the police more representative of the community they serve'; and 'protect and vindicate the human rights and human dignity of all?' (p. 6). In all, the report made 175 recommendations, but equally significant are the principles underpinning the Commission's broad approach. This is particularly evident in relation to the two themes that drive the report's analysis: human rights, and the relationship between the police and the public.

## Human rights

Throughout the report, the authors stress that their recommendations should serve as a template for the 'protection and vindication of the human rights of all'. To that end, the report recommended the introduction of 'a comprehensive programme of action to focus policing in Northern Ireland on a human rights-based approach.' The recommendations to reflect this explicit human rights approach included a new oath of office, a new code of ethics, increased training in human rights[3] (including updating as necessary) as well as the full integration of human rights throughout the training curriculum. As the report noted: 'such an approach goes beyond a series of specific actions. It is more a matter of the philosophy, and should inspire everything that a police service does. It should be seen as *the core of this report*' (p. 20; emphasis added).

## Policing with the community

Concerning the relationship between the police and the public, the Patten Report recognized the contested environment of policing in Northern Ireland. The approach it took, however, was not to call for the communities of Northern Ireland to 'get in line' with the expectations of the police or the demands of government; rather, it proposed a 'genuine' partnership between police and community. As the report noted: 'It is not so much that the police need support and consent, but rather that policing is a matter for the whole community, not something that the community leaves to the police to do. Policing should be a collective community responsibility: a partnership for community safety' (p. 8).

By focusing on 'policing' rather than 'the police', the Commission sought to promote a broad-based vision of how safety would be ensured, one that extended beyond the boundaries of traditional police-centred activity and provided scope for consideration of new partnerships and networks, of which the public police would be only one part (see also Shearing 2001, 2000; Kempa and Shearing 2002). Even in so far as police activity was concerned, the report stated that 'policing with the community should be the core function of the police service and the core function of every police station' (p. 43). Moreover, responsibility for policing should be devolved to police district commanders as much as possible, and these commanders should have 'fully devolved authority over the deployment of personnel within their command, devolved budgets, authority to purchase a range of goods and services, and to finance local policing initiatives' (pp. 58–9). Additionally, 'every neighbourhood (or rural area) should have a dedicated policing team with lead responsibility for policing its area' (p. 43). These neighbourhood policing teams should be 'empowered to determine their own local priorities and set their own objectives, within the overall Annual Policing Plan and in consultation with community representatives'. The emphasis would be on foot patrols, with all officers trained in problem-solving techniques and 'appraised as to their performance in doing so' (p. 45). Police training was to be overhauled to inculcate this new emphasis on policing with the community.

These twin orientations gave rise to a broad programme of further recommendations that covered a wide range of issues, including accountability mechanisms, organization and structure, composition and recruitment, and symbolism of the police.

## Accountability

In terms of new policing institutions, the report's recommendations concerning accountability were the most significant. First, the report proposed that 'everything should be available for public scrutiny unless it is in the public interest – not the police interest – to hold it back' (p 36). Second, the report expressed dissatisfaction with the manner in which the doctrine of operational independence inhibited police disclosure of the rationale for its actions. It suggested that this doctrine be replaced by one of *operational responsibility* (pp. 32–3), which maintained the independent quality of its predecessor, but supplemented this by requiring the police to explain their decisions and thus take responsibility for their actions in doing so.

In terms of specific recommendations, the report proposed the establishment of several new institutions. First, it called for a 'Policing Board' to replace the Police Authority for Northern Ireland, the primary function of which would be 'to hold the Chief Constable and the police service publicly to account' (p. 28). The report was critical of PANI's narrow understanding of its responsibilities, observing that the relationship between the police and PANI was more akin to 'that between executive collaborators rather than one between a service provider and a regulator' (p. 24). Unlike PANI whose membership was entirely appointed by the Secretary of State, the Board would comprise a combination of elected and non-elected members. Ten members would be elected members of the Northern Ireland Assembly (allocated to parties on the same d'Hondt basis used to appoint the assembly's executive), while a further nine 'independent members' would be drawn from a variety of fields with a view to being representative of the community as a whole.

The report noted the limited powers available to PANI and the failure of government and the Chief Constable to take it seriously, and it was adamant that the Board should be more than a silent partner in the delivery and regulation of policing. The report recommended that the Board should be able to set medium-term objectives and priorities (over a 3–5 year basis), that these should be adopted in a policing strategy over a similar timeframe, and that it should also adopt an Annual Policing Plan on the basis of these. The Board would also have responsibility for negotiating the annual budget with government, allocating it to the Chief Constable, and then monitoring 'police performance against the Annual Policing Plan and the 3–5 year strategy' (pp. 28–9). The Board would also have 'the power to require the Chief Constable to report on any issue pertaining to the performance of his functions or those of the police service', an obligation which 'should extend to explaining operational decisions'. The Board would also have the power 'to follow up on any report from the Chief Constable by initiating an inquiry into any aspect of the police service or police conduct' (p. 33). The thrust of the commission's approach was also evident in its 'deliberate' choice of 'policing' rather than 'police' in its title: 'We see the role of the new body going beyond supervision of the police service itself, extending to the wider issues of policing and the contributions that people and organizations other than the police can make towards public safety' (p. 29). Accordingly, the role of the Board was envisaged as being a key regulator for all actors and agencies involved in the provision of public safety, not just the public police.

Second, the ICP recommended that at the local authority level of district council, District Policing Partnership Boards (DPPBs) be established to provide a measure of local accountability (and it recommended that Belfast have four DPPBs). The membership of DPPBs would follow the same principle as the PB, involving a combination of local elected representatives and 'independent' members. DPPBs were envisaged as providing a vital element of local accountability and as being active partners in community safety provision. Reflecting this role, they were also to be given the powers to impose a local tax of up to three per cent to purchase additional services, whether from the police or other agencies.

Third, the ICP warmly endorsed the establishment of a Police Ombudsman as recommended in the 1997 Hayes Report. This office has already been established under the Police (Northern Ireland) Act 1998, legislation whose passage 'mystified' the Commission given that it had been established to consider closely related matters. The Patten Report specifically recommended that the Ombudsman should have the power 'to initiate inquiries or investigations even if no specific complaint has been received' (p. 37), and 'to investigate and comment on police policies and practices, where these are perceived to give rise to difficulties, even if the conduct of individual officers may not in itself be culpable' (p. 38).

The report also proposed the establishment of an oversight commissioner to monitor and report on the extent to which the report was implemented. While this was consistent with the attentiveness to accountability and transparency evident throughout the report, it was also a shot across the bows of the British government to the extent that it implicitly queried whether the government would willingly implement the report.

## Organization, structure and environment

As discussed above, the report proposed a decentralized and streamlined organizational structure with community policing at its core. To secure greater availability of police officers, the report called for a large programme of civilianization to be initiated. The report also considered the possibility of tiered police services, but rejected it on the basis of the potential negative consequences of policing fragmentation (although these were not fully outlined in the report). On that basis, the report stated that 'a decentralized but unified police service is greatly to be preferred' (p. 70; see also Brogden 1998, 2001; McGarry 2004). The ICP made further recommendations concerning cooperation with other forces, particularly An Garda Síochána (the police force in the Irish Republic), in relation to joint protocols and personnel exchanges.

The report recommended several 'normalization' measures, including – in so far as the security situation allowed this – the replacement of armoured Land-Rovers with police cars, measures to make police stations 'less forbidding' (p. 47), the closure of the holding centres used to detain suspects held under emergency legislation and the introduction of video recording into the police custody suites which would henceforth hold all detainees (p. 49). Concerning emergency legislation, the commission noted that because no records were kept of such measures as roadblocks and stops and searches it was not able to assess properly the persistent concerns raised about them. Its sole recommendations concerning emergency legislation were that 'the law in Northern Ireland should be the same as that in the rest of the United Kingdom', and that 'records should be kept of all stops and searches and other such actions taken under emergency powers' (pp. 48–9). In relation to plastic baton rounds (PBRs), the report noted that: 'All of us began our work wanting to be able to recommend that they be dispensed with straight away.' However, the Commission felt unable to do so, apparently on the basis that removing PBRs from the alternatives available to police would encourage resort to live ammunition sooner than would be the case otherwise (p. 54). Instead the report called for research into 'an acceptable, effective and less potentially lethal alternative to the PBR', and for the police to 'be equipped with a broader range of public order equipment than the RUC currently possess' (p. 55).

The report called for greater scrutiny to be applied to counter-insurgency policing activities, including the appointment of a 'commissioner for covert law enforcement'. Observing that the Special Branch was widely viewed as 'a force within a force' – a complaint which one commissioner noted was most frequently made by other officers[4] – Patten recommended that it be folded in with the Criminal Branch, under one senior officer (a recommendation also made in the RUC's *Fundamental Review of Policing*). The report also noted that Police District Commanders should be consulted regarding Special Branch activities (the report noted that previously local commanders generally were given little knowledge of Special Branch activities underway in their area).

### Composition and recruitment

The report called for recruitment procedures to be established that would make the force fully representative of the community it served. The report's main recommendations on issues of composition and recruitment involved scaling down the force considerably while simultaneously increasing Catholic participation within it. It called for the force to decrease in size from almost 13,000 to 7,500 full-time officers over a ten-year period. Some of this would occur through the phasing out of the Full-Time Reserve (then comprising nearly 3,000 officers), but the report also called for a substantial programme of early retirement (including a generous severance package). For a ten-year period, future recruits would be drawn from a pool of qualified candidates on a 50:50 basis of Catholics and non-Catholics (mirroring the demographic background of people in their 20s) with the goal of achieving 30 per cent Catholic participation by that time. The report recommended that the Part-Time Reserve be expanded from 1,300 to 2,500 officers, with these additional recruits being recruited from those areas that currently were underrepresented, the implication being that this would increase nationalist representation within it.

### Symbols

Tucked away in Chapter 17 towards the end of the report, the commissioners recommended that 'while we have not accepted the argument that the Royal Ulster Constabulary should be disbanded, it should henceforth be named the Northern Ireland Police Service'. In order to ensure that the force could command the support of all sections of the community, the report specifically called for the new police service to 'adopt a new badge and symbols which are entirely free from any association with either the British or Irish states'. It also recommended that 'the Union flag should no longer be flown from police buildings', and that when a flag was to be flown on such buildings that it should be the flag of the new force. The colour of the existing uniform should be retained, although a 'new, more practical style of uniform' should be adopted (p. 99).

## Reception and response

When the Patten Report was published on 9 September 1999, it sparked enormous and heated debate. The report itself obviously generated criticism, both from those who felt it went too far in its recommendations and from those who felt it should have gone further. While anticipating some of the furore that greeted the report, the commissioners were still somewhat surprised by the lack of considered debate it generated, at least immediately following its publication. As Peter Smith, one of the commissioners, noted, 'my skin has been thickened [by] . . . my experience over the last six weeks or so [involving] many people who haven't read the report being extremely anxious to criticize' (CAJ 1999: 15). The British and Irish governments generally gave it a positive welcome, while nationalists became more vocal in their praise for its recommendations in the months following its publication. The SDLP soon was calling for its immediate and complete implementation (SDLP 1999) while, from 2000 onwards Sinn Féin also was demanding that 'the Patten recommendations be implemented in full' (Sinn Féin 2003: 1; see also Sinn Féin 2002; Hillyard and Tomlinson 2000; McGarry 2004).

In contrast, unionists vilified the report. The UUP leader, David Trimble, described it as a 'gratuitous insult' to the RUC and the 'most shoddy piece of work I have seen in my entire life' (*Irish Times*, 10 September 1999). Other UUP politicians criticized the 'republican Patten report' for its 'scant and fleeting' acknowledgement of RUC officers' sacrifice (*Irish Times*, 15 October 1999), describing it as 'superficial and quite honestly unworthy of the people who sat on the commission' (*Irish Times*, 2 December 1999). When an Irish government minister urged unionists to accept the report, the DUP leader Ian Paisley retorted that 'this female slanderer of the RUC should keep her lying mouth shut'. Describing the report as 'the death-knell of the RUC', he claimed that the RUC 'is now to be offered as a final sacrificial lamb, to appease Roman Catholic Republican murderers and their nationalist fellow travellers . . . Patten's programme is that Protestants have to be ethnically cleansed' (DUP press release, 9 September 1999). The unionist *News Letter* gave its response in a one-word front-page headline: 'Betrayed' (10 September 1999). Within the broader unionist constituency, various 'Save the RUC' rallies were held across Northern Ireland, while a 'Defend the RUC' campaign associated with the *Daily Telegraph* was set up to thwart the 'great betrayal' of the commission's proposals. The PFNI launched a petition in October 1999 'seeking one million signatures to defend the

RUC against the Patten Report' (nearly 400,000 were delivered to the British Prime Minister in January 2000).

Patten and other commissioners challenged the position of politicians who had signed up to the terms of reference, but who subsequently expressed surprise or outrage when significant changes were recommended. After all, as one commissioner noted: 'Setting up an independent commission is hardly to be taken as a recipe for protection of the status quo' (interview). According to McGarry (2004: 389): 'The most charitable interpretation of Trimble's reaction is that he had thought when he signed up to the Agreement's terms of reference that he was endorsing the status quo: that is, the RUC was already impartial, free from partisan control, imbued with a human rights culture, and so on.' Certainly, this does appear to be the case, as unionist figures identified few failings within the prevailing policing arrangements. Instead the vision of reform they articulated resonated closely with that of the RUC: evolutionary organizational adjustments in light of the changing security situation. As the UUP stated: 'Beyond that the only change that is really needed is to have many more Catholics serving the community in the police. All that is needed to achieve that is an end to intimidation. Positive support from the Catholic community for Catholics who join the police is the most important change' (UUP press release, 9 September 1999).

### Mobilizing the reform agenda

Subsequent to the report's publication, the commissioners did not embark on a widespread campaign of advocacy or persuasion. Nor did they engage in the flurry of media interviews that so often accompanies the publication of a major report. Beyond the press conference at the report's launch, there were some presentations made by commission members (Patten and Hayes addressed a US House of Representatives subcommittee, and Hayes and Smith addressed a CAJ conference in Belfast). Generally though the report was left to speak for itself, a situation that undermined the generation of momentum necessary to mobilize 'local constituencies of interest' (Beirne 2001: 303).

The commissioners unambiguously advised against 'cherry-picking' from the report on the basis that 'we felt that we had put together a package, and that the whole thing would unravel if people were to accept one part of it but not another' (interview with ICP member). In this regard, the report may have oversold itself, for the radical changes it proposed surely would have benefited from greater attention to the very rationale for change. Strikingly, Trimble's criticisms of the report made much of what he termed its 'manner and style', and the fact that it 'proceeds by bald assertion' (Millar 2004: 94–5).[5] In addition to analysis of existing studies, the ICP commissioned its own research, including public attitude surveys, focus groups and a 'cultural audit' of the RUC.

Nevertheless, their discussion of public perceptions of policing was largely confined to a little over four pages of text (pp. 13–17). Here, the commission made some important, if familiar, observations: that respondents' evaluations of local police performance was often at variance with their political orientation towards the police; that many concerns surrounding policing and crime were shared by nationalists and unionists alike; and that 'in the lower income groups, Protestants could be as alienated from the police as were their Catholic counterparts' (p. 16). Nevertheless, as Beirne (2001: 303) notes, the report did not outline in any concrete detail the basis of people's experiences of policing, such that it 'failed to give the people of Northern Ireland a sufficiently clear analysis of the current problems, and mobilize them around the necessity for change.' As such, the commissioners' claims that their recommendations stood as a coherent package that should be accepted in its entirety were not established through empirical analysis. Instead the new beginning that was proposed emerged from an evident reluctance to outline, except in the most general terms, the nature of the problem to begin with.

### Symbolism and ownership

Despite the fundamental changes proposed in a range of areas, the changes to the symbolism of the RUC – particularly the name change – generated most debate.[6] Ryder described the name change as the report's 'most fundamental, controversial and headline-grabbing' recommendation (Ryder 2000: 512). Although, when launching the 'Save the RUC' petition, PFNI chairman Les Rodgers stated that 'as a professional and operationally independent police service we should be claimed by no-one as "their RUC" ',[7] such an appeal belied the realities of support for and affiliation with the RUC across the communities of Northern Ireland. 'Ownership' of the police was one the historical legacies of the situation in Northern Ireland and one of the key fault lines of the reform debate. The proposed changes to the RUC's symbolism was a key dimension of the ICP's efforts to address this point, an issue which they noted in the report:

> While many people regardless of their religious background may have similar expectations and experiences of policing, they may take a different view of the RUC as an institution – a view owing more to political considerations than to policing concerns. We had a stark example of this at one of our public meetings in a Unionist/Loyalist area when, after an hour or so of discussing difficulties facing local policing, one speaker made a statement of unqualified support for 'our' police force and the mood of the meeting was abruptly transformed as nearly all subsequent speakers rallied behind the same, essentially political, position. (p. 16)

As the report noted, their research found no examples of Catholics referring to the RUC as 'our' police (p. 16). Thus the ICP accepted the argument that the symbolism, ethos and composition of the RUC served to reinforce and maintain Catholics' 'feelings of secondary membership in Northern Irish society' (Kempa and Shearing 2002: 39). Nevertheless, the report's recommendations on these issues were perceived by most RUC officers and many unionists as a blatant insult in the face of the sacrifice the force had given. The PFNI's response to Patten captured the emotion associated with the name change:

> His report is, of course, a betrayal of the proud tradition of the Royal Ulster Constabulary. He tosses our name and history aside with a casual disregard for the sacrifice of brave men and women. The absence of tribute from the report on 9th September told us all we needed to know about how much he understood what the police service and their families had been through over the past 30 years. A sincere acknowledgement was needed in his presentation if he were to convince us that he understood the scale of the hurt which his recommendations on the name and associated symbols would mean. He called his report 'A New Beginning'. I can tell you that if implemented in full as it stands, it would be the cruellest of endings for one of the finest police forces in the world. (Speech by PFNI Chairperson, November 1999)

Given the relationship between the RUC and unionism – one which increasingly had come to be expressed in terms of tacit rather than overt allegiance, but which remained a powerful link nonetheless – changing the symbolism of the RUC was perceived as tantamount to an attack on the activities and role of the RUC, and on unionism itself. The broad-based ownership of policing which the ICP had sought to engender was eclipsed by unionists' sense that what the report was proposing was not a win-win situation, but a further erosion of their identity. As Trimble noted, 'it wasn't clear until the end that we were going to lose everything on the symbolic front' (in Millar 2004: 93), a 'loss' that other unionists blamed on Trimble specifically (DUP 2003a; Godson 2004). Peter Smith, an ICP member who in the past had been involved in unionist politics, noted that unionist obsession with the perceived symbolic slight overshadowed other dimensions of ownership which the report had advanced – creating not just a symbolism to which all could affiliate, but institutions which the wider community could actively support. As he put it:

> ... after having listened (as I have) to unionist meetings over many years where people complained bitterly about policing being under the control (as they saw it) of unaccountable Westminster ministers, I thought, perhaps naively thought – that our proposals for the

remission of policing to democratic institutions in Northern Ireland would have struck a chord among thinking unionists ... It is a source of immense surprise to me that no one, as far as I am aware, in that unionist political community has actually addressed – whether negatively or positively – those very recommendations which to my mind, lie very much at the core of our report ... that is to say, democratic accountability. I am amazed that they haven't welcomed those recommendations – above all others. I'm amazed that they would not have balanced their angst about the badge and flag issues with recognition of the importance to the unionist community of the return of true accountability through democratic mechanisms of policing to the people of Northern Ireland. (CAJ 1999: 15)

Given the history of policing in Northern Ireland, it was not unexpected that the radical changes proposed in the report would generate enthusiasm among nationalists and outrage among unionists. While these responses generally reflected the extent to which the report meshed with the political standpoint of the respective commentators, in the following section I focus on the report itself and highlight a number of issues to be considered in assessing it.

## Assessing the Patten Report

In addition to the issues raised above, several other aspects of the Patten Report drew criticism. Commentators raised concerns over the report's treatment of gender (Moore and O'Rawe 2001); its rejection of a tiered policing service – which McGarry (2004: 385) described as 'the least convincing part of the report' given its failure to outline a rationale for taking this position; and the manner in which many issues were left dependent on security assessments from the Chief Constable and the Secretary of State, the very bodies whose hegemony on policing matters was now being challenged (McGarry 2004). The report was also criticized for its failure to comment in greater detail on emergency legislation – the report only devoted two paragraphs to this issue – given the security excesses which had so frequently been associated with emergency powers, and the ICP's own emphasis on human rights (Beirne 2001; Hillyard and Tomlinson 2000; McGarry 2004; Moore and O'Rawe 2001; O'Rawe 2003). In addition to these concerns, there are two further aspects of the report worth noting.

### Best practice

While the Patten Report was often described in terms of extremes – a prophetic voice of hope on the one hand, an apocalyptic vision of doom on the other – it is useful to demystify it from this sacred/heretical opposition and recognize its congruence with many of the current notions of 'best practice'. Commission members certainly believed that it represented 'a statement of international best practice as far as policing is concerned' (interview with ICP member). Moreover, the belief prevailed within RUC circles that Patten was in large part merely a further outing for proposals already developed in-house but shelved while the commission was underway. One senior officer noted that the RUC's *Fundamental Review of Policing* (1997) was the basis for almost the entirety of the Patten Report's recommendations on operational policing matters (fieldnotes), a view echoed by the Chief Constable on several occasions (Hillyard and Tomlinson 2000). As Ryder (2004: 278) suggested: '165 of its 175 recommendations, the "nuts and bolts" issues which were universally accepted as necessary, directly mirrored those already identified by Flanagan's frozen fundamental review.'

As such, it is worth pointing out that the report's concerns were not ethereal, but solidly grounded in the banal dimensions of policing and the governance of security. It sought to synthesize current best practice in policing and apply these to address everyday policing concerns, issues often far removed from the conflicts over policing which had been such a feature of public debate in Northern Ireland, although ones which continued to confound police organizations around the world (the commissioners noted that 'there is no perfect model for us'; p. 3). In that regard, the report brought policing in Northern Ireland to resemble that in Britain more closely than hitherto, and its proposals were more readily amenable to adoption since, as Walker noted, 'they fit with discourses of managerialism and service delivery which have prevailed for some years within the realm of British policing' (2001: 160). In evidence to a US House of Representatives subcommittee, Hayes outlined the pragmatic organizational concerns that underpinned their recommendations:

> I think this is largely a managerial document. It imposes its controls in a managerial way. It may not be melodramatic enough for people who wanted to see blood on the floor, but I can assure you that a careful reading of that will show you that accountability is intended for the establishment and the maintenance of professional policing practices. (Hayes 1999)

Similarly, in one discussion of the report, Shearing stated that he had 'nothing to say' about a number of proposals that were 'extremely consequential for the transformation of policing in Northern Ireland' (concerning 'culture and symbols, the organization of the new policing service, and the importance of partnerships in police'). His position reflected the fact that 'these proposals, while very significant for

Northern Ireland, are unexceptional – they apply principles that are routinely embraced elsewhere' (Shearing 2000: 386–7).

### Dealing with the past

The second issue I want to highlight is the Commission's decision to outline the framework for 'a new beginning' for policing in Northern Ireland without seeking to lay bare its past. As discussed earlier in the chapter, RUC officers viewed the absence of a eulogy for the force or a detailed account of its sacrifices as a fundamental flaw in the report. For others, however, the report's failure to examine the controversies in which it had been involved was an equally serious omission (Hillyard and Tomlinson 2001; Moore and O'Rawe 2001; O'Rawe 2003). As Bell *et al.* (2004: 314) note, the report was 'an attempt to address the *legacy* of institutional delegitimation without an exploration of the *process* of delegitimation that an examination of the past might have produced' (original emphasis). The report, nevertheless, *did* explicitly acknowledge such issues:

> We are in no doubt that the RUC has had several officers within its ranks over the years who have abused their position. Many supporters of the RUC and both serving and retired officers have spoken to us about 'bad apples'. It is not satisfactory to suggest, as some people have, that one should somehow accept that every organization has such 'bad apples'. They should be dealt with. (p. 26)

How that should happen, the report did not explain. Instead, it justified its approach in three main ways: its terms of reference, the procedures it was establishing and the need to face the future.

First, the report noted that investigating specific allegations of misconduct was beyond its remit: 'We were not charged with a quasi-legal investigation of the past. If there is a case for such inquiries it is up to the government to appoint them, not for us to rewrite our terms of reference' (p. 3). Second, through the establishment of appropriate oversight mechanisms and the infusion of a human rights culture into every aspect of policing, the report noted that at a general level its proposals were designed 'to minimise as far as possible any prospect of abuses such as those alleged to have taken place in the past' (p. 26). Third, the report itself was driven by a concern with outlining positive ways forward, rather than embarking on an exegesis of the past, with all that would entail in terms of laying judgement and assigning blame: 'it was ... clear to us that we would never be able to fashion a fresh start out of a series of judgments about who was culpable for each of the tragedies and mistakes of the past.' Accordingly, the Commission saw its approach as 'restorative, not retributive' (p. 4). As Hayes noted in testimony to a US House of Representatives subcommittee:

> The Good Friday Agreement itself is a forward-looking document. It does tend to draw a line on the past. It does base the whole future of society on mutual respect, on equality of respect for the different traditions in Northern Ireland. That is why we have looked forward ... It seemed to us that the spirit of the Agreement was one of looking forward, and it would seem odd under those circumstances, where you are letting prisoners out of jail, to be proposing to put policemen in. We didn't give anybody amnesty. There is nobody who is immune to the law, to the prosecution of cases; and some of the cases you mentioned are being investigated and may well lead to prosecution and appearances in the court. It would have been wrong for us, I think, to have become involved in that. (Hayes 1999)

The Commission's efforts to ensure that the future of policing in Northern Ireland would be brighter than its past are significant and coherent. However, the report's self-characterization as 'restorative' rather than 'retributive' is not entirely accurate, for no matter how laudable their efforts to avoid blame games and all the political fallout associated with that, restorative justice has at its core a commitment to information-sharing, if not truth-telling. Restorative justice typically begins from the premise that the parties involved are given an opportunity to outline their version of events, to articulate their sense of any harm suffered and to respond to the positions of others. The Patten Report steadfastly avoided analysis of such issues – despite their prominence in the Commission's public meetings – and as such its approach is more accurately described as 'prospective' rather than restorative in outlook. However, the failure to examine the past – or even explain the differing interpretations of same – may, in large part, have been at the root of continued institutional resistance within government and the police, and of 'foot dragging' by unionists. With no justifications offered for the need for radical change, it is hardly surprising that many wondered why it was at all necessary, and why anything more than implementation of the force's *Fundamental Review* proposals was required. Past controversies would, however, remain perhaps the dominant feature in public debate about the report's implementation (discussed in the next two chapters).

## Conclusion

The Report of the Independent Commission on Policing emerged from a context of profound socio-political division. In seeking to resolve the policing question of Northern Ireland, the report proposed a model of policing derived from the 'first principles' of the protection of human rights, and constructive partnerships between the police and the public. Inquiries into the justice system in Northern Ireland were often depicted as solely engaged with repair duties to the state's legitimacy (Burton and Carlen 1979; Scraton 2004; see also Gilligan and Pratt 2004). Nevertheless, as the dust settled and gut-reaction gave way to considered analysis, the Patten report came to be recognized as an insightful, progressive and far-reaching document, both for the detail of its recommendations and the vision of policing it articulated. Although the report offered itself as a model that met universal needs regarding policing and community safety and so could be implemented in any jurisdiction, it arose from the specific context of Northern Ireland and it would be measured against its impact on that society. In the following chapter, I consider the report's implementation and its consequences for police–community relations.

## Notes

1 For further discussion of the 1998 Belfast Agreement, see Harvey (2001) and O'Leary (2004).
2 For analysis of unionist approaches to the peace process, see Cochrane (2001). Detailed discussions of Trimble's role during the GFA negotiations are provided in Millar (2004) and Godson (2004).
3 The report noted that of the 700 training sessions that RUC officers received, only two of those were dedicated to human rights issues, compared with 40 for drill and 63 for firearms training (p. 19).
4 As one commissioner noted (interview): 'We got more complaints about Special Branch from uniformed officers than from anyone else. "They're wrecking us out there, searching 100 houses when two would do." You need Special Branch, or at least the skills of Special Branch. What you don't need is people making up the rules as they go along, being a force within a force.' As a result of his investigation into the shoot-to-kill allegations, Stalker (1988: 56–7) noted in relation to Special Branch that: 'I had never experienced, nor had any of my team, such an influence over an entire police force by one small section.'
5 Stephen King, one of Trimble's closest advisors, wrote favourably of 'pulping' the Patten Report, noting: 'I have read his [Patten's] solutions; now I want to know what the problem is?' (*Belfast Telegraph*, 16 September 1999).
6 The name 'Northern Ireland Police Service' had already made a legislative appearance in the 1998 Police Act, section 2(2) as an umbrella term for all public policing agencies in Northern Ireland.
7 This refers to the fact that the DUP had included the RUC's badge on some of its election material. The 2005 elections also featured former PFNI chairman Jimmy Spratt running as a DUP candidate.

# Chapter 9

# Implementing the reform programme: the new institutional framework of policing

Establishing the new institutional framework of policing in Northern Ireland was, by any standards, a massive endeavour. The Inspector of Constabulary described it as 'probably the single largest change process undertaken by any police force' (HMIC 2001: 2). The NIO established a 'Patten Action Team' and the PSNI a 'Change Management Team' to coordinate their respective activities,[1] but the network of agencies comprising the Policing Board, District Policing Partnerships and Office of the Police Ombudsman were key components of 'the new beginning' envisaged by the Patten Commission and the most visible expression of reforms which extended beyond the police organization. Their success was crucial in ensuring that the police would be held accountable to the public and in establishing mechanisms through which the ethos of 'policing with the community' would be enacted and regulated. The political divisions in Northern Ireland, however, inevitably asserted themselves in terms of the operation of these organizations. This chapter builds on the analysis of the Patten Report outlined in the previous chapter and addresses three interrelated issues. First, I examine the implementation of the Patten reform programme. Second, I consider the establishment and operation of the Policing Board, the District Policing Partnerships and the Office of the Police Ombudsman. Third, I analyse the impact of these changes on operational policing and on public attitudes to the PSNI.

## The implementation process

Following the report's publication, discussion of its implementation was dogged by conflict over the weight that should be attached to its recommendations. As UUP leader David Trimble stated, 'commissions don't decide . . . I found it quite astonishing when it later became clear that the British government got itself into a situation where the commission's report was treated as Holy Writ' (quoted in Millar 2004: 88). From the outset, the ICP stressed the overall coherence of the package it offered and called for its recommendations to be implemented 'comprehensively and faithfully': 'We advise in the strongest terms against cherry-picking from this report or trying to implement some major elements in it in isolation from others' (p. 105). As one of its members noted, this was the firm purpose behind the recommendations to appoint an Oversight Commissioner: 'We knew how things work. If you don't like parts of the report then you fillet it. You accept things at no cost. The ones you stall on are crucial to the whole thing.' The ICP's fears were well-founded. Following a period of consultation over the report, the British Secretary of State for Northern Ireland, Peter Mandelson (who had taken over the post from Mo Mowlam in late 1999), made a statement to the House of Commons in January 2000 noting that the government accepted the Patten Report 'in principle' (2000: 2). When the Police (Northern Ireland) Bill was published later that year, the principled acceptance of the report announced by Mandelson yielded, in practice, a pale shadow of the vision of policing articulated by Patten and his colleagues (see, for example, Statewatch 2000). Over the course of its passage, the legislation was subject to significant change. Mandelson's initial claims that the Bill was faithful to Patten was undermined by the fact that the SDLP alone tabled some 150 amendments of which approximately 100 were accepted (Ryder 2004: 308).

Several of the commissioners publicly criticized the Bill, stating that it reflected neither the details nor the spirit of the report. One commissioner observed that the drafting process was equivalent to 'the rats gnawing at it [the report]' (confidential source). The strongest criticism came from Clifford Shearing who stated that the report had been:

> . . . undermined everywhere. The district policing partnership boards that are so vital to the Patten Commission's vision have been diluted. So have its recommendations in the key areas outlined in its terms of reference – composition, recruitment, culture, ethos and symbols. The Patten Report has not been cherry-picked, it had been gutted . . . It will not serve the people of Northern Ireland. Nor will it serve the many, many dedicated persons within the RUC who

have been looking for a new vision for policing that will move and inspire them to police in partnership with the community they serve. (*Guardian*, 14 November 2000)

However, after extensive parliamentary debate and scrutiny, some former commission members rallied behind the legislation. As Maurice Hayes put it, 'The only way you can influence things is from the inside ... Basically the nationalist parties have to decide if they want 90 per cent of something or 100 per cent of nothing' (*Irish Times*, 25 November 2000). Chris Patten also entered the debate. Although when launching the report he had pointedly called for the recommendations to be implemented in their entirety, on this occasion he refused to be drawn into a debate on the Bill's inadequacies and simply called for people to support it (*Belfast Telegraph*, 28 November 2000).

The Police (Northern Ireland) Act 2000 was enacted in November of that year. Some Patten recommendations were omitted from the legislation and instead were included in an 'implementation plan' published by the Northern Ireland Office (2000), with responsibility for introducing these measures resting with the Chief Constable, the Northern Ireland Office or the Secretary of State and dependent on their assessments of the security situation. In terms of the Patten recommendations on police symbols, the 2000 Act retained the name of the RUC in the title deeds of the 'new' force, although for operational purposes the force would be known as the Police Service of Northern Ireland.[2] The key differences between the Act and the Patten Report were most evident in relation to the powers of the new institutions.

The powers of the Policing Board were significantly reduced. Whereas the Patten Report had emphasized that the Chief Constable had a right and duty to take operational decisions, it also emphasized that he/she 'must be capable of being held to account afterwards for the manner in which he/she exercises them' (p. 33), and accordingly much weight was invested in the authority of the Board to require reports from the Chief Constable. The Patten Report had suggested that the Chief Constable's grounds for questioning the Board's right to call for reports be 'strictly limited to issues such as those involving national security, sensitive personnel matters and cases before the courts'. The 2000 Act changed 'sensitive personnel matters' to 'sensitive *personal* matters' (emphasis added) and added a fourth ground on which such a request might be referred to the Secretary of State: that the report 'would, or would be likely to, prejudice the prevention or detection of crime or the apprehension or prosecution of offenders' (section 59(3)(d)). Such an open-ended qualification greatly extended the range of circumstances under which a call for a report might be refused, and correspondingly eroded the oversight powers of the Board (McGarry 2004), a situation that even

PANI described as 'ludicrous and totally unacceptable' (PANI press release, 17 May 2000). The Ombudsman's oversight powers were also restricted. The Patten Report had recommended that the Ombudsman has the power to 'investigate' police policies and practices, but the legislation only specified the power to 'carry out research' on those issues.

The DPPBs became District Policing Partnerships (DPPs) rather than 'boards', reflecting a shift away from executive functions towards a purely consultative role. Belfast would have one DPP rather than the four recommended by Patten. The recommendation that DPPBs should be able to impose a local tax of up to 3 per cent to purchase additional policing services generated considerable alarm among unionists and within British governmental circles. For them, it raised the prospect of the police being potentially supplanted by 'service providers' drawn from paramilitary organizations. Although in illustrating this provision the report had given the examples of installing security cameras or funding youth club schemes (p. 35) – one commissioner also suggested a potential further use of this provision as 'cleaning up graffiti' - the British government considered this level of autonomy deeply problematic and deferred any decision on this until the Criminal Justice Review (CJR) reported, given that it also was considering the issue of community safety. When the CJR subsequently reported, it recommended the establishment of a system of Community Safety Partnerships (CSPs) which would play the role that the Patten Report had envisaged for DPPs (CJR 2000: 273). It also recommended that CSPs should have the power to finance community safety initiatives through the 3 per cent tax proposed by the Patten Report (p. 277). The government did establish CSPs, but it declined to grant them that tax-raising power; instead the NIO established a Community Safety Unit to which CSPs could submit funding bids for specific initiatives. In these combined ways, the report's broad vision of 'policing' as 'everybody's business' fell victim to the implementation process. This was very much a 'police' Act (McGarry 2004; O'Rawe 2003).

Neither the SDLP nor Sinn Féin endorsed the legislation, and even the Irish premier, Bertie Ahern, stated that he could not call on the nationalist parties to do so in light of this divergence from the Patten agenda (*Irish Times*, 25 November 2000). The failure to resolve policing was itself related to ongoing disputes over the implementation of the Belfast Agreement and, given the centrality of policing to this process, it was inevitable that it would be revisited. Further political negotiations were held, and following one key bout of talks at Weston Park in Shropshire in July 2001, an updated implementation plan was issued (NIO 2001) and further amending legislation was agreed, resulting in the Police (Northern Ireland) Act 2003. The 2003 Act included a stronger statement of the importance attached to 'policing with the community': 'Police officers shall carry out their functions with the aim – (a) of securing the support of the local community, and (b) of acting in cooperation with the local community' (section 31A(1)). It also specified that, when setting long-term policing objectives, the Secretary of State's requirement simply to 'consult' with the Policing Board was replaced by a requirement that such consultation should be undertaken 'with a view to obtaining its agreement to the proposed objectives' (section 1(2)). The Policing Board's powers to commission reports and initiate inquiries were extended, and the Police Ombudsman was given the additional power to 'investigate police practices and policies' if s/he was of the belief that it was 'in the public interest' to do so (section 60(1)(b)). The changes agreed at the Weston Park negotiations met the immediate concerns of the SDLP which took up its seats on the Policing Board when this was established in November 2001 and on the DPPs when these were eventually established in 2003. Sinn Féin refused to endorse or participate in the new institutions (Sinn Féin press release, 25 August 2001), a position it holds up to the time of writing, although this may well change in light of the IRA's statement in July 2005 that it was ending its armed campaign.[3] Sinn Féin's position was closely tied to the wider implementation of the GFA, but it ensured a less than auspicious beginning for the new institutions.

## The new institutional framework

In this section, I examine the operation of the network of agencies central to the vision of policing outlined in the Patten Report – the Northern Ireland Policing Board, the District Policing Partnerships and the Office of the Police Ombudsman for Northern Ireland. While these various bodies have only been in existence for a relatively short period, their activities were crucial in shaping the unfolding reform programme.

### The Northern Ireland Policing Board

The composition of the Policing Board reflected the broader political divisions surrounding policing. Sinn Féin – which in the 2003 Assembly elections overtook the SDLP as the largest nationalist party – refused to participate in the Board, and as a consequence its two allocated seats were redistributed according to the d'Hondt principles, giving one additional seat each to the UUP and the DUP. Additionally, the Board also included within it unionists bitterly opposed to the Belfast Agreement and to the Patten Report. Ian Paisley, the DUP leader, had earlier stated that the DUP was 'totally dedicated to the destruction of this report' (Ryder 2004: 277), and its 2003 'Fair Deal' election manifesto highlighted the determined manner in which it had gone about doing so:

> The DUP has worked tirelessly to block those Patten proposals which were not based on the principle of good policing, but on political judgements. The DUP took its seats on the Police [sic] Board and the work of Ian Paisley Jnr, Sammy Wilson and William Hay has prevented many of the Patten Recommendations from being realized. (DUP 2003a: 24)

These divergent positions were reflected in some breaches of confidentiality from Board members (including over the appointment of Orde as Chief Constable), which in turn undermined its relationships with both the PSNI and the Ombudsman (NIAC 2005a; Ryder 2004).

As CAJ noted, the Board 'quickly established itself as a more accountable and effective body' than the Police Authority had been (2003: 4). It held its monthly meetings with the Chief Constable in public (although 'virtually no decisions' were taken in these public fora; NIAC 2005a: 17), it reached agreement on the symbols to be included in the PSNI's emblem, created a new code of ethics for PSNI officers and a new framework for monitoring human rights issues, and published policing plans. Although it focused more on 'police' matters than on 'policing' more generally, early assessments of the Board were on the whole positive. The Oversight Commissioner found that the Policing Board 'performs its governance and accountability functions well, often under difficult circumstances' (2004: 6), and the Northern Ireland Affairs Committee (2005a: 23) reported that the Board had made 'solid progress in establishing its role and had developed sound mechanisms for holding the police service to account.'

There were, however, a number of issues that clouded this picture. One such instance concerned the secrecy surrounding the purchase of CS spray by the PSNI. The Board endorsed the PSNI's proposal to obtain the spray, and stated that it did so on the basis of presentations made to it by the PSNI and other information made available by a number of official policing bodies. However, no information was made available explaining the rationale for obtaining the spray, nor did the Board consult with human rights organizations on this issue or obtain independent scientific assessments on the effects of using CS spray. A second issue was the manner in which the Board appeared to position itself more as advocate for the police than an independent accountability mechanism. While some evidence of this was apparent in the Board's stance on the Ombudsman's report on the Omagh bomb (discussed further below), Board members also appeared keen to support the PSNI when the Ombudsman published research on the legal profession, including claims by 55 lawyers that they had experienced harassment or threats from police officers. The Board wrote to the Ombudsman asking her to 'reflect on the negative impact that unbalanced commentary can have on those who need little to be convinced that your office is the preserve of nationalists and exists only to "give the police a hard time" ' (quoted in CAJ 2003: 12). Such an approach appeared to focus more on defending the police from criticism rather than holding them to account.

### District Policing Partnerships

District Policing Partnerships were established in March 2003 – their delay due mainly to the large-scale public appointments exercise involved – and within a short period of time they were acclaimed as a major success story of the new policing arrangements in Northern Ireland. The PBNI vice-chairman Denis Bradley suggested that DPPs had 'helped to transform the culture of policing in Northern Ireland' and that 'the reintegration of police ... into the normal community is actually being led by district policing partnerships' (NIAC 2005a: Ev. 27). This optimistic assessment was echoed within the police. The PSNI Deputy Chief Constable, Paul Leighton, described DPPs as 'one of the biggest steps forward in policing in a long time' (NIAC 2005a: Ev. 39). Even the PFNI claimed that DPPs 'have turned into an excellent community sounding board ... providing a useful channel of communication between the police service and the community' (speech by PFNI Chairman at a House of Commons reception, 16 November 2004).

However, a survey in May 2004 suggested this assessment should be strongly qualified. It found that of the 67 per cent of respondents who had heard of DPPs, only 2 per cent were 'very confident' while a further 32 per cent were 'confident' that their local DPP was helping to address local problems. By contrast, 49 per cent of respondents were 'not confident' and a further 9 per cent were 'not at all confident' that DPPs were of use in that context (in each response category, the views of Catholic and Protestant respondents were almost identical; NIPB 2004a: tables 6, 8a). The survey also found that only 48 per cent of respondents 'were prepared to contact their local DPP regarding local policing' (table 10a). Another survey conducted in April 2005 found that 4 per cent of respondents were 'very confident', 19 per cent were 'confident', 51 'had some confidence', 15 per cent had 'little confidence' and 3 per cent had 'none at all' (again, with very little difference between the stated views of Catholic and Protestant respondents) (NIPB 2005a: table 17). This survey found that 58 per cent of respondents had heard of DPPs, and of these only 31 per cent felt their local DPP had 'helped to improve policing in your local area', while 36 per cent felt it had not (table 19).[4]

The views and experiences of DPP members also suggest a more complex reality than the glowing assessments of DPPs offered by the

Policing Board and others. At a CAJ-organized conference on DPPs held in Belfast in June 2004, DPP members were deeply critical of a number of aspects of their structure and organization (CAJ 2005a).[5] DPP members spoke of feeling 'abandoned' by the Policing Board, in terms of a failure to provide them with support (especially training) and even basic information. The often-stilted formality that characterized many DPP meetings was also seen as inhibiting its development as a consultation forum, particularly through requirements that questions from the public be submitted in advance 'in order to have a written answer prepared by the police read to them at the public meeting' (p. 16). Difficulties over this were compounded by the failure to even allow follow-up questions in many instances. Thus one person described DPP meetings as 'talking shops stage-managed to avoid controversy' (p. 16), while a CPLC member stated that he declined an offer to join a DPP on the basis that 'It stood for everything that I had worked against as a community activist: it was disempowering people. I just thought it was awful that a member of the public has to submit a question in writing and wait fourteen days before receiving an answer' (p. 57).

One of the structural impediments to the success of DPPs was the establishment of Community Safety Partnerships under the auspices of the Northern Ireland Office. This perplexing development was roundly criticized for undermining the mandate and scope of DPPs. Limiting locally established DPPs to the role of consulting with the police – while providing CSPs with the capacity to finance local community safety initiatives from NIO funds – undermined the ICP's efforts to maximize local capacity. It was, in effect, the reinsertion of the state into a space that the ICP believed properly belonged to local communities. In addition to constituting a significant dilution of the powers and scope of DPPs, this arrangement was also widely viewed as ineffective. PBNI vice-chairman Denis Bradley characterized the two-tier system as 'wasteful', 'burdensome', 'expensive', 'confusing' and 'bad on the ground level' (NIAC 2005a: Ev. 29). The PSNI Deputy Chief Constable and the Inspector of Constabulary for the PSNI also criticized this system (NIAC 2005a: Ev. 40, Ev. 46; HMIC 2004: 47). At a local level, some measures had already been introduced to overcome the forced division of labour, such as a sharing of support services between DPPs and CSPs in a number of district councils (although the Northern Ireland Office had declined the proposal to establish common secretariats formally; NIAC 2005a: Ev. 30), but in other instances relations were rather more distant: one CSP had refused to allow DPP members to join it (CAJ 2005a: 21). The creation of separate structures for policing on the one hand and community safety on the other was widely viewed as evidence of political interference by the NIO to hamstring the DPPs. As one member of the ICP observed in relation to CSPs: 'I think it's to ensure that the DPPs wither on the vine' (interview).

Aside from concerns about their powers (particularly the view that government wished to contain them within specific parameters), one of the immediate features of their operation was the manner in which they reflected wider conflicts over policing. Conflict between nationalists and republicans was a prominent aspect of this. Following the publication of the 'updated implementation plan' in August 2001, the SDLP began formally participating in the new policing arrangements while Sinn Féin did not. In some local authority settings, this generated considerable tension between councillors of different parties (SDLP 2003), and it also impacted on DPPs' effectiveness. The consequences of Sinn Féin's failure to participate in DPPs were most evident in Belfast. The Belfast DPP had sub-groups corresponding to the electoral districts of the city (the Patten Report had recommended that each area should have its own DPP). The West Belfast sub-group – covering an area in which Sinn Féin holds a strong electoral majority – was composed of 'one SDLP councillor – with the remaining political members being unionist – and four independent Catholics, none of whom lived in the area . . . On security grounds the sub-group does not meet in the area' (CAJ 2005a: 16–17). Additionally, across Northern Ireland there were several attacks and threats by dissident republicans in the Real IRA against DPP members (particularly nationalists), resulting in a small number of them resigning.[6] DPPs were, therefore, both a promising local initiative and a reflection of continuing political conflict.

## The Office of the Police Ombudsman

The establishment of the Police Ombudsman was widely recognized as a major step towards greater accountability and scrutiny of the police. Nuala O'Loan, a legal academic at the University of Ulster and a member of the Police Authority, was appointed to the post. Although the creation of the Office was provided for in the Police (Northern Ireland) Act 1998, it did not become operational until November 2000 and did not receive official guidance as to its activities until May 2001.

The Office was functioning for less than a year when it had its most significant challenge. This concerned an investigation by the Ombudsman into allegations that the police had had prior warning of a republican plan to bomb Omagh town, but – to safeguard the identity of an informant – had taken no action. The Ombudsman investigation produced a report critical of the use of intelligence information by police officers, and it criticized the Chief Constable and another senior officer for 'defective leadership, poor judgement and a lack of urgency' (OPONI 2001a: 12). The Chief Constable had asked for a delay in the report's publication given its inclusion of what he described as 'many significant factual inaccuracies, unwarranted assumptions and material omissions'. Flanagan expressed outrage at the suggestion that the RUC would fail to take such a bomb threat seriously or pursue the investigation with insufficient commitment, and he stated that he would resign and 'publicly commit suicide' should the allegations be proven. Mandelson publicly criticized the Ombudsman's report, calling it a 'very poor piece of work indeed', and even the British prime minister intervened, stating that Flanagan had his 'full support', while simply noting that the Ombudsman has 'done her duty.' (CAJ 2003: 21–4; see also CAJ 2005b). Despite the controversy, most of the Ombudsman's substantive recommendations were accepted and pursued, including an independent evaluation of the PSNI investigation. In an effort to improve communication channels between the PSNI and the Ombudsman's office, protocols were established concerning how future reports would be handled.

The high profile of the Ombudsman's investigations, and her apparent willingness to hold the police to account irrespective of any embarrassment it might cause them, led to an enormous backlash in some circles. Unionist politicians, including some members of the Policing Board, denounced the Ombudsman and called for her resignation. The NIPB Chairman, Desmond Rea, noted that: 'The personalized nature of some of the commentary in the Ombudsman's Omagh Report has left a residue of distrust that we continue to deal with to this day' (NIAC 2005b: Ev. 52). Within the police also, feelings ran high. The PSNI Deputy Chief Constable Paul Leighton stated that as a result of the new protocols and working relationships that had been established, relations between the PSNI and the Ombudsman's Office had 'improved dramatically in the past couple of years' (NIAC 2005b: Ev. 55), but other police representatives were less positive. A spokesperson for the PSNI Superintendents' Association stated that the Ombudsman's 'very positive effect on public confidence in policing' was offset by a general police perception that 'the Ombudsman's staff are blinded by a search for evidence of collusion or corruption' and 'that over-zealous approach has led to inappropriate or unprofessional conduct by some of the Ombudsman's investigators, and that obviously has an effect on the confidence of police officers in the system' (NIAC 2005b: Ev. 64, 72). Terry Spence, the PFNI secretary, went further, claiming that police confidence in the Ombudsman's office 'is at an all-time low' (Ev. 66).

Research undertaken by the Ombudsman's Office in 2003 found that 58 per cent of officers thought that complaints against the police should be independently investigated, and 41 per cent thought that an independent complaints system would increase public confidence in the police. However, police attitudes towards the Office of the Ombudsman were deeply negative. The survey found that '44% of police officers think that the Police Ombudsman is not doing a good job in dealing with complaints against the police' and that '43 per cent of police officers think that the Police Ombudsman's Office will not help ensure that the police do a good job'. In terms of the activities of the Police Ombuds-man's Office and the professionalism of its investigators, 70 per cent of respondents thought that the Ombudsman's Office did not approach the investigation with an open mind, 63 per cent thought that the investiga-tors were more likely to believe a complainant than the officer being complained about and 42 per cent of police officers believed that 'the Police Ombudsman's Office is out to get them'. The findings of the survey were contradictory in certain respects. For example, while 48 per cent of officers who had been in contact with the Ombudsman's Office said they were dissatisfied with the way they had been dealt with during the investigation, 64 per cent were satisfied with the outcome of the investigation' (OPONI 2004a). Nevertheless, these findings were so negative that a working group comprised of representatives of the Ombudsman's Office and police staff associations was formed in search of ways to improve matters.

The Ombudsman's role and powers in relation to retrospective cases was a particularly contentious issue. In a submission to the Northern Ireland Affairs Committee, Ian Paisley Jr (the DUP's justice/policing spokesperson and a member of the Policing Board) claimed that: 'The Police Ombudsman should be prevented from investigating historic cases. The Police Ombudsman [is] supposedly about drawing a line in the sand. The current operating system is more like a witch-hunt of police officers' (NIAC 2003: appendix 3, p. 2). The UUP also noted that the Ombudsman's powers to examine retrospective cases had brought it into 'disrepute' among unionists, who viewed it 'as being out to punish the security forces, RUC and Army and to rewrite history on behalf of republicanism' (NIAC 2005b: Ev. 108). The ability to investigate retro-spective cases was, nevertheless, one of the crucial functions available to it. Some of the cases it investigated substantiated complaints that the original investigation had not been adequate (for example, the investiga-tion into the 1997 murder of Sean Brown; OPONI 2004b), and addressed long-standing grievances involving such celebrated cases as the police assault on Samuel Devenny in 1969 (OPONI 2001b). Providing the Ombudsman with powers to address such issues had been viewed by Sinn Féin and the SDLP as crucial in attracting the support of nationalists. Certainly, the Ombudsman viewed the ability to investigate retrospective cases as a particularly important matter and, moreover, one of which Northern Ireland was sorely in need:

> What we will do (and do) is say to the Chief Constable, 'In this investigation we believe there are unexplored evidential opportuni-ties . . . and therefore we believe that you would wish to revisit these opportunities and to see whether you can bring this case to closure for people.' Conversely, we can go back to people and say, 'Actually

the case in which you were involved, the death of a loved one, is one in which the police did as thorough a job as possible.' We have done that and we have gone back to people and we have had the response, which was, 'For the first time in 15, 20 years I am able to sleep at night.' I think that is enormously important because we are a very wounded community in Northern Ireland, as well as a very divided community. (NIAC 2005b: Ev. 33)

## Operational policing and the reform programme

When launching the ICP Report, Patten stated that: 'We are transforming the RUC, not disbanding it' (Patten 1999b). As the Police Service of Northern Ireland officially came into being on 4 November 2001, some unionists claimed that the transformation was a complete one, and that the RUC had effectively been 'lost'. The DUP, for instance, noted that 'the Belfast Agreement destroyed the force which stood against terrorism for 30 years' (2003a: 33). However, in strikingly similar ways, some political figures of opposing hues claimed that little of significance had changed. For UUP leader David Trimble, the PSNI was 'the same men wearing much the same uniform enforcing exactly the same law' (quoted in Millar 2004: 94), while for Martin McGuinness (Sinn Féin's chief negotiator), it was 'a tarted up RUC' (*Irish Times*, 27 November 2000).[7]

The task of monitoring the scale of the reforms was largely left to the Oversight Commissioner,[8] who regularly published reports on the implementation of the measures agreed by government. Although the Oversight Commissioner repeatedly criticized the delay in implementing particular aspects of the Patten Report and noted that this had the air of 'cherry picking' about it (2003a: 12, 15), this criticism related to fairly discrete recommendations. Some of these were infrastructural, including the establishment of a new police training college, the upgrading of police premises and the 'de-fortification' of police stations. Others, however, were closely related to organizational structure and central to the overall thrust of the Patten Report. These latter issues included an extensive civilianization process, addressing the future of the Full-Time Reserve, the establishment of formal arrangements to facilitate devolution of policing to the District Command level, the registration of members' interests, the establishment of an effective 'early warning' mechanism in relation to complaints against the police, and the Oversight Commissioner was especially critical of the delays in the integration of Special Branch with the Crime Branch (see, for example, 2003b: 5–7) (which were brought together in a newly established Crime Operations Department in March 2004).

The Oversight Commissioner noted that 'large numbers of officers' found the reforms 'unsettling and at times threatening' (2003b: 7), and it is clear that such changes did not occur without resistance.[9] When giving evidence in January 2003 to the US National Committee on Foreign Policy, the Chief Constable Hugh Orde noted that: 'There are people who want me to fail. Some of those people are within my organization' (*Irish Times*, 10 January 2003). Responding to the ensuing outcry, he stated that 'anyone who believed that all 9,000 police officers were in favour of reform should "wake up" ' (*Irish Times*, 11 January 2003). Republicans' concerns over such matters were reinforced in October 2002 by a police raid on Sinn Féin's offices at Stormont, amid claims by the Deputy Chief Constable that the police had disrupted 'a major intelligence unit within the IRA'. The Chief Constable subsequently apologized for the 'heavy-handed' and high-profile nature of the raid, television footage of which was widely broadcast. An Ombudsman's report into the raid found no evidence that it was 'politically motivated', although it did note that 'the scale and manner of the raid' – which at one stage involved 25 officers in public order uniforms – 'was totally disproportionate', and that insufficient attention was given to the fact that it was an office within the legislative assembly (OPONI press release, 1 August 2004).

Furthermore, institutional changes did not necessarily equate to changes in police practice. As the Oversight Commissioner noted in December 2004, 'there are many areas in which the impact and outcomes of changes made, particularly as those influence behaviour and police culture, have yet to be fully demonstrated' (2004: 2). Moreover, the impact of some initiatives was clearly open to question. One senior officer claimed in 2004 that the Patten Report recommendations had 'no effect' on the culture within the police, on the grounds that the force's culture was not a problem in the first place (fieldnotes). Evaluations of the PSNI's training programmes also noted that the delivery of these programmes was problematic in several respects. An assessment of the PSNI's Student Officer Training Programme found that despite a stated commitment to human rights and problem-oriented training scenarios, the training included little material based on the realities of policing in Northern Ireland (Northern Ireland Human Rights Commission 2002). As a consequence students had little or no opportunity to consider such significant issues as how to address sectarianism. On several occasions, trainers explicitly shied away from any discussion of the big 'no-go' issues of religion or politics (p. 16). Moreover, several instances were observed in which the focus was sharply on learning the script of human rights rather than using it as a tool to shape the delivery of policing. As the programme evaluator noted, such an approach ran the risk of students being 'trained to say the right thing, rather than do the right thing' (p. 30). For example, training in restraint techniques and the use of force included advice to students that, 'if a person needs to be struck, always hit them as hard as you possibly can, because one hard blow could be one assault whereas twenty softer ones could be twenty assaults' (p. 30). Similarly, a review of the two-day 'Course for All' programme delivered to approximately 11,000 police staff in 2002–03 noted a clear sense that 'human rights' had been foisted on the police, rather than being a core component of policing in itself (NIHRC 2004).

Overall, it seems indisputable that the architecture and organization of policing changed in significant and far-reaching ways. There were numerous claims, too, that these changes were yielding concrete improvements in public support for the police. The PFNI Chairman noted that: 'The core principle of policing and the greatest aspiration of any police service must be to enjoy policing with consent. In Northern Ireland we are almost there. At ground level, where police officers daily have engagement with the public on an individual basis, I believe, we have that consent' (speech at a House of Commons reception, 16 November 2004). Desmond Rea, chairman of the Policing Board, also noted the scale of the issues involved: 'Let there be no doubt there has been a tanker turned. There have been times when one has been nervous of what has been demanded of the PSNI but it has happened and I think that the justification of that statement is seen from the surveys in terms of the communities' (NIAC 2005a: Ev. 27).

One complicating factor in terms of securing public support was, as the Inspector of Constabulary noted, that the public's expectations of the PSNI were 'very high, and in many cases, wholly unrealistic'. Moreover, the failure to deliver policing of the kind sought by public representatives often led to 'robust' criticism of the police (HMIC Report for 2001–02: 19, 2). The Patten Report certainly appeared to filter into routine contact between the police and local representatives. One police commander noted that when some local politicians and community representatives met with him, they often brought with them a copy of the Patten Report, which he termed 'their bible'. During such meetings, individuals would sometimes point to specific passages of the report to inform him of how they believed policing in the area should be conducted: 'But Patten says you have do this' (fieldnotes).

The voluntary severance programme had a significant impact on the PSNI's effectiveness. Between January 2001 and March 2003, 1,786 officers left the force under this scheme (483 in the first three months of 2001, 791 in the financial year 2001–02 and 512 in 2002–03). If its purpose was to provide an exit route for those individuals unwilling to countenance the reform measures and expedite the increase in Catholic recruits, it also ensured that at one stroke considerable expertise was lost to the force (as a consequence, the voluntary severance scheme was suspended for the financial year 2003–04; see PSNI Annual Report for 2003–04: 12). This had implications for some aspects of the implementation of Patten's recommendations, as the Chief Constable retained 680 of the Full-Time Reserve to meet a shortfall in front-line officers. Personnel shortages were widely attributed as the cause of the decline in the number of routine patrols and crime prevention activities. The HMIC inspection for 2001–02 found 'whilst there has been progress in some areas, the Service, as a whole, was largely failing to deliver the community policing service articulated within the Patten Report and expected by the public' (HMIC 2001–02: 1). The clearance rate for recorded crime dropped from 30.2 per cent in 1999/00 to 20.1 per cent in 2001/02, although by 2004/05 it had risen to 28.2 per cent. Many of the difficulties surrounding police effectiveness were due to 'serious resource deficiency', particularly the loss of experienced detectives, as well as the diversion of officers into public order duties (mostly in relation to a number of high-profile incidents in Belfast in 2001).

### Recruitment and participation

Increasing Catholic participation in the police was one of the goals of the ICP. As one of its members observed, this was the 'holy grail' they sought: 'A test of our recommendations will be that young Catholic and young Protestant youth can stand up at youth clubs in their own district and say "I am going to join the police", without being jeered out of existence or being kicked out' (Hayes 1999). Prior to the 1994 ceasefires, Catholics comprised about 11 per cent of applications. This rose to 22.3 per cent immediately after the ceasefires, dropping to 17 per cent by 1997 and then rising to 22.3 per cent in 1998 (although acceptance rates averaged 13.4 per cent of recruits in this period; *Belfast Telegraph*, 11 January 1999). Following the Patten Report, an independent agency, Consensia, was given responsibility for all recruitment to the PSNI. In what the Policing Board described as 'hugely successful recruitment campaigns' (2002–03 Annual Report: 10), applications from Catholics and women increased considerably. The recruitment campaign in November 2001 received nearly 5,000 applications, of which approximately 40 per cent were from Catholics, while 38 per cent were from women (NIPB 2001–02 Annual Report: 26). In 2003, 36 per cent of applicants were Catholic and 37 per cent were women (O'Rawe 2003).

In April 2002 the first officers recruited under the 50:50 Catholic/non-Catholic model graduated. The proportion of Catholic recruits within the force increased visibly as a consequence of the new recruitment procedures, from 8.9 per cent in 2002, to 11.7 per cent in 2003, 13.9 per cent in 2004 and 18.22 per cent by July 2005 (figures from PBNI and PSNI). The Full-Time and Part-Time Reserves historically tended to have a smaller proportion of Catholics within them,[10] and when these Full-Time Reserves are taken into account, total Catholic representation within the combined branches of the police drops somewhat, but the overall figures still show Catholic participation increasing to 16 per cent by May 2005 (Oversight Commissioner 2005: 10). The gender composition of the force also registered significant changes, the numbers of women rising to 19.37 per cent of the regular PSNI in 2005.

**Table 9.1**  Public perceptions of local police performance

| *Taking everything into account, do you think that police in this area do a good job or a poor job?* | 2000 | | 2001 | | 2002 | | 2003 | | 2004* | | 2005* | |
| --- | --- | --- | --- | --- | --- | --- | --- | --- | --- | --- | --- | --- |
| | *C* | *P* | *C* | *P* | *C* | *P* | *C* | *P* | *C* | *P* | *C* | *P* |
| Very/fairly good | 59 | 79 | 55 | 79 | 57 | 76 | 59 | 69 | 45 | 57 | 53 | 62 |
| Neither good nor poor | 14 | 11 | 20 | 10 | 16 | 11 | 19 | 14 | 22 | 17 | 26 | 21 |
| Fairly/very poor | 23 | 7 | 21 | 8 | 22 | 10 | 19 | 14 | 31 | 23 | 17 | 13 |
| Don't know/refusal | 5 | 2 | 4 | 2 | 5 | 3 | 3 | 3 | 2 | 2 | 5 | 3 |

*Source*: NIPB (2003. table 4; 2005a: table 1).
*For 2004–05 Surveys: 'Do you think that the PSNI does a good job or a poor job in your area?'

## Public attitudes towards the PSNI

Survey data on public attitudes towards the PSNI found that a majority of Catholic and Protestant respondents each rated the police as doing a very good or fairly good job (Table 9.1). Catholic and Protestant respondents also rated police performance across Northern Ireland slightly higher than police performance in their own area (NIPB 2005a: Table 2), but irrespective of the sphere of policing in question, Catholics were considerably less positive and more critical of the police than Protestants were.

When respondents were asked about their confidence in the police's ability, first, 'to provide an ordinary day-to-day policing service for all of the people of Northern Ireland', and second, 'to deal with public disorder situations such as riots', Catholics also expressed less confidence in the police than did Protestants, although the differences were not great. For example, in relation to public order policing, 27 per cent of Catholics had 'a lot' or 'total' confidence in the police compared to 34 per cent of Protestants, while 29 per cent of Catholics and 19 per cent of Protestants had 'little' confidence or 'none at all' in the police's ability to deal with public disorder and riots (NIPB 2004b: table 8).

In relation to issues of 'fairness' and 'equality', surveys found that an overall majority both of Catholics and Protestants responded that the PSNI treats Catholics and Protestants equally, although Protestants are

**Table 9.2** Public perceptions of police fairness

| Would you say that the police deal fairly with everyone? | 2000 | | 2001 | | 2002 | | 2003 | |
|---|---|---|---|---|---|---|---|---|
| | C | P | C | P | C | P | C | P |
| Yes | 63 | 81 | 57 | 83 | 61 | 78 | 66 | 78 |
| No | 28 | 13 | 33 | 12 | 30 | 13 | 26 | 15 |
| Don't know/refusal | 8 | 6 | 9 | 5 | 9 | 9 | 8 | 8 |

*Source*: NIPB (2003) Community Attitude Survey 2003; table 3.

considerably more likely to maintain this. A quarter or more of Catholics believe that the police do not deal fairly with everyone (Table 9.2).

When asked their views on how the police treat Catholics and Protestants (Table 9.3), a substantial minority of Catholics believe that Protestants are treated better by the police both in their local area as well as across Northern Ireland as a whole, although this view appears to be declining. Only half of Catholic respondents believed that the PSNI treated Catholics and Protestants equally across Northern Ireland as a whole (although the proportion of Catholics who think the police treat Protestants better than Catholics is noticeably less than that found in surveys during the conflict; see Table 4.1 in Chapter 4).

These results are broadly confirmed by Hamilton, Radford and Jarman's (2003) survey of 1,163 respondents aged 16–24, which found that strong differences were evident in the attitudes of Catholics and Protestants towards the police (albeit that a large proportion of respondents opted for the 'neither agree not disagree' response to each question). Catholics were *less likely* than Protestants to agree with statements that the police are professional (36 per cent and 58 per cent), fair (22 per cent and 44 per cent), acceptable (35 per cent and 55 per cent) and representative of their community (14 per cent and 36 per cent). However, Catholics were *more likely* than Protestants to agree that policing had improved (23 per cent and 12 per cent). The survey also found that 38 per cent of Catholic respondents stated that they 'do not' support the police, compared to 27 per cent of Protestant respondents (Hamilton *et al*. 2003: 38, 48).

### Continuity and change

Overall, then, these data confirm both continuity and change. In relation to the scale of these changes, the reform programme was widely depicted as a major success. According to the Oversight Commissioner, the goals of the Patten Commission 'in large measure are being achieved. The degree of change already accomplished over a relatively short period, from the autumn of 2001 to the autumn of 2004, is both remarkable and unparalleled in the history of democratic policing reform

**Table 9.3**  Public perceptions of police impartiality, 2003–05

| How do the PSNI treat Catholic and Protestant members of the public in your area? | 2003 | | 2004 | | 2005 | |
|---|---|---|---|---|---|---|
| | Cath. | Prot. | Cath. | Prot. | Cath. | Prot. |
| Catholics better | 4 | 5 | 2 | 6 | 3 | 5 |
| Both equally | 58 | 79 | 60 | 80 | 63 | 82 |
| Protestants better | 24 | 4 | 28 | 2 | 14 | 3 |
| Don't know/refusal | 10 | 12 | 10 | 11 | 20 | 11 |
| *How do the PSNI treat Catholic and Protestant members of the public in Northern Ireland as a whole?* | | | | | | |
| Catholics better | 2 | 8 | 6 | 5 | 2 | 8 |
| Both equally | 50 | 76 | 51 | 75 | 55 | 77 |
| Protestants better | 38 | 8 | 31 | 10 | 27 | 4 |
| Don't know/refusal | 10 | 9 | 12 | 9 | 17 | 10 |

*Source*: Omnibus Survey, April 2003, October 2004 and April 2005 (NIPB 2004b: tables 3 and 4; NIPB 2005a: tables 3 and 4).

... the desired fundamental transformation of policing is taking place' (Oversight Commissioner 2004: 1). In March 2005 a report conducted on behalf of the Policing Board found that the PSNI 'has done more than any other police service anywhere else in the UK to achieve human rights compliance' (NIPB 2005b: ii). The Police Ombudsman described the creation of her Office as 'part of a wider strategy to ensure a level of accountability and transparency, which was hitherto unknown anywhere in the world' (NIAC 2005b: Ev. 25). Patten also asserted that the desired change had taken place and that the new institutions were now established (*Guardian*, 18 August 2003). Irwin (2003: 4) noted that policing reform dropped from being Catholics' first priority in May 2000 to their eighth priority by February 2003, suggesting that Catholics saw their concerns being dealt with, partly at least. As the above surveys demonstrate, Catholic perceptions of policing were, in relation to specific spheres of activity, broadly positive.

In other respects, however, continuity was the order of the day as concerns over policing remained live issues. In 2003, Sir John Stevens's third report on collusion was published in which he stated that collusion *had* occurred in the murders of Finucane and Lambert, and roundly criticized the manner in which his investigation had been actively impeded by a number of official agencies. Additionally, police involvement in controversial public order situations had always been a drain on its public support, and the policing of such events – particularly in Belfast during this period – maintained a clear link between contemporary and historical events. As one audience member at a policing conference in Belfast in 2004 claimed:

> The reason that nationalist people cannot get involved with DPPs is to be found not in history books, but was seen here last Saturday. On Saturday, the PSNI got into their full riot gear, had three water cannons, had lots and lots of Jeeps, and faced down the nationalist people who were peacefully in their own area. I was also over on the other side of the barrier and there the police wore their baseball caps, were walking along with the marchers – joking and behaving in a totally different way. The DPPs need to recognize that the RUC [sic] have a totally different attitude to the two communities – until this reality is recognized and dealt with, people will not be able to cooperate. (Quoted in CAJ 2005a: 59).

Moreover, it was not only among nationalists that policing reform proved controversial. Irwin's (2003) survey found that 72 per cent of DUP supporters and 24 per cent of UUP supporters considered it unacceptable to have Sinn Féin representatives sit on the Policing Board (30 per cent of Sinn Féin supporters also considered it unacceptable for that party to take up its seats on the Board). Furthermore, 62 per cent of DUP supporters and 29 per cent of UUP supporters viewed it as unacceptable that 'the reform of the PSNI should be completed' (p. 10).

## Conclusion

As the Patten Report emphasized, the full impact of its recommendations could only be realized in conditions of political stability and with an end to paramilitary violence. Other strands of the Belfast Agreement were implemented – including prisoner release – but policing remained problematic. The institutional and organizational reforms that were implemented reflected the contingencies of the peace process, and their operation and activities were inevitably constrained by the broader political environment. The Northern Ireland executive was suspended on several occasions and remains so at the time of writing, while allegations that the IRA carried out a £26.5 million bank robbery in Belfast in December 2004 and that some of its members were involved in the murder of Robert McCartney in January 2005 put the process under further strain. The 2005 British general election results also saw considerable gains for the DUP, largely at the expense of the UUP. David Trimble lost his seat and resigned as UUP leader, and the UUP retained only one MP while the DUP increased its representation to nine seats.

On 28 July 2005, after much media speculation, the IRA 'formally ordered an end to the armed campaign'. In September 2005, in a further significant event, the International Independent Decommissioning Commission reported that the IRA had decommissioned its weapons, and ordered its members to support political and democratic programmes 'through exclusively peaceful means' and to desist from all other activity. The statement also noted that the IRA would engage with the Independent International Commission on Decommissioning 'to put its arms beyond use' in a verifiable way. The British government quickly announced a number of 'security normalization' measures, including the dismantling of some particularly contentious army bases and watchtowers, the disbandment of the Northern Ireland-based battalions of the Royal Irish Regiment, and a large reduction in troop numbers in Northern Ireland (to what would amount to a 'peacetime' garrison).

While the IRA's statement and the British government's response seemed a clear signal that the conflict was over – although the future of loyalist and dissident republican paramilitaries remains unresolved – the political consequences of this are unclear. Unionist politicians were enraged at the scale of the security normalization measures and the speed with which they were announced, and they argued that a lengthy period (up to two years) of verification was required before they would participate with Sinn Féin in devolved government when the Northern Ireland assembly was restored. The DUP also threatened to disrupt the activities of the NIPB unless its concerns were addressed. Moreover, the electoral gains for the DUP meant that its composition on the NIPB would increase considerably when the Board was reconstituted after its current term of office expired (although the British government allowed it to continue in its present format for a further year, on the stated grounds of continuity and stability). Whatever difficulties lie ahead, in light of the IRA statement, the day when Sinn Féin formally participates in the Policing Board and DPPs, and presumably also when control over policing and justice matters is devolved to the Northern Ireland assembly, seemed to draw significantly nearer.

While this 'new beginning' may not have had as easy a birth or made as much progress as the Patten Commission hoped for, it undeniably represented a fundamental shift in the institutional landscape of policing, one that also impacted on police–community relations in significant ways. Initiatives were launched that previously would have been discarded by government, and other symbolic events (including a meeting held between Chief Constable Orde and Adams in November 2004) took place in their shadows. Much of this was down to the vision of policing articulated in the Patten Report, and its efforts to advance an agenda for policing to which all could claim allegiance.

## Notes

1 As these terms indicate, this process was persistently described in official statements as 'change' rather than 'reform'. For instance, the reports of the Oversight Commissioner were titled: *Overseeing the Proposed Revisions to the Policing Services of Northern Ireland.*

2 In March 2000 the UUP stated it would refuse to join any future devolved political structures unless the RUC's name was retained (Beirne 2001: 302). Section 1(1) of the Act subsequently stated: 'The body of constables known as the Royal Ulster Constabulary shall continue in being as the Police Service of Northern Ireland (incorporating the Royal Ulster Constabulary).'

3 Rejecting calls to support the new institutions, in 2004 Sinn Féin president Gerry Adams noted: 'It has to be remembered that during the worst years of collusion, torture and human rights abuses these governments actively defended and praised the RUC, authorized co-operation with it and urged nationalists to join it. People have a right to a first-class policing service. This does not exist at this time' (*Irish Times*, 11 March 2004).

4 While these figures may seem low, they compare favourably with the public's knowledge of CPLCs. The Patten Commission's research found that only 29 per cent of respondents 'were aware of CPLCs', and nearly 40 per cent of these said 'they did not know what the CPLCs actually did' (Patten Report 1999: 34).

5 I gratefully acknowledge CAJ's generosity in making available to me draft copies of its reports on the DPPs and the Ombudsman (2005a, 2005b).

6 See *Irish Times*, 11 January 2005, 1 October 2004, 8 August 2004, 11 March 2004, 6 October 2003, 24 September 2003, 11 September 2002. On at least one occasion, loyalists threatened DPP members concerning possible rerouting of parades (*Irish Times*, 20 June 2004).

7 In evidence to the Northern Ireland Affairs Committee (2005a: Ev. 106), Sinn Féin highlighted the continuity between the two forces and pointedly called for 'the provision of effective powers to root out human rights abusers, who have transferred en masse from the RUC into the PSNI.'

8 Tom Constantine, formerly head of the US Drug Enforcement Agency, was appointed Oversight Commissioner on 31 May 2000. He retired on 31 December 2003, and was succeeded by Al Hutchinson, who formerly had served as the Constantine's Chief of Staff.

9 As Detective Chief Superintendent Eric Anderson, an experienced and prominent officer within the force, noted: 'The sterling service of the past and present members of the RUC is being subverted by Patten and as a matter of principle I will not be serving under his new scheme of things' (*Irish Times*, 2 December 2000).

10 The Patten Report recommended the expansion of a part-time policing service, with these new recruits being largely drawn from geographical areas currently underrepresented within the police. This began on a pilot basis in four District Command Units, and 108 new part-time officers commenced training in 2004 (see PSNI Annual Report for 2003–04: 12; 2004–05: 8).

# Chapter 10

# Conclusion: conflict, legitimacy and reform

Few issues have dominated the social and political landscape of Northern Ireland to the extent that policing has. Through a violent conflict and an uneasy peace process, successive programmes of reform sought to enhance the police's legitimacy by securing the full support of the communities most antagonistic to it. Significant inroads were made into this legitimacy deficit, but institutional changes in themselves could not overcome the material legacy of police actions and the political opposition emanating from the police's role as a key institution of a disputed state. This book has attempted to explain the dynamics of this process by analysing police reform and representational strategies, and public responses to these.

The debate about the future of policing in Northern Ireland was a debate about its past. The official and oppositional discourses outlined in this book drew on divergent readings of Northern Irish history that highlighted different memories, experiences and understandings of policing. The organizational memory of the RUC highlighted the professionalization programme it undertook, and officers argued that this yielded considerable improvements in terms of police impartiality, accountability and relations with the public. As the peace process developed, this discourse was supplemented by the vocal claims that any difficulties surrounding policing were the result of the distortions resulting from the demands of the conflict, and that, given the sacrifice and suffering of the RUC, what peace should bring was recognition rather than reform. Among nationalists and republicans, a different reading of police history was evident. This highlighted the continuing concerns surrounding policing even after the RUC's professionalization from the 1970s onwards. Following the ceasefires, the narratives articulating this oppositional discourse highlighted 'signal' and 'everyday' events, and the links between them. The implementation of the Patten reform agenda was also hostage to this contested backdrop.

My discussion of these issues leaves unanswered two questions of clear importance. The first of these is the obvious issue concerning the long-term development of policing in Northern Ireland. Despite its status as one of the most extensive and far-reaching programmes of change in the history of organized policing, this remains a nascent process. While there is general consensus that the changes arising from the Patten Report have yielded sizeable benefits in terms of the general structures of policing and the development of community relations, these are early days. Full consideration of the impact of these changes will require a longer timeframe and more detailed empirical investigation of them than has been provided here. Second, the often-strained relationship between the police and unionist and loyalist communities has been highlighted in a number of studies (Ellison 2001; McVeigh 2004; O'Mahony *et al.* 2000; Weitzer 1995) as well as in the Patten Report (1999a: 16), but there remains a need for sustained research on different aspects of this important issue.[1]

In this concluding chapter, I highlight two broad issues: the lessons that policing in Northern Ireland may have for broader criminological debates; and the specific role that police reform plays in ongoing processes of conflict resolution in Northern Ireland.

## Lessons from the Northern Ireland conflict?[2]

As some social commentators express the view that globalization has led to the demise of the nation state as the locus of social organization and regulation (Castells 2000), criminological writing increasingly has taken to heart a concern about the links between crime and locale, posing questions about the nature, extent and consequences of policy 'flow' or 'transfer' and 'lessons-drawing' between jurisdictions. It has not only teased out the specificity of criminal justice systems in the new global order (Crawford 2002), but has also considered the dynamics of 'the global travel of crime policies' (Karstedt 2002). The salience of this approach derives from the fact that political regimes appear increasingly attentive to criminal justice developments in other jurisdictions, and also from the often implicit or untested assumptions that the importation and adoption of such developments is both desirable and feasible (Newburn and Sparks 2004). Moreover, the establishment of supranational institutions to promote and coordinate criminal justice developments on a transnational basis raises fundamental questions of governance and accountability (Loader 2002; Walker 2003).

The Patten Report has placed the context of Northern Ireland centre-stage in such debates. As the Report was gradually implemented, it was seen not only as an example of best practice in terms of its relevance for Northern Ireland, but was also characterized as a programme of reform that warranted transfer to and duplication in other contexts and jurisdictions. As the Oversight Commissioner (2003b: 1) noted:

> With each passing oversight review it has become increasingly apparent that the Patten Commission not only identified the critical areas in need of reform, but proposed solutions that are clearly representative of 'best practices' in policing. The recommendations of the Patten Commission and the success of the Police Service of Northern Ireland in implementing them are now being seen as models for many police forces around the world.

The Chairperson of the Northern Ireland Policing Board also claimed that the Patten Report provided a 'blueprint for modern policing worldwide' (seminar on 'Police/Community Relations', Dublin, 22 April 2005). Even the Police Federation, which initially had denounced the Patten Report in unambiguous terms (PFNI 1999), remarked that 'much of what has been introduced in Northern Ireland would serve as an excellent role model for elsewhere in the UK and the rest of the world' (speech by PFNI Chairman, House of Commons, 16 November 2004). Other accounts of policing in Britain, Ireland and elsewhere, have acclaimed the Patten Report as 'a model for reform in the future' (Newburn 2003: 99) due to its extensive focus on accountability and on community involvement in 'policing' in its broadest sense (Bowling and Foster 2002: 1019; Connolly 2002; Irish Council for Civil Liberties 2003; Reiner 2000: 198). In this section I consider the lessons to be learnt, both historically and in the contemporary period, from debates and developments about policing and police reform in Northern Ireland.

### Critical criminology and the 'contagion thesis'

For many years, developments in Northern Ireland occupied an ambivalent position in criminological writing. Despite a recent growth in research on crime and justice issues in Northern Ireland (McEvoy and Ellison 2003), most criminologists tended to 'ignore' the conflict (Brewer *et al.* 1997: 4). As a result, few sustained analyses emerged that considered developments in Northern Ireland in relation to broader criminological debates in Britain, the Irish Republic or elsewhere. The most notable appearance that Northern Ireland *did* make in this regard was in the work of critical criminologists. A number of authors writing in this vein frequently highlighted developments in the administration of justice in Northern Ireland as evidence of the growing power of the 'authoritarian state' (Bunyan 1977; Hillyard 1997, 1993, 1987, 1985; Sim *et al.* 1987). This argument articulated what may be described as a 'contagion thesis' (Mulcahy 2005), which held that Northern Ireland essentially served as a testing ground for the repressive technologies and practices through which the power of the authoritarian state would be extended to 'normal' societies: sooner or later, the policies and practices evident in Northern Ireland (such as heavily armed police, non-jury courts, emergency powers) would visit Britain's shores and, indeed, Europe generally (Farrell 1993; Tomlinson 1993). Rather than remaining confined to the management of political violence and thus peripheral to the rest of the criminal justice system, the 'emergency' measures enacted in response to the conflict – such as the Prevention of Terrorism (Temporary Provisions) Act 1974 – were increasingly being treated as part of the 'ordinary' legal landscape. Their 'temporary' description belied their marked longevity, while their 'emergency' character was at odds with their gradual 'normalization' (Hillyard, 1987, 1993; Ní Aoláin, 2000). With senior British police officers particularly attentive to the public order-oriented and militarized mode of policing being developed in Northern Ireland, Hillyard (1985) argued that the 'lessons from Ireland' were profoundly depressing ones, with grave implications for civil liberties and the character of criminal justice. While a number of factors suggest the flow of policy and expertise was more nuanced that this uniformly oppressive and one-directional model would suggest (Mulcahy 2005), the Patten Report has given new impetus to Northern Ireland's role in these debates on policy transfer. Two issues in particular highlight potentially positive 'lessons from Ireland': human rights, and the relationship between police and public.

## Human rights, accountability and oversight

Despite the rapid growth of interest in issues of 'policy transfer', this body of work has largely bypassed the important question of the impact that violent upheaval in one jurisdiction may have on neighbouring jurisdictions. Despite some incisive and troubling analyses of the exportation of police technology and expertise (Huggins 1998; Marenin 1996; see also Brogden and Nijhar 2005), issues of human rights and their abuse have played a relatively 'subdued role in the cross-national exchange of crime policies' (Karstedt 2002: 121). Debate on the impact of security measures enacted following the 11 September 2001 attacks has brought these issues into sharper focus, if only to highlight the minimal role that human rights play in these policy responses whose emphasis instead is firmly on security (Scraton 2002). This general omission from policy transfer debates is all the more significant as human rights abuses are likely to be more prevalent in circumstances of violent conflict, and potential transfer to other societies of strategies and technologies developed and employed in those contexts is an issue of self-evident concern.

The Patten Report has, however, dramatically changed the role that Northern Ireland plays in human rights debates. In terms of formal structures and powers, the framework of accountability established in Northern Ireland still stands as perhaps the most progressive and extensive model of oversight yet established. In a world post-11 September 2001, where laws on torture are being rewritten to legalize violent interrogation techniques provided these do not lead to organ failure or death, there is much that is comforting within the covers of the Patten Report. Its steadfast promotion of policing as 'the protection and vindication of the human rights of all' brings a counterbalance against the predictable pressures to infringe on human rights during conflict situations. Rolston (2002a) notes that developments in Northern Ireland have been implicated in US security measures taken in response to the 11 September 2001 attacks. In this context where international collaboration explicitly underpins security policies in the new global order, it is important to recognize that the history of Northern Ireland provides an object lesson in the potentially counterproductive impact of security measures (Campbell and Connolly 2003; Ellison and Smyth 2000).[3] There is, clearly, a distinction to be drawn between rhetorical and actual commitment to such principles, and it is clear from the grudging manner in which the report was implemented that state interests remained reluctant to loosen their grip on control of policing. Every single significant proposal that sought to open policing up to greater scrutiny was – initially at least – resisted and significantly watered down in the subsequent legislation and associated implementation plans. Nevertheless, this formal adherence to a human rights-based model of policing is surely an essential first step in delivering such policing, and – if only as a declaration of intent – it must be welcomed.

### Police, public and nodal governance

The Patten Report also offers important lessons on the relationship between the police and the public. As the history of Northern Ireland shows, the police and other criminal justice organizations play a key role in mediating the relationship between communities and the state (and, indeed, relationships with other communities). As Frank Wright noted: 'In national conflicts, law, order and justice are not issues that happen to arise from other causes. National conflicts, once they are fully developed, revolve around these issues' (cited in McGarry and O'Leary 1999: 3).

This view is supported by Whyte's (1990: 86) observation that Catholics and Protestants disagree more over policing and security measures than over constitutional issues. The significance of the Patten Report in this regard derives from the very recognition it provides to the public, and the importance it attaches to their role in policing (McEvoy *et al.* 2002).

In seeking to reorient policing 'towards the support of active and equal citizenship rather than the support of a sovereign statehood' (Walker 2001: 146), the Patten Report outlines a democratic vision of policing in which the police are seen as partners with the public in the joint production of safety and security. This is, of course, a fine balancing act. The weight of criminological research suggests that the 'core practice' of policing (Cain 1979) remains the maintenance of social order, that in crisis situations this dominates over other aspects of policing (particularly the development of good community relations) and that in practice the coercive powers of policing are directed against individuals and groups who feature low down the social hierarchy. In conflict situations where the legitimacy of the state is at issue, reform programmes may provide better training, oversight and so on, but if the police are tasked with enforcing the laws of a state which is overtly challenged, then police actions will inevitably be directed against those who dispute the state's legitimacy. In conditions of political stability, however, when issues of state are – on a day-to-day basis at least – settled, new possibilities emerge for how policing may be structured. Such was the case with the Patten Report. Its proposals were not ones directed against conditions of widespread political violence, but ones which sought to establish a framework for a 'new beginning' in Northern Ireland in which policing would no longer be a source of conflict. As the commissioners noted, their purpose was to remove policing from politics. However, in recognizing that only in conditions of political stability could policing be fully 'depoliticized' (ICP 1999: chapter 8), the report paradoxically confirmed the key associations between these two spheres.

Beyond the emphasis on human rights and accountability discussed above, the most distinctive aspect of the report was in terms of its steadfast commitment to 'policing' rather than the 'police'. In focusing on the activity rather than the state institution, the Patten Report sought to outline a model for policing and its regulation that recognized the state's limited capacity in terms of security provision, and that simultaneously maximized local involvement and capacity in terms of the delivery and governance of security. Shearing and his colleagues (2000, 2001; Kempa and Shearing 2002; see also Johnston and Shearing 2003) believed the report's most significant contribution was not those measures which dominated debate in Northern Ireland – particularly those concerning police symbolism – but rather the template it provided for a 'nodal conception of governance'. This model called for policing to be decentred from the traditional state monopoly and instead provided by and regulated through a network of 'nodes' or organizations in which the public are actively involved. Shearing argued that the 'golden thread' (2000: 388) of the report was the manner in which, first, it recognized the limits of the traditional state-centred model of policing (the 'public' police) and absorbed the lessons from changes taking place in policing worldwide, particularly through the emergence of private policing and various public-private hybrids; and second, applied these to Northern Ireland by establishing mechanisms that would enhance and regulate public capacity to contribute to the provision of security. Shearing (2000: 393) highlighted as particularly significant the recommendations for a 'policing' rather than a police board, the establishment of functional rather than institutional budgets (ones not restricted to funding the 'public' police), and the principle of 'operational responsibility' to replace that of 'operational independence'. These would ensure greater responsiveness and adaptability in the provision of policing, enhance local capacity in shaping the policing that communities received (or co-generated) and, ultimately, 'deepen democracy' (Kempa and Shearing 2002: 25).

The nodal governance model advanced in the Patten Report and strongly advocated by Shearing and others is not without its critics. Loader and Walker (2004, 2006) in particular have criticized this model's decisive shift away from a state-centred framework of policing, and questioned whether the proposed alternatives can fulfil the 'solidarity-nourishing role' (2004: 227) that hitherto rested with the state and its agencies. While they too recognize the dramatic changes taking place worldwide in relation to policing, they remain sceptical that the market model advanced by Shearing and others can adequately address the 'social' nature of security in a way that contributes to 'civic solidarity' rather than to 'levelled-up tribalism' (pp. 226–7). Several commentators in Northern Ireland have also considered the difficulties of establishing the 'active partnerships' envisaged in the Patten Report given the state's grudging approach to these issues (Hillyard and Tomlinson 2000; McEvoy et al. 2002; O'Mahony et al. 2000). Here too it must be noted that the full import of the nodal governance model outlined in the report was undermined in the implementation programme. For example, the recommendations concerning the tax-raising powers of DPPs did not materialize in the enacting legislation, and the focus of the Policing Board and the DPPs remains very much on the public police rather than on the delivery and regulation of 'policing' more generally. As noted in the previous chapter, a longer time-frame than is available here is needed to provide a more considered evaluation of the Patten Report and its impact. Nevertheless, the future lessons that policing in Northern Ireland provides may well be in terms of how a nodal framework of governance develops there.

## Conflict resolution and police reform

In periods of conflict resolution and political transition, law and legal institutions assume a heightened importance and become key chapters in narratives of social change (Glaeser 2003). Their status as pillars of the former regime is generally replaced by one that reflects the scale of the political changes underway and that requires a more expansive role for these institutions than previously was the case (Teitel 2000). This process is undeniably complex and multi-faceted, but it is most often manifested in demands for extra-institutional measures rather than recourse to a model of institutional 'modernization' (Campbell *et al.* 2003; O'Rawe 2003). In that regard, the requirements of transitional justice serve as a useful antidote to uncritical acceptance of the discourse of 'professional' policing as an adequate response to the demands of this key moment. As evident from discussions in earlier chapters, legitimacy must be distinguished from instrumental judgements concerning effectiveness and other intra-organizational measures of police performance. People's belief in the appropriateness of police behaviour is closely related to the legitimacy they accord the police and the levels of support they provide them with (Tyler 2004). Policing, however, is never 'just' about issues of technical efficiency and effectiveness. These issues certainly have their own logic and significance, but policing can never be reduced to them. Public understandings of policing are profoundly implicated in issues of affect, affiliation and identity. In the absence of a shared narrative of legitimacy, the police may turn inwards and focus instead on internally derived measures. Ultimately, though, these measure organizational activity rather than public acceptance, and it is the former rather than the latter that is the most significant dimension of the legitimation process. Police professionalization must therefore be regarded as a strategy to secure legitimacy rather than evidence of its achievement.

What the police do and how policing develops plays a key role in the production of 'collective memory' among different sectors of society (Glaeser 2003; Innes 2003; Loader and Mulcahy 2003). Collective memory is a reconstruction of the past, albeit one fashioned in light of understandings of the present. In this interpretive process, however, the momentum of the past is indisputable. As Halbwachs (1992: 183) argues:

It is undoubtedly difficult to modify the present, but is it not much more difficult in certain respects to transform the image of the past that is also – at least virtually – in the present, since society always carries within its thoughts the frameworks of memory? After all, the present, if we consider the area of collective thought that it occupies, weighs very little in comparison to the past.

Transitional justice is complicated by the general 'lack of a shared narrative by all parties on the causes of conflict and its manifestations' (Bell *et al.* 2004: 313). Accordingly, such periods are often characterized by a clash of competing and antagonistic histories – often ones that were, respectively, prescribed and proscribed under the previous regime – rather than the articulation of a mutually shared one. As Memmi (1990) suggests, conflict over the past reflects broader conflicts over the need to legitimize power relations. He argues that 'domination' immediately implicates the 'victor' in an unending process of justification:

> to possess victory completely he needs to absolve himself of it and the conditions under which it was attained. This explains his strenuous insistence, strange for a victor, on apparently futile matters. He endeavours to falsify history, he rewrites laws, he would extinguish memories – anything to succeed in transforming his usurpation into legitimacy. (p. 52)

The complexities of the legitimation process thus highlight the contentiousness of history. They also demonstrate that memory and amnesia function strategically to plot reality, to set its limits and to circumscribe the imagination within specific horizons of understanding. This is a function of both officially sanctioned histories and the oppositional histories that would disrupt them. Each set of narratives is resilient in the face of refutation, and through a variety of discursive strategies maximizes the veracity of their own accounts while simultaneously undermining the material bases of the others (Boyarin 1994).

The uncertainty of transitional periods ensures that these competing histories are often expressed with even greater ardour than during the conflict itself; but a process of conflict resolution also gives rise to more considered reflection as former combatants and others take stock, and are forced to reckon with the human costs of conflict. Moreover, the demand for progress is often accompanied by a demand to address allegations of past abuses and the impact these had not just on individuals, but on entire communities (Osiel 1997). As Teitel (2000: 6) notes, in contexts of political transformation, 'Law is caught between the past and the future, between backward-looking and forward-looking, between retrospective and prospective, between the individual and the collective.'

This was the case in Northern Ireland, as the violence of the Troubles largely gave way to an emphasis during the peace process on charting the victimhood and loss that had occurred over the previous decades. This 'flurry of recognition' (Rolston 2000: x) took various forms, including general audits of the conflict (McKittrick *et al.* 2004; Fay *et al.* 1999; Smyth and Fay 2000) as well as more specifically local commemoration activities (Ardoyne Commemoration Project 2002).

Under the provisions of the Good Friday Agreement, a Victim's Commisison was also established (Bloomfield 1998). As these developments confirmed, the legacy of the past yielded a profound sense of victimhood and grievance across Northern Ireland, and the peace process was characterized by an unparalleled expression of this. What issued forth, though, was not an agreed-upon shared history, but rather the articulation of anxiety and grief, anger and resentment, as individuals and groups feared that their stories would be the final casualties of the conflict, or, as that, as the PFNI feared, they would be 'airbrushed from history' (*Police Beat*, September 2001). Such accounts of the past are deeply embedded in wider political struggles over the nature and legitimacy of the Northern Irish state.

Among nationalists, the peace process provided an opportunity to address long-standing grievances over policing, articulated most often in relation to the 'signal events' and 'everyday' policing issues discussed in Chapter 7. Scott (1990) suggests that, rather than an opportunity for the development of some commonly agreed upon history, transitional periods are better characterized as an opportunity for previously hidden histories to be forcefully articulated in public settings. In Northern Ireland, however, an oppositional history of the police could only have been described as a 'hidden history' in the loosest sense of the term. This was, after all, a history celebrated in visible and accessible ways through murals and parades (Jarman 1997), as well as through local media and the routine channels of community life (Burton 1978; Matassa 1999; Sluka 1989). Rather, in a context of conflict resolution, the concerns that animated nationalist and republican suspicion and/or hostility towards the police now became part of the mainstream political agenda, and were established as key aspects of the peace process. It involved recognition of their claims concerning policing, claims which underpinned the demand that police reform would be central to any political settlement.

For unionists, the peace process and the prominent role of police reform within it raised a different set of concerns, ones that were profoundly shaped by the British state's strategy of conflict management that had characterized the conflict *solely* as 'terrorism' and criminality to be addressed through the normal (if enhanced) criminal justice system. In those circumstances, participating in a peace process may have been seen as politically pragmatic, and even as a necessary undertaking, but the dominant unionist definition of the conflict also ensured that it was regarded as a morally compromised exercise. As McEvoy (2001) convincingly argues in relation to the release of paramilitary prisoners, while this proved traumatic for many nationalists, it was less so for them than for unionists because within nationalism – irrespective of whether one agreed with the rationale that paramilitary groups offered for engaging in violence – there was a general acceptance that the state was problematic at best, if not inherently exclusionary as far as their cultural/national identity and political participation was concerned. Within this framework, it made 'sense' to nationalists that prisoner release would have to form part of an overall settlement to bring an end to the conflict, just as policing would too. For many unionists, however, police reform generated massive ideological dissonance. The terrorist discourse promoted by the British government as the *sole* sanctioned perspective on the conflict was not a tawdry fiction they had idly bought into; it was a fundamental component of unionist identity. In these terms, the state was legitimate, it was necessary to protect unionists, it was assailed by a vicious campaign of often indiscriminate violence, and peace had been secured through the dedication and sacrifice of the RUC and security forces generally. The police had been cast in heroic terms, suffering terrible casualties, enduring terrible traumas to maintain law and order and to preserve the integrity of the state, and ultimately to maintain the status quo. Against that background, police reform was a none-too-subtle challenge to unionist readings of the state, its history, and the conflict. Its 'implicit narrative of institutional failure' (Bell *et al*. 2004: 315) generated what was, in effect, an ontological crisis for unionism and unionists, shaking the institutions with which they had so closely affiliated and aligned themselves, and that had reflected their identity and protected their state. A political solution challenged their view that a security solution was what was required. As with prisoner release, police reform made this apolitical characterization of the conflict 'increasingly untenable' (McEvoy 2001: 352).

## Reconciliation and redress

Dealing with the past is often the most onerous aspect of conflict resolution. This is due not only to the wholesale violence and destruction evident in conflict situations, but also to the ideological divisions that often give rise to those very conflicts (Osiel 1997; Teitel 2000) and the complex difficulties of acknowledging and commemorating unpalatable truths (Young 1993; see also McEvoy and Conway 2004). While Northern Ireland is a profoundly segregated society in terms of residence and education, it is no less segregated in terms of discursive space. Echoing the findings of many other anthropological studies of Northern Ireland, Kelleher (2003: 205) found that 'Conversations between Catholics and Protestants often stopped when the state was invoked.' This avoidance of controversial yet basic issues reinforced the other social pressures that inhibited movement outside of particular (usually familiar) discursive circles. While this may have its own consequences for the particular dynamics of conflict – through all of the consequences that flow from a preoccupation with identifying threatening 'others' through various strategies of 'telling' (Burton 1978) – it also impacts on processes of conflict resolution. This was particularly the case given the differential impact that the conflict had on the everyday lives of people, a process most significantly mediated by geographical area and community profile (Fay *et al.* 1999). Different experiences meshed with different political ideological standpoints to produce different historical accounts of the conflict.

The unrelenting tension between divergent histories of policing in Northern Ireland is part of a larger debate about reconciliation and redress that itself reflects the sheer scale of the conflict, both in terms of the prevalence of suffering, as well as the magnitude of specific events. The scale of some events simply does not have a ready equivalent in adjacent jurisdictions. For instance, while the British police service was rocked by the Macpherson Inquiry (1999) into the 1993 murder of Stephen Lawrence and the wide-ranging criticisms it made of the police investigation into his death, most of the criticisms made related to acts of omission rather than commission. Yet in Northern Ireland, allegations of collusion between members of the security forces and loyalist paramilitaries have been long-standing features of the conflict (see the discussion in Chapter 4). Sir John Stevens's investigations not only confirmed that collusion had occurred, but his first investigation into these issues was undermined to the extent that the building where the investigation was based was burnt down in what he described as 'a deliberate act of arson' (Stevens 2003: 13), presumably on the part of one or more branches of the state security forces. The oppositional history of policing celebrated within nationalist and republican communities demonstrates that unresolved questions concerning past events – allegations of collusion in the cases of Pat Finucane and others prominent among these – remained a huge obstacle to the RUC's, and latterly the PSNI's, legitimation efforts.[4] The discursive prominence and political significance of these histories is indisputable. What is less clear is what to do about them.

Silence and denial have been familiar state responses to allegations of past misconduct (Cohen 2001). Although these strategies may succeed in preventing any formal recognition being given to those alleging victimization, that does not necessarily resolve the issue. In so far as people's beliefs are sincerely held and, in their own eyes, based on plausible and compelling evidence, to ignore a complaint or issue a denial does not in these circumstances undermine those beliefs, and may actually bolster them. Denials may be counterproductive if they are perceived as false, and merely as further evidence that the initial claim is so revealing of issues at the heart of the state that to acknowledge it, and thereby 'accommodate' it, is a step the state is unwilling to take.

While silence and denial may be 'business as usual' for the state, in situations of political transition dealing with the past becomes a vocal enterprise in which demands for truth and disclosure are equated with broader processes of reconciliation. Formal 'reconciliation' events may be held, apologies given and so on, but the recognition that occurs under such conditions may veer towards the abstract: general harm done by unspecified protagonists to anonymous others. Such abstract gestures give no full sense of the harm caused, the victims created, the consequential actions then taken which are now so regretted. Moreover, the tone of such recognition may also be questionable, perhaps expressed through bland expressions of regret, particularly ones that simultaneously reiterate the suffering that one's own constituency endured. During the Northern Ireland peace process, several prominent apologies were made, including ones by loyalist and republican paramilitaries, as well as by the British Prime Minister.[5] Yet the format of apology is inevitably a ritual entity and, given that it involves a specific mode of presentation of self, it is subject to all the concerns relating to the sincerity of such an exercise. If an apology is perceived to be devoid of sincerity, offered as a strategic response to a demand made rather than a felt expression of remorse, it runs the risk of undermining itself, adding fresh insult to existing injury (Rolston 2000: 322). Moreover, there is the related issue that if an apology is demanded as the basis for humiliation, this is likely to impede rather than advance reconciliation.[6] As Scott argues (1990: 58): 'Remorse, apologies, asking forgiveness, and generally, making symbolic amends are a more vital element in almost any process of domination than punishment itself.' Such actions do not merely demonstrate compliance; they repair the symbolic order by demanding 'a show of *discursive affirmation from below*' (original emphasis).

The issue of reconciliation is further complicated by the fact that the very nature of the conflict is itself such a disputed issue (McGarry and O'Leary 1996). Throughout the peace process, nationalists and unionists sought recognition for competing litanies of grievance.[7] Northern Ireland is hardly unique in this respect, and truth commissions have emerged in the aftermath of many violent conflicts in an effort to address similar concerns (Hayner 1994). While the precise format they take may vary from context to context, they share in common a view that the truth plays an important role in political transition, whether with a view to prosecution, reconciliation or remembrance (Booth 2001). In Northern Ireland, some commentators have opposed a truth commission on the basis that it will not secure the full participation of the British government (Rolston 2002b), others on the grounds that it 'would serve only to hold those who served in the Crown Forces to account for their actions while terrorists can hide behind the cloak of anonymity' (DUP 2003b: 9). It is difficult to gauge what such a process would yield, but some effort 'to find a common history by treating the various antagonistic relationships seriously' (McEvoy 2001: 359) is entirely warranted.

This is not to suggest that full disclosure or uncontested readings of the past are possible. To advocate such an enterprise misrepresents the constructed quality of all understandings of the past. Moreover, even the most committed efforts to assemble evidence and information about particular events face daunting challenges.[8] Northern Ireland has been described as 'the most heavily researched area on earth' (Whyte 1990: viii), but knowledge is not 'truth', and many questions remain unanswered and many experiences unacknowledged. Recent developments in Northern Ireland constitute an opportunity for policing to be unshackled from the burden of securing a state whose legitimacy was never established in any conclusive way, and for its publics to have institutions with which they can productively engage to address human needs and which at a political level they can affiliate with. One of the key elements of the Patten Report was its understanding of policing as 'everybody's business'. No less can be said about the past. Memory and amnesia, remembering and forgetting, are as much political as historical phenomena. But it is not a case of choosing one to the exclusion of the other. Reconciliation is partly about forgetting, but justice is partly about remembering. They both have a role to play in developing a better understanding of the histories of policing in Northern Ireland and in securing a more positive future for it.

## Notes

1  Four aspects of relations between unionists/loyalists and the police seem especially significant. First, how was identification with the RUC at a nationalistic level absorbed, understood, expressed and enacted, and with what level of cohesion or fractiousness? Second, how did unionist and loyalist communities respond to the changing relationship between them and the RUC as the force sought to distance itself from its historical role as a key symbol of an overtly unionist state and establish itself as an impartial police force equidistant from the 'immature communities' (*Police Beat*, July 2004) it policed? If this was about the RUC refashioning and repackaging itself, how did unionists reflect on this process, and with what consequences for their relations with the force as well as for the nature and coherence of their socio-political identity? Third, how did unionists and loyalists resolve the tension between, on the one hand, their criticisms and concerns over the policing they received, and on the other, their frequently expressed desire not to undermine the force's role in addressing republican paramilitary violence? How prevalent was this concern not to rock the boat, what forms did it take and with what consequences? Fourth, how have these combined issues evolved during the ongoing reform programme, and what is their likely impact on relations between unionists/loyalists and the police into the future?

2  This section draws on material from Mulcahy (2005).

3  The new security climate has also affected paramilitary activities. For example, the unionist politician Jeffrey Donaldson considered it extremely unlikely that, 'post 9/11, republicans could ever try to bomb the heart of London again, because it just would not be tolerated internationally' (*Irish Times*, 5 August 2004).

4 As part of the 2001 Weston Park negotiations, retired Canadian Judge Peter Cory was tasked with inquiring into a number of high-profile cases in which collusion was alleged, including the Finucane case (Cory 2004). On the basis of his reports, the British and Irish governments undertook to hold inquiries into these particular cases. When the British government published its draft legislation to establish these inquiries, the *Inquiries Bill*, Cory roundly criticized its narrow scope, stating that 'I cannot contemplate any self-respecting Canadian judge accepting an appointment to an inquiry constituted under the new proposed act'. Despite widespread criticism of the proposed inquiry format, the Bill was passed in April 2005. Further details of these issues are available from the CAIN website (www.cain.ulst.ac.uk) and the Pat Finucane Centre website (www.serve.com/pfc/). See also Rolston and Scraton (2005).

5 For example, the British Prime Minister Tony Blair apologized in February 2005 in relation to miscarriages of justice in the case of the Guildford Four and the Maguire Seven (http://www.cain.ulst.ac.uk/issues/politics/docs/pmo/tb090205.htm). Paramilitary organizations also expressed apologies, including that by the Combined Loyalist Military Command when announcing the loyalist paramilitary ceasefire in October 1994 (http://cain.ulst.ac.uk/events/peace/docs/clmc131094.htm) and by the IRA in 2002 (http://www.cain.ulst.ac.uk/events/peace/docs/ira160702.htm).

6 In November 2004, at a rally in his political heartland of Ballymena, Ian Paisley stated that 'the IRA needs to be humiliated. And they need to wear their sackcloth and ashes, not in a backroom but openly. And we have no apology to make for the stand we are taking' (*Irish Times*, 30 November 2004). This occurred during tense political negotiations relating to arms decommissioning and, while the negotiations broke down over a failure to reach agreement on how this process would be guaranteed, the explicit call for humiliation was seen as a further factor blocking progress.

7 While a sense of grievance and victimhood was a prominent aspect of republican identity, unionist identity was also shaped by litanies of signal events that often shadowed those of nationalists (see, for example, DUP 2003b). While this was evident from the outset of the conflict (Ó Dochartaigh 2005), it was particularly prominent during the peace process when debates about respective levels of victimization were at their height.

8 The Police Ombudsman noted some of the concrete difficulties involved in investigating the past: 'The forensic science lab was blown up, lots of police stations were blown up, a lot of evidence has gone, people have died, memories have changed, locations have changed. Those investigations are difficult' (NIAC 2005b: Ev. 38). The exercise of state agency by 'proxy' has further clouded matters (Jamieson and McEvoy 2005). In addition, the sheer scale of the unanswered questions of the conflict is vast. In March 2005, the PSNI Chief Constable Hugh Orde announced the establishment of a 'murder review group' tasked with examining unsolved murders from the conflict. Dating back to 1969, this amounted to approximately 1,800 deaths, including 211 police officers. See also his newspaper article, 'North's legacy of unsolved crimes must be addressed' (*Irish Times*, 23 October 2004).

# References

Allen, K. (2004) *Max Weber: A Critical Introduction*. London: Pluto.

Alliance Party (1995) *The Police Authority Consultation Process: The Alliance Party Response*. Belfast: Alliance Party.

Altheide, D. and Johnson, J. (1980) *Bureaucratic Propaganda*. Beverly Hills, CA: Sage.

Amnesty International (1978) *Report of an Amnesty International Mission to Northern Ireland*. London: Amnesty International.

Amnesty International (1994) *Political Killings in Northern Ireland*. London: Amnesty International.

Anderson, D. (1994) *14 May Days: The Inside Story of the Loyalist Strike of 1974*. Dublin: Gill & Macmillan.

Anderson, P. (1977) 'The antinomies of Gramsci', *New Left Review*, 100: 5–78.

Annesley, H. (1992) 'Police Foundation lecture – July 21 1992', *Police Journal*, 65: 287–96.

Ardoyne Association (1994) *Policing in Ardoyne: Community Conference on Policing*. Belfast: Ardoyne Association.

Ardoyne Association (1996) *Ardoyne: A Neighbourhood Police Service*. Belfast: Ardoyne Association.

Ardoyne Commemoration Project (2002) *Ardoyne: The Untold Truth*. Belfast: Beyond the Pale.

Balbus, I. (1977) *The Dialectics of Legal Repression* (2nd edn). New Brunswick, NJ: Transaction.

Barker, A. (2004) *Shadows: Inside Northern Ireland's Special Branch*. Edinburgh: Mainstream.

Barker, T. and Carter, D. L. (eds) (1994) *Police Deviance* (3rd edn). Cincinnati, OH: Anderson.

Baxter, N. S. J. (2001) *Policing the Line: The Development of a Theoretical Model for the Policing of Conflict*. Aldershot: Ashgate.

Bayley, D. and Shearing, C. (1996) 'The future of policing', *Law and Society Review*, 30(3): 586–606.

Bayley, D. and Shearing, C. (2001) *The New Structure of Policing: Description, Conceptualization, and Research Agenda*. Washington, DC: National Institute of Justice.

Bayley, D. H. (1977) 'The limits of police reform', in D. H. Bayley (ed.), *Police and Society*. Beverly Hills, CA: Sage.

Beetham, D. (1991) *The Legitimation of Power*. London: Macmillan.

Beirne, M. (2001) 'Progress or placebo? The Patten Report and the future of policing in Northern Ireland', *Policing and Society*, 11(3–4): 297–319.

Bell, C., Campbell, C. and Ní Aoláin, F. (2004) 'Justice discourses in transition', *Social and Legal Studies*, 13(3): 305–28.

Bennett Committee (1979) *Report of the Committee of Inquiry into Police Interrogation Procedures in Northern Ireland* (Cmnd. 7497). London: HMSO.

Bew, P., Gibbon, P. and Patterson, H. (1996) *Northern Ireland 1921–1996: Political Forces and Social Classes* (rev. edn). London: Serif.

Bittner, E. (1980) *The Functions of the Police in Modern Society*. Cambridge, MA: Oelgeschlager, Gunn & Hain.

Black Committee (1976) *The Handling of Complaints Against the Police: Report of the Working Party For Northern Ireland* (Cmnd. 6475). London: HMSO.

Bloomfield, K. (1998) *We Will Remember Them: Report of the Northern Ireland Victims Commissioner, Sir Kenneth Bloomfield*. Belfast: Stationery Office.

Blumberg, M. (1989) 'Controlling police use of deadly force', in R. G. Dunham and G. P. Alpert (eds), *Critical Issues in Policing*. Prospect Heights, IL: Waveland Press.

Bobock, R. (1986) *Hegemony*. New York: Tavistock.

Booth, W. J. (2001) 'The unforgotten: memories of justice', *American Political Science Review*, 95(4): 777–91.

Bourdieu, P. (1977) *Outline of a Theory of Practice*, trans. Richard Nice. Cambridge: Cambridge University Press.

Bowling, B. and Foster, J. (2002) 'Policing and the police', in M. Maguire, R. Morgan and R. Reiner (eds), *Oxford Handbook of Criminology* (3rd edn). Oxford: Oxford University Press.

Bowyer-Bell, J. (2000) *The IRA 1968–2000: An Analysis of a Secret Army*. London: Frank Cass.

Boyarin, J. (1994) 'Space, time and the politics of memory', in J. Boyarin (ed.), *Remapping Memory: The Politics of TimeSpace*. Minneapolis, MN: University of Minnesota.

Boyce, D. G. (1979) ' "Normal policing": public order in Northern Ireland since partition', *Eire-Ireland*, 14: 35–52.

Boyle, K., Hadden, T. and Hillyard, P. (1980) *Ten Years on in Northern Ireland: The Legal Control of Political Violence*. London: Cobden Trust.

Breathnach, S. (1974) *The Irish Police*. Dublin: Anvil.

Brewer, J. (1990) *The RIC: An Oral History*. Belfast: Institute for Irish Studies.

Brewer, J. (1991) 'Policing in divided societies', *Policing and Society*, 1(3): 179–91.

Brewer, J. (1992) 'The police and the public', in P. Stringer and G. Robinson (eds), *Social Attitudes in Northern Ireland: The Second Report, 1991–1992*. Belfast: Blackstaff Press.

Brewer, J. (1993) 'Public images of the police in Northern Ireland', *Policing and Society*, 3(3): 163–76.

Brewer, J., Guelke, A., Hume, I., Moxon-Browne, E. and Wilford, R. (1996) *Police, Public Order and the State* (2nd edn). London: Macmillan.

Brewer, J., Lockhart, B. and Rodgers, P. (1997) *Crime in Ireland 1945–95*. Oxford: Clarendon.

Brewer, J., Lockhart, B. and Rodgers, P. (1998) 'Informal social control and crime management in Belfast', *British Journal of Sociology*, 49(4): 570–85.

Brewer, J., with Magee, K. (1991) *Inside the RUC: Routine Policing in a Divided Society*. Oxford: Clarendon.

British Irish Rights Watch (1999) *Deadly Intelligence: State Involvement in Loyalist Murder in Northern Ireland*. London: British Irish Rights Watch.

Brogden, M. (1998) *Two-Tiered Policing: A Middle Way for Northern Ireland?* Belfast: Democratic Dialogue.

Brogden, M. (2001) 'The Patten Report: a unitary solution to a multi-dimensional problem', *Policing and Society*, 11(3–4): 273–95.

Brogden, M. and Nijhar, P. (2005) *Community Policing: National and International Models and Approaches*. Cullompton: Willan.

Brogden, M. and Shearing, C. (1993) *Policing for a New South Africa*. New York: Routledge.

Bruce, S. (1992) *The Red Hand: Protestant Paramilitaries in Northern Ireland*. Oxford: Oxford University Press.

Bruce, S. (1994) *Edge of the Union: The Ulster Loyalist Political Vision*. Oxford: Oxford University Press.

Bryett, K. (1997) 'What does Drumcree tell us about the RUC?', *Critical Criminology*, 8(1): 49–62.

Bunyan, T. (1977) *The History and Practice of the Political Police in Britain*. London: Quartet.

Burton, F. (1978) *The Politics of Legitimacy: Struggles in a Belfast Community*. London: Routledge & Kegan Paul.

Burton, F. and Carlen, P. (1979) *Official Discourse: On Discourse Analysis, Government Publications, Ideology and the State*. London: Routledge & Kegan Paul.

Cain, M. (1979) 'Trends in the sociology of police work', *International Journal of the Sociology of Law*, 7(2): 143–67.

Cain, M. (1983), 'Gramsci, the state and the place of law', in D. Sugarman (ed.), *Legality, Ideology and the State*. New York: Academic Press.

Callaghan, J. (1973) *A House Divided: The Dilemma of Northern Ireland*. London: Collins.

Cameron Committee (1969) *Disturbances in Northern Ireland: Report of the Commission Appointed by the Governor of Northern Ireland* (Cmnd. 532). London: HMSO.

Campaign for Social Justice in Northern Ireland (1972) *Northern Ireland – The Mailed Fist: A Record of Army and Police Brutality from August 9 – November 9, 1971*. Dungannon: Campaign for Social Justice in Northern Ireland.

Campbell, C. and Connolly, I. (2003) 'A model for the "war against terrorism"? Military intervention in Northern Ireland and the 1970 Falls Road curfew', *Journal of Law and Society*, 30(3): 341–75.

Campbell, C., Ní Aoláin, F. and C. Harvey (2003) 'The frontiers of legal analysis: reframing the transition in Northern Ireland', *Modern Law Review*, 66(3): 317–45.

Castells, M. (2000) *End of Millenium: The Information Age, Vol. 3*. Oxford: Blackwell.

Central Citizens' Defence Committee (1973) *The Black Paper: Northern Ireland – The Story of the Police*. Belfast: Central Citizens' Defence Committee.

Chan, J. (1997) *Changing Police Culture: Policing in a Multi-Cultural Society*. Cambridge: Cambridge University Press.

Choongh, S. (1997) *Policing as Social Discipline*. Oxford: Oxford University Press.

Cochrane, Fergal. (2001) *Unionist Politics and the Politics of Unionism Since the Anglo-Irish Agreement* (rev. edn). Cork: Cork University Press.

Cohen, S. (2001) *States of Denial: Knowing about Atrocities and Suffering*. Cambridge: Polity.

Coicaud, J.-M. (2002) *Legitimacy and Politics*, trans. D. A. Curtis. Cambridge: Cambridge University Press.

Committee on the Administration of Justice (1992) *Inquests and Disputed Killings in Northern Ireland*. Belfast: CAJ.

Committee on the Administration of Justice (1993) *Adding Insult to Injury? Allegations of Harassment and the Use of Lethal Force by the Security Forces in Northern Ireland.* Belfast: Committee on the Administration of Justice.

Committee on the Administration of Justice (1996) *The Misrule of Law: A Report on the Policing of Events During the Summer of 1996 in Northern Ireland*. Belfast: Committee on the Administration of Justice.

Committee on the Administration of Justice (1999) *The Patten Commission: The Way Forward for Policing in Northern Ireland?* Report of a CAJ Conference, 8 October. Belfast: Committee on the Administration of Justice.

Committee on the Administration of Justice (2003) *Commentary on the Northern Ireland Policing Board*. Belfast: Committee on the Administration of Justice.

Committee on the Administration of Justice (2005a) *Commentary on District Policing Partnerships*. Belfast: Committee on the Administration of Justice.

Committee on the Administration of Justice (2005b) *A Commentary on the Office of the Police Ombudsman for Northern Ireland – Draft Document*. Belfast: Committee on the Administration of Justice.

Compton Committee (1971) *Report of an Enquiry into the Allegations against the Security Forces of physical brutality in Northern Ireland arising out of events on the 9th August 1971* (Cmnd. 4823). London: HMSO.

Connerton, P. (1989) *How Societies Remember*. Cambridge: Cambridge University Press.

Connolly, J. (2002) 'Policing Ireland: past, present and future', in P. O'Mahony (ed.), *Criminal Justice in Ireland*. Dublin: Institute of Public Administration.

Connolly, W. (1984a) 'Introduction: legitimacy and modernity', in W. Connolly (ed.), *Legitimacy and the State*. New York: New York University Press.

Connolly, W. (1984b) 'The dilemma of legitimacy', in W. Connolly (ed.), *Legitimacy and the State*. New York: New York University Press.

Cory Report (2004) *Cory Collusion Inquiry Report – Patrick Finucane* (HC 470). London: Stationery Office.

Crawford, A. (ed.) (2002) *Crime and Insecurity: The Governance of Safety in Europe*. Cullompton: Willan.

Crawford, A. (2003) 'The pattern of policing in the UK: policing beyond the police', in T. Newburn (ed.), *Handbook of Policing*. Cullompton: Willan.

Criminal Justice Review (2000) *Review of the Criminal Justice System in Northern Ireland*. Belfast: HMSO.

Curtis, L. (1984) *Ireland: The Propaganda War*. London: Pluto Press.


De Baróid, C. (1999) *Ballymurphy and the Irish War* (2nd edn). London: Pluto.

Democratic Unionist Party (2003a) *A Fair Deal: DUP Manifesto 2003*. Belfast: DUP.

Democratic Unionist Party (2003b) *A Voice for Victims*. Belfast: DUP.

Dewar, M. (1996) *The British Army in Northern Ireland* (rev. edn). London: Arms & Armour.

Dickson, B. and Millar, R. (1990) 'Complaints against the police', in B. Dickson (ed.), *Civil Liberties in Northern Ireland: The CAJ Handbook* (2nd edn). Belfast: Committee on the Administration of Justice.

Diplock Committee (1972) *Report of the Commission to Consider Legal Procedures to Deal with Terrorist Activities in Northern Ireland* (Cmd. 5185). London: HMSO.

Dixon, B. and van der Spuy, E. (eds) (2004) *Justice Gained: Crime and Crime Control in South Africa's Transition*. Cullompton: Willan.

Doherty, R. (2004) *The Thin Green Line: The Histroy of the Royal Ulster Constabulary GC.* Barnsley: Pen and Sword.

Ellison, G. (1997) 'Professionalism in the Royal Ulster Constabulary: An Examination of the Institutional Discourse'. Unpublished DPhil thesis, University of Ulster.

Ellison, G. (2000) 'Reflecting all shades of opinion: public attitudinal surveys and the construction of police legitimacy in Northern Ireland', *British Journal of Criminology*, 40(1): 88–110.

Ellison, G. (2001) 'Young people and the Royal Ulster Constabulary: a study of inter-communal attitudes', *Policing and Society*, 11(3–4): 321–36.

Ellison, G. (2005 in press) 'Fostering a dependency culture: the commodification of community policing in a global marketplace', in A. Goldsmith and J. Sheptycki (eds), *Crafting Global Policing*. Oxford: Hart.

Ellison, G. and Martin, G. (2000) 'Policing, collective action and social movement theory', *British Journal of Sociology*, 51(4): 681–99.

Ellison, G. and Mulcahy, A. (2001) 'Policing and social conflict in Northern Ireland', *Policing and Society*, 11(3–4): 243–58.

Ellison, G. and Smyth, J. (1995) 'Bad apples or rotten barrels? Policing in Northern Ireland', in O. Marenin (ed.), *Policing Change, Changing Police: International Perspectives*. New York: Garland.

Ellison, G. and Smyth, J. (2000) *The Crowned Harp: Policing Northern Ireland*. London: Pluto.

Emsley, C. (1992) 'The English bobby: an indulgent tradition', in R. Porter (ed.), *Myths of the English*. Cambridge: Polity.

English, R. (2003) *Armed Struggle: A History of the IRA*. Basingstoke: Macmillan.

Enloe, C. (1980) *Ethnic Soldiers: State Security in a Divided Society*. Harmondsworth: Penguin.

Ericson, R. V. and Haggerty, K. (1997) *Policing the Risk Society*. Oxford: Clarendon.

Faligot, R. (1983) *Britain's Military Strategy in Ireland: The Kitson Experiment*. London: Zed Books.

Farrell, M. (1980) *Northern Ireland: The Orange State* (2nd edn). London: Pluto.

Farrell, M. (1983) *Arming the Protestants*. Dingle, Ireland: Brandon.

Farrell, M. (1993) 'Anti-terrorism and Ireland: the experience of the Irish Republic', in T. Bunyan (ed.), *Statewatching the New Europe*. London: Statewatch.

Faul, D. and Murray, R. (1975) *The RUC: The Black and Blue Book*. Dungannon: Authors.

Fay, M.-T., Morrissey, M. and Smyth, M. (1999) *Northern Ireland's Troubles: The Human Costs*. London: Pluto.

Feenan, D. (2002) 'Community justice in conflict: paramilitary punishments in Northern Ireland', in D. Feenan (ed.), *Informal Justice*. Aldershot: Ashgate.

Fentress, J. and Wickham, C. (1992) *Social Memory*. Oxford: Basil Blackwell.

Findlay, M. (1984) 'Organized resistance, terrorism and criminalization in Ireland: the state's construction of the control equation', *Crime and Social Justice*, 21/22: 95–115.

Findlay, M. (1985) ' "Criminalisation" and the detention of "political prisoners" – an Irish perspective', *Contemporary Crises*, 9(1): 1–17.

Fisher, C. (ed.) (1995) *Policing in a New Society*. Belfast: Centre for Research and Documentation/Belfast Community Forum on Policing.

Fishman, M. and Cavender, G. (eds) (1998) *Entertaining Crime: Television Reality Programmes*. New York: Aldine de Gruyter.

Fisk, R. (1975) *The Point of No Return*. London: Deutsch.

Fitzgerald, G. (1992) *All in a Life*. Dublin: Gill & Macmillan

Forum for Peace and Reconciliation. (1995) *Transcript of Oral Submissions on Policing in Northern Ireland*. Dublin: Forum for Peace and Reconciliation.

Foucault, M. (1980) 'Two lectures', in C. Gordon (ed.), *Power/Knowledge*. New York: Pantheon.

Foucault, M. (1990) *The History of Sexuality, Vol. One*. New York: Vintage Books.

Foucault, M. (1991) 'Governmentality', in G. Burchell, C. Gordon and P. Miller (eds), *The Foucault Effect*. Chicago: University of Chicago Press.

Fyfe, J. (1988) 'Police use of deadly force: research and reform', *Justice Quarterly*, 5(2): 165–205.

Gardiner Committee (1975) *Report of a Committee to Consider, in the Context of Civil Liberties and Human Rights, Measures to Deal with Terrorism in Northern Ireland* (Cmnd. 5847). London: HMSO.

Garland, D. (1996) 'The limits of the sovereign state: strategies of crime control in contemporary society', *British Journal of Criminology*, 36(4): 335–71.

Gilligan, G. and Pratt, J. (eds) (2004) *Crime, Truth and Justice: Official Inquiry, Discourse, Knowledge*. Cullompton: Willan.

Gillis, J. (ed.) (1994) *Commemorations: The Politics of National Identity*. Princeton, NJ: Princeton University Press.

Glaeser, A. (2003) *Divided in Unity: Identity, Germany and the Berlin Police*. Chicago: University of Chicago Press.

Godson, D. (2004) *Himself Alone: David Trimble and the Ordeal of Unionism*. London: HarperCollins.

Goffman, E. (1959) *The Presentation of Self in Everyday Life*. New York: Anchor Books.

Goldsmith, A. J. (1991) 'External review and self-regulation: police accountability and the dialectic of complaints procedures', in A. J. Goldsmith (ed.), *Complaints Against the Police*. Oxford: Oxford University Press.

Goldstein, H. (1977) *Policing a Free Society*. Cambridge, MA: Ballinger.

Goldstein, H. (1990) *Problem-Oriented Policing*. New York: McGraw-Hill.

Gordon, P. (1987) 'Community policing: towards the local police state?', in P. Scraton (ed.), *Law, Order and the Authoritarian State*. Milton Keynes: Open University Press.

Gramsci, A. (1971) *Selections from the Prison Notebooks*, trans. Q. Hoare and G. N. Smith. New York: International Publishers.

Greene, J. R. and Mastrofski, S. D. (eds) (1988) *Community Policing: Rhetoric or Reality?* New York: Praeger.

Greer, S. (1994) *Supergrasses*. Oxford: Oxford University Press.

Gregory, E. (2004) *Not Waving but Drowning*. Edinburgh: Mainstream.

Grimshaw, R. and Jefferson, T. (1987) *Interpreting Policework*. London: Allen & Unwin.

Habermas, J. (1975) *Legitimation Crisis*, trans. T. McCarthy. Boston: Beacon Press.

Halbwachs, M. (1992) *On Collective Memory*, ed. and trans. L. Coser. Chicago: University of Chicago Press.

Hall, S. (1977) 'Culture, the media, and the "ideological effect" ', in J. Curran, M. Gurrevitch and J. Woollacott (eds), *Mass Communication and Society*. London: Edward Arnold.

Hall, S. (1988) 'The toad in the garden: Thatcherism among the theorists', in C. Nelson and L. Grossberg (eds), *Marxism and the Interpretation of Cultures*. Urbana, IL: University of Illinois Press.

Hall, S., Critcher, C., Jefferson, T., Clarke, J. and Roberts, B. (1978) *Policing the Crisis: Mugging, the State and Law and Order*. London: Macmillan.

Hamill, D. (1986) *Pig in the Middle: The British Army in Northern Ireland, 1969–1985*. London: Metheun.

Hamilton, A., Moore, L. and Trimble, T. (1995) *Policing a Divided Society: Issues and Perceptions in Northern Ireland*. Coleraine: Centre for the Study of Conflict.

Hamilton, J., Radford, K. and Jarman, N. (2003) *Policing, Accountability and Young People*. Belfast: Institute for Conflict Research.

Hart, W. (1980) 'Waging peace in Northern Ireland', *Police Magazine*, 3(3): 22–32.

Harvey, C. (ed.) (2001) *Human Rights, Equality and Democratic Renewal in Northern Ireland*. Oxford: Hart.

Hayes, B. and McAllister, I. (2001) 'Sowing dragons' teeth: public support for political violence and paramilitarism in Northern Ireland', *Political Studies*, 49(5): 901–22.

Hayes, M. (1997) *A Police Ombudsman for Northern Ireland?* Belfast: HMSO.

Hayner, P. (1994) 'Fifteen truth commissions – 1974 to 1994: a comparative study', *Human Rights Quarterly*, 16(4): 598–655.

Held, D. (1989) *Political Theory and the Modern State*. Cambridge: Polity.

Helsinki Watch (1991) *Human Rights in Northern Ireland*. New York: Human Rights Watch.

Helsinki Watch (1992) *Children in Northern Ireland: Abused by Security Forces and Paramilitaries*. New York: Human Rights Watch.

Her Majesty's Inspectorate of Constabulary (2001) *Inspection of the Royal Ulster Constabulary, 2000/2001*. London: HMSO.

Her Majesty's Inspectorate of Constabulary (2004) *Baseline Assessment of the Police Service of Northern Ireland*. London: HMSO.

Her Majesty's Inspectorate of Constabulary. (1995) *Primary Inspection for the Royal Ulster Constabulary*. London: HMSO.

Hermon, J. C. (1997) *Holding the Line: An Autobiography*. Dublin: Gill & Macmillan.

Hillyard, P. (1985) 'Popular justice in Northern Ireland: continuities and change', in S. Spitzer and A. T. Scull (eds), *Research on Law, Deviance, and Social Control, Vol. 7*. Greenwich, CT: JAI Press.

Hillyard, P. (1987) 'The normalization of special powers: from Northern Ireland to Britain', in P. Scraton (ed.), *Law, Order and the Authoritarian State*. Milton Keynes: Open University Press.

Hillyard, P. (1993) *Suspect Community: People's Experience of the Prevention of Terrorism Acts in Britain*. London: Pluto.

Hillyard, P. (1997) 'Policing divided societies: trends and prospects in Northern Ireland and Britain', in P. Francis, P. Davies and V. Jupp (eds), *Policing Futures*. London: Macmillan.

Hillyard, P. and Tomlinson, M. (2000) 'Patterns of policing and policing Patten', *Journal of Law and Society*, 27(3): 394–415.

Holdaway, S. (1983) *Inside the British Police*. Oxford: Basil Blackwell.

Holland, J. and Phoenix, S. (1996) *Phoenix: Policing the Shadows*. London: Hodder & Stoughton.

Hollywood, B. (1997) 'Dancing in the dark: ecstasy, the dance culture and moral panic in post-ceasefire Northern Ireland', *Critical Criminology*, 8(1): 62–77.

Huggins, M. (1998) *Political Policing: The United States and Latin America*. Durham, NC: Duke University Press.

Human Rights Watch (1997) *Without Fear or Favour*. New York: Human Rights Watch.

Hunt Committee (1969) *Report of the Advisory Committee on Police in Northern Ireland* (Cmnd. 535). London: HMSO.

Hutchinson, B. (1995) 'Policing in loyalist areas', in C. Fisher (ed.), *Policing in a New Society*. Belfast: Centre for Research and Documentation/Belfast Community forum on Policing.

Innes, M. (2003) *Investigating Homicide*. Oxford: Oxford University Press.

Innes, M. (2004) 'Signal crimes and signal disorders: notes on deviance as communicative action', *British Journal of Sociology*, 55(3): 335–55.

Irish Congress of Trade Unions (1981) *Supplementary Report No. 3: Police Authority for Northern Ireland*. Belfast: ICTU.

Irish Council for Civil Liberties (2003) *Police Reform: Why Patten Should Apply Here and How This Can be Achieved*. Dublin: ICCL.

Irwin, C. (2003) *Devolution and the State of the Peace Process*. See: http://www.peacepolls.org/Resources/NIPoll9A.pdf.

Jamieson, R. and McEvoy, K. (2005) 'State crime by proxy and judicial othering', *British Journal of Criminology*, 45(4): 504–27.

Jarman, N. (1997) *Material Conflicts: Parades and Visual Displays in Northern Ireland*. London: Berg.

Jefferson, T. and Grimshaw, R. (1984) *Controlling the Constable*. London: Cobden Trust.

Jennings, A. (1990a) 'Shoot to kill: the final courts of justice', in A. Jennings (ed.), *Justice Under Fire: The Abuse of Civil Liberties in Northern Ireland*. London: Pluto.

Jennings, A. (1990b) 'Bullets above the law', in A. Jennings (ed.), *Justice Under Fire: The Abuse of Civil Liberties in Northern Ireland*. London: Pluto.

Johnston, L. and Shearing, C. (2003) *Governing Security: Explorations in Policing and Justice*. London: Routledge.

Jones, T. (2003) 'The governance and accountability of policing', in T. Newburn (ed.), *Handbook of Policing*. Cullompton: Willan.

Jones, T. and Newburn, T. (2000) *Widening Access: Improving Police Relationships with 'Hard to Reach' Groups*. London: HMSO.

Karstedt, S. (2002) 'Durkheim, Tarde and beyond: the global travel of crime policies', *Criminal Justice*, 2(2): 111–23.

Keith, M. (1993) *Race, Riots and Policing: Lore and Disorder in a Multi-Racist Society*. London: University College London Press.

Kelleher, W. (2003) *The Troubles in Ballybogoin: Identity and Memory in Northern Ireland*. Ann Arbor, MI: University of Michigan Press.

Kelling, G. L. and Moore, M. H. (1988) 'From political to reform to community: the evolving strategy of police', in J. R. Greene and S. D. Mastrofski (eds), *Community Policing*. New York: Praeger.

Kempa, M. and Shearing, C. (2002) 'Microscopic and macroscopic responses to inequalities in the governance of security: respective experiments in South Africa and Northern Ireland', *Transformation*, 49: 25–54.

Kennally, D. and Preston, E. (1971) *Belfast, August 1971: A Case to be Answered*. London: Independent Labour Party.

Kennedy, L. (ed.) (1995) *Crime and Punishment in West Belfast*. Belfast: West Belfast Summer School.

Kitson, F. (1989) *Low Intensity Operations: Subversion, Insurgency and Peacekeeping* (2nd edn). London: Faber & Faber.

Knox, C. (2002) 'See no evil, hear no evil: insidious paramilitary violence in Northern Ireland', *British Journal of Criminology*, 42(1): 164–85.

Latham, R. (2001) *Deadly Beat: Inside the Royal Ulster Constabulary*. Edinburgh: Mainstream.

Lawyers Committee for Human Rights (2002) *Beyond Collusion: The UK Security Forces and the Murder of Pat Finucane*. Washington: Lawyers' Committee for Human Rights.

Lea, J. and Young, J. (1993) *What Is to Be Done About Law and Order?* (rev. edn). London: Pluto.

Lee, J. (1981) 'Some structural aspects of police deviance in relations with minority groups', in C. Shearing (ed.), *Organisational Police Deviance*. Toronto: Butterworth.

Lennon, B. (1995) *After the Ceasefires: Catholics and the Future of Northern Ireland*. Dublin: Columba Press.

Liberty (1992) *Broken Covenants: Violations of International Law in Northern Ireland*. London: Liberty.

Liberty (1995) *Northern Ireland: Human Rights and the Peace Dividend*. London: Liberty.

Lloyd, D. (1993) *Anomalous States: Irish Writing and the Post-Colonial Moment*. Durham, NC: Duke University Press.

Loader, I. (2002) 'Policing, securitization and democratisation in Europe', *Criminal Justice*, 2(2): 125–53.

Loader, I. and Mulcahy, A. (2003) *Policing and the Condition of England: Memory, Politics, and Culture*. Oxford: Oxford University Press.

Loader, I. and Walker, N. (2001) 'Policing as a public good: reconstituting the connections between policing and the state', *Theoretical Criminology*, 5(1): 9–35.

Loader, I. and Walker, N. (2004) 'State of denial: rethinking the governance of security – review of *Governing Security*', *Punishment and Society*, 6(2): 221–8.

Loader, I. and Walker, N. (2006 in press) 'Necessary virtues: the legitimate place of the state in the production of security', in B. Dupont and J. Wood (eds), *Democracy, Society and the Governance of Security*. Cambridge: Cambridge University Press.

Lucy, G. (1996) *Stand-Off! Drumcree: July 1995 and 1996*. Lurgan: Ulster Society Publications.


Macpherson, W. (1999) *The Stephen Lawrence Inquiry: Report of an Inquiry by Sir William Macpherson of Cluny* (Cm. 4262). London: Stationery Office.

Magee, K. (1991) 'The dual role of the Royal Ulster Constabulary in Northern Ireland', in R. Reiner and M. Cross (eds), *Beyond Law and Order*. London: Macmillan.

Mandelson, P. (2000) *Statement by the Secretary of State for Northern Ireland, Peter Mandelson MP, on the Implementation of the Patten Report, 19 January 2000*. See: http://www.cain.ulst.ac.uk/issues/police/patten/pm19100.htm.

Manning, P. K. (1988) 'Community policing as a drama of control', in J. R. Greene and S. D. Mastrofski (eds), *Community Policing*. New York: Praeger.

Manning, P. K. (1992) *Organizational Communication*. New York: Aldine de Gruyter.

Manning, P. K. (1997) *Police Work: The Social Organization of Policing* (2nd edn). Prospect Heights, IL: Waveland.

Manning, P. K. (2003) *Policing Contingencies*. Chicago: University of Chicago Press.

Mapstone, R. (1992) 'The attitudes of police in a divided society: the case of Northern Ireland', *British Journal of Criminology*, 32(2): 183–92.

Mapstone, R. (1994) *Policing in a Divided Society: A Study of Part Time Policing in Northern Ireland*. Aldershot: Avebury.

Marenin, O. (ed.) (1996) *Policing Change, Changing Police*. New York: Garland.

Mark, R. (1978) *In the Office of Constable*. London: Collins.

Mastrofski, S. D. (1988) 'Community policing as reform: a cautionary tale', in J. R. Greene and S. D. Mastrofski (eds), *Community Policing*. New York: Praeger.

Matassa, M. (1999) 'The Social Construction of Security and Control in a North Belfast Community'. Unpublished PhD thesis, University of Leeds.

Matassa, M. and Newburn, T. (2003) 'Policing and terrorism', in T. Newburn (ed.), *Handbook of Policing*. Cullompton: Willan.

Mawby, R. C. (2002) *Policing Images: Policing, Communication and Legitimacy*. Cullompton: Willan.

McCann, E. (1980) *War and an Irish Town* (2nd edn). London: Pluto.

McEvoy, K. (2001) *Paramilitary Imprisonment in Northern Ireland*. Oxford: Oxford University Press.

McEvoy, K. and Conway, H. (2004) 'The dead, the law and the politics of the past', *Journal of Law and Society*, 31(4): 539–62.

McEvoy, K. and Ellison, G. (2003) 'Criminological discourses in Northern Ireland: conflict and conflict resolution', in T. Newburn and K. McEvoy (eds), *Criminology, Conflict Resolution and Restorative Justice*. London: Palgrave.

McEvoy, K. and Mika, H. (2001) 'Punishment, policing and praxis: restorative justice and non-violent alternatives to paramilitary punishments in Northern Ireland', *Policing and Society*, 11(3–4): 359–82.

McEvoy, K., Gormally, B. and Mika, H. (2002) 'Conflict, crime control and the "re-construction" of state–community relations in Northern Ireland', in G. Hughes, E. McLaughlin and J. Muncie (eds), *Crime Prevention and Community Safety*. London: Sage.

McGarry, J. (2004) 'The politics of policing reform in Northern Ireland', in J. McGarry and B. O'Leary (eds), *The Northern Ireland Conflict: Consociational Engagements*. Oxford: Oxford University Press.

McGarry, J. (2000) Police reform in Northern Ireland, *Irish Political Studies*, 15: 183–92.

McGarry, J. and O'Leary, B. (1995) *Explaining Northern Ireland: Broken Images*. Oxford: Blackwell.

McGarry, J. and O'Leary, B. (1999) *Policing Northern Ireland: Proposals for a New Start*. Belfast: Blackstaff Press.

McGinty, R. (1999) 'Policing and the Northern Ireland peace process', in J. Harrington and E. Mitchell (eds), *Politics and Performance in Contemporary Northern Ireland*. Amherst, MA: University of Massachusetts Press.

McGuffin, J. (1973) *Internment*. Tralee: Anvil.

McGuffin, J. (1974) *The Guinea Pigs*. London: Penguin.

McKittrick, D., Kelters, S., Feeney, B. and Thornton, C. (2004) *Lost Lives: The Story of the Men, Women and Children who Died as a Result of the Northern Ireland Troubles* (2nd edn). Edinburgh: Mainstream.

McLaughlin, E. (2005) 'From real to ideal: the Blue Lamp and the popular cultural construction of the English "bobby" ', *Crime, Media, Culture*, 1(1): 11–30.

McLaughlin, E. and Murji, K. (1998) 'Resistance through representation: "storylines", advertising and Police Federation campaigns', *Policing and Society*, 8(4): 367–400.

McMichael, G. (1995) 'Policing in Northern Ireland', *New Ulster Defender*, 1(13): 22–3.

McNiffe, L. (1997) *A History of the Garda Síochána*. Dublin: Wolfhound.

McVeigh, R. (1994) *'It's part of life here . . .': The Security Forces and Harassment in Northern Ireland*. Belfast: Committee on the Administration of Justice.

McWilliams, M. (1995) 'Masculinity and violence: a gender perspective on policing and crime in Northern Ireland', in L. Kennedy (ed.), *Crime and Punishment in West Belfast*. Belfast: West Belfast Summer School.

Memmi, A. (1990) *The Colonizer and the Colonized*, trans. H. Greenfeld. London: Earthscan.

Millar, F. (2004) *Trimble: The Price of Peace*. Dublin: Liffey Press.

Miller, D. (1994a) *Don't Mention the War: Northern Ireland, Propaganda and the Media*. London: Pluto.

Miller, D. (1994b) 'The Northern Ireland Information Service and the media: aims, strategies, tactics', in Glasgow University Media Group (eds), *Getting the Message*. London: Routledge.

Miller, D. (1998) 'Colonialism and academic representations of the Troubles', in D. Miller (ed.), *Rethinking Northern Ireland*. Harlow: Longman.

Moloney, E. (2003) *A Secret History of the IRA*. London: Penguin.

Moore, L. and O'Rawe, M. (2001) 'A new beginning for policing in Northern Ireland?', in C. Harvey (ed.), *Human Rights, Equality and Democratic Renewal in Northern Ireland*. Oxford: Hart.

Morgan, R. (1989) 'Policing by consent: legitimating the doctrine', in R. Morgan and D. J. Smith (eds), *Coming to Terms with Policing*. London: Routledge.

Morgan, R. and Newburn, T. (1996) *The Future of Policing*. Oxford: Oxford University Press.

Morrissey, M. and Pease, K. (1982) 'The black criminal justice system in West Belfast', *Howard Journal*, 21: 159–66.

Mulcahy, A. (1995) 'Claims-making and the construction of legitimacy: media coverage of the 1981 Northern Irish hunger strike', *Social Problems*, 42(4): 449–67.

Mulcahy, A. (1999) 'Visions of normality: peace and the reconstruction of policing in Northern Ireland', *Social and Legal Studies*, 8(2): 277–95.

Mulcahy, A. (2000) 'Policing history: the official discourse and organisational memory of the Royal Ulster Constabulary', *British Journal of Criminology*, 40(1): 68–87.

Mulcahy, A. (2002) 'The impact of the Northern "Troubles" on criminal justice in the Irish Republic', in P. O'Mahony (ed.), *Criminal Justice in Ireland*. Dublin: Institute of Public Administration.

Mulcahy, A. (2005) 'The "other" lessons from Ireland? Policing, political violence and policy transfer', *European Journal of Criminology*, 2(2): 185–209.

Mulcahy, A. and Ellison, G. (2001) 'The language of policing and the struggle for legitimacy in Northern Ireland', *Policing and Society*, 11(3–4): 383–404.

Munck, R. (1984) 'Repression, insurgency, and popular justice: the Irish case', *Crime and Social Justice*, 21–22: 81–94.

Munck, R. (1988) 'The lads and the hoods: alternative justice in an Irish context', in M. Tomlinson, T. Varley and C. McCullagh (eds), *Whose Law and Order?* Belfast: Sociological Association of Ireland.

Murray, R. (1990) *The SAS in Ireland*. Dublin: Gill & Macmillan.

Murray, R. (1998) *State Violence in Northern Ireland, 1969–1997*. Cork: Mercier.


Newburn, T. (2003) 'Policing Since 1945', in T. Newburn (ed.), *Handbook of Policing*. Cullompton: Willan.

Newburn, T. and Sparks, R. (eds) (2004) *Criminal Justice and Political Cultures*. Cullompton: Willan.

Newman, K. (1978) 'Prevention in extremis: the preventative role of the police in Northern Ireland', in *The Cranfield Papers*. London: Peel Press.

Ní Aoláin, F. (2000) *The Politics of Force: Conflict Management and State Violence in Northern Ireland*. Belfast: Blackstaff.

Northern Ireland Affairs Committee (1998) *Composition, Recruitment and Training of the RUC* (HC 337-I). London: Stationery Office.

Northern Ireland Affairs Committee (2003) *The Police (Northern Ireland) Bill: List of Conclusions and Recommendations*. London: Stationery Office.

Northern Ireland Affairs Committee (2005a) *The Functions of the Northern Ireland Policing Board* (HC 108). London: Stationery Office.

Northern Ireland Affairs Office (2005b) *The Functions of the Office of the Police Ombudsman for Northern Ireland* (HC 344). London: Stationery Office.

Northern Ireland Human Rights Commission (2002) *An Evaluation of Human Rights Training for Student Police Officers in the Police Service of Northern Ireland.* Belfast: Northern Ireland Human Rights Commission.

Northern Ireland Human Rights Commission (2004) *Human Rights in Police Training – Report Four: Course for All.* Belfast: Northern Ireland Human Rights Commission.

Northern Ireland Office (1989) *'The Day of the Men and Women of Peace Must Surely Come . . .'* Belfast: Northern Ireland Office.

Northern Ireland Office (1994a) *Community Attitudes Survey – A Report of the First 12 Months, November 1992-October 1993*, Policy, Planning and Research Unit, Occasional Paper No. 26. Belfast: NIO.

Northern Ireland Office (1994b) *Policing in the Community: Policing Structures in Northern Ireland.* Belfast: HMSO.

Northern Ireland Office (1995a) *Community Attitudes Survey – The Second Report, November 1993 – October 1994*, Policy, Planning and Research Unit, Occasional Paper No. 29. Belfast: NIO.

Northern Ireland Office (1995b) *Building the Peace in Northern Ireland* (2nd edn). Belfast: Northern Ireland Information Service.

Northern Ireland Office (1996) *Foundations for Policing: Proposals for Policing Structures in Northern Ireland* (Cmnd. 3249). London: HMSO.

Northern Ireland Office (2000) *The Patten Report: Secretary of State's Implementation Plan.* Belfast: HMSO.

Northern Ireland Office (2001) *The Community and the Police Service: Report of the Independent Commission on Policing for Northern Ireland. Updated Implementation Plan.* Belfast: HMSO.

Northern Ireland Policing Board (2003) *Community Attitudes Survey: The Northern Ireland Policing Board Module 2003.* Belfast: Northern Ireland Policing Board.

Northern Ireland Policing Board (2004a) *DPP Public Consultation Survey May 2004.* Belfast: NIPB.

Northern Ireland Policing Board (2004b) *Public Perceptions of the Police and the Northern Ireland Policing Board* (Omnibus Survey, October 2004). Belfast: NIPB.

Northern Ireland Policing Board (2005a) *Public Perceptions of the Police, DPPs and the Northern Ireland Policing Board.* Belfast: NIPB.

Northern Ireland Policing Board (2005b) *Human Rights Annual Report.* Belfast: NIPB.

Ó Dochartaigh, N. (1997) *From Civil Rights to Armalites: Derry and the Birth of the Irish Troubles.* Cork: Cork University Press.

Ó Dochartaigh, N. (2005) *From Civil Rights to Armalites: Derry and the Birth of the Irish Troubles* (2nd edn). London: Macmillan/Palgrave.

O'Brien, C. C. (1994) *Ancestral Voices: Religion and Nationalism in Ireland.* Dublin: Poolbeg.

O'Doherty, M. (1992) 'Fear and loathing on the Falls Road', *Fortnight*, 304 (March).

O'Doherty, M. (1998) *The Trouble With Guns: Republican Strategy and the Provisional IRA.* Belfast: Blackstaff.

O'Leary, B. (2004) 'The nature of the Agreement', in J. McGarry and B. O'Leary (eds), *The Northern Ireland Conflict: Consociational Engagements.* Oxford: Oxford University Press.

O'Leary, B. and McGarry, J. (1996) *The Politics of Antagonism: Understanding Northern Ireland* (2nd edn). London: Athlone.

O'Mahony, D., Morison, J., Geary, R. and McEvoy, K. (2000) *Crime, Community and Locale: The Northern Ireland Communities Crime Survey*. Aldershot: Ashgate.

O'Rawe, M. (2003) 'Transitional policing arrangements in Northern Ireland: the can't and the won't of the change dialectic', *Fordham International Law Journal*, 26(3): 1015–73.

O'Rawe, M. and Moore, L. (1997) *Human Rights on Duty: Principles for Better Policing – International Lessons for Northern Ireland*. Belfast: Committee for the Administration of Justice.

O'Rawe, M. and Moore, L. (2000) 'Accountability and police complaints in Northern Ireland: leaving the past behind?', in A. Goldsmith and C. Lewis (eds), *Civilian Oversight of Policing*. Oxford: Hart.

Office of the Police Ombudsman of Northern Ireland (2001a) *Statement by the Police Ombudsman of Northern Ireland on her Investigation of Matters Relating to the Omagh Bombing of August 15 1998*. Belfast: OPONI (see: http://www.policeombudsman.org//Publicationsuploads/omaghreport.pdf).

Office of the Police Ombudsman of Northern Ireland (2001b) *Police Ombudsman Releases Findings on Devenny Investigation*. Belfast: OPONI (see: http://www.policeombudsman.org//Publicationsuploads/devenny.pdf).

Office of the Police Ombudsman of Northern Ireland (2004a) *A Study of the Attitudes of Members of the Police Service of Northern Ireland to the Office of the Police Ombudsman for Northern Ireland and the New Complaints System*. Belfast: OPONI (see: http://www.policeombudsman.org//Publicationsuploads/main%20findings.doc).

Office of the Police Ombudsman of Northern Ireland (2004b) *The Investigation by the Police of the Murder of Mr Sean Brown on 12 May 1997*. Belfast: OPONI (see: http://www.policeombudsman.org//Publicationsuploads/Sean%20Brown%20report.pdf).

Osiel, M. (1997) *Mass Atrocity, Collective Memory and the Law*. New Brunswick, NJ: Transaction.

Oversight Commissioner (2003a) *Overseeing the Proposed Revisions to the Policing Services of Northern Ireland, 8th Report*. Belfast: Oversight Commissioner.

Oversight Commissioner (2003b) *Overseeing the Proposed Revisions to the Policing Services of Northern Ireland, 9th Report*. Belfast: Oversight Commissioner.

Oversight Commissioner (2004) *Overseeing the Proposed Revisions to the Policing Services of Northern Ireland, 12th Report*. Belfast: Oversight Commissioner.

Oversight Commissioner (2005) *Overseeing the Proposed Revisions to the Policing Services of Northern Ireland, 13th Report*. Belfast: Oversight Commissioner.

Paisley, I. (1999) *Statement Issued by Ian Paisley, leader of the Democratic Unionist Party, on the publication of the Patten Report, Thursday 9 September*. See: http://www.cain.ulst.ac.uk/issues/police/patten/.

Paisley, I. Jr (1995) 'Policing in Northern Ireland', in L. Kennedy (ed.), *Crime and Punishment in West Belfast*. Belfast: West Belfast Summer School.

Palmer, S. H. (1988) *Police and Protest in England and Ireland, 1780–1850*. Cambridge: Cambridge University Press.

Parker Committee (1972) *Report of the Privy Counsellors Appointed to Consider Authorised Procedures for the Interrogation of Persons Suspected of Terrorism* (Cmnd. 4901). London: HMSO.

Pat Finucane Centre (1995) *One Day in August*. Derry: Pat Finucane Centre.

Pat Finucane Centre (1996) *In the Line of Fire*. Derry: Pat Finucane Centre.

Patten Report (1999a) *A New Beginning: Policing in Northern Ireland. The Report of the Independent Commission on Policing in Northern Ireland*. Belfast: Stationery Office.

Patten, C. (1999b) *Statement by Chris Patten on the Publication of the Patten Report on the future of Policing in Northern Ireland*. See: http://www.cain.ulst.ac.uk/issues/police/.

Patten, C. (1999c) *Testimony given to the Subcommittee on International Operations and Human Rights of the Committee on International Relations House of Representatives, One Hundred Sixth Congress, First Session, September 24, 1999 (Serial No. 106-103)*. See: http://www.access.gpo.gov/congress/house/house09.html.

Pickering, S. (2002) *Women, Policing and Resistance in Northern Ireland*. Belfast: Beyond the Pale.

Pockrass, R. M. (1986) 'The police response to terrorism: the Royal Ulster Constabulary', *Police Journal*, 59(2): 143–57.

Police Authority for Northern Ireland (1988) *Working Together to Police Northern Ireland*. Belfast: PANI.

Police Authority for Northern Ireland (1995) *Annual Report for 1995*. Belfast: PANI.

Police Authority for Northern Ireland (1996a) *'Everybody's Police': A Partnership for Change*. Belfast: PANI.

Police Authority for Northern Ireland (1996b) *'A Partnership for Change': A Report on Further Consultation by the Police Authority for Northern Ireland*. Belfast: PANI.

Police Authority for Northern Ireland (1998) *Reflecting All Shades of Opinion*. Belfast. PANI.

Police Federation for Northern Ireland (1999) *Independent Commission on Policing in Northern Ireland: Submission to Government by the Police Federation for Northern Ireland*. Belfast: PFNI.

Portelli, A. (1991) *The Death of Luigi Trastulli and Other Stories: Form and Meaning in Oral History*. New York: State University of New York Press.

Porter, N. (2003) *The Elusive Quest: Reconciliation in Northern Ireland*. Belfast: Blackstaff Press.

Progressive Unionist Party (1995) *Submission to the Northern Ireland Office by the Progressive Unionist Party on Policing and Related Matters*. Belfast: Progressive Unionist Party.

Punch, M. (1985) *Conduct Unbecoming*. London: Tavistock.

Punch, M. (ed.) (1983) *Control in the Police Organisation*. Cambridge, MA: MIT Press.

Rees, M. (1985) *Northern Ireland: A Personal Perspective*. London: Methuen.

Reiner, R. (2000) *The Politics of the Police* (3rd edn). Oxford: Oxford University Press.

Relatives for Justice (1995) *Collusion*. Derry: Relatives for Justice.

Religious for Justice and Peace (1995) *Policing in Northern Ireland – Options for the Future*. Belfast: Author.

Rolston, B. (2000) *Unfinished Business: State Killings and the Quest for Truth*. Belfast: Blackstaff.

Rolston, B. (2002a) 'Resistance and terror: lessons from Ireland', in P. Scraton (ed.), *Beyond September 11: An Anthology of Dissent*. London: Pluto.

Rolston, B. (2002b) 'Assembling the jigsaw: truth, justice and transition in the North of Ireland', *Race and Class*, 44(1): 87–105.

Rolston, B. and Scraton, P. (2005) 'In the full glare of English politics: Ireland, inquiries and the British State', *British Journal of Criminology*, 45(4): 547–64.

Rose, R. (1971) *Governing Without Consensus*. London: Faber & Faber.

Royal Ulster Constabulary (1988) *Professional Policing Ethics*. Belfast: RUC.

Royal Ulster Constabulary (1992a) *Strategic Statement 1992–1995*. Belfast: RUC.

Royal Ulster Constabulary (1992b) *Statement of Purpose and Values*. Belfast: RUC.

Royal Ulster Constabulary (1993) *RUC Charter*. Belfast: RUC.

Royal Ulster Constabulary (1996) *A Fundamental Review of Policing: Summary and Key Findings*. Belfast: RUC.

Royal Ulster Constabulary (1997) *Strategic Statement 1997–2000*. Belfast: RUC.

Royal Ulster Constabulary (n.d.) *The RUC*. Belfast: RUC.

Royal Ulster Constabulary (various) *Chief Constable's Annual Reports*. Belfast: HMSO.

Royal Ulster Constabulary Museum (1995) *The Royal Ulster Constabulary Museum: A Guide to the Collection*. Belast: RUC Historical Society.

Ruane, J. and Todd, J. (2005 in press) *The Dynamics of Conflict in Northern Ireland* (2nd edn). Cambridge: Cambridge University Press.

Ryder, C. (2000) *The RUC 1922–2000: A Force Under Fire* (4th edn). London: Arrow.

Ryder, C. (2004) *The Fateful Split: Catholics and the Royal Ulster Constabulary*. London: Methuen.

Ryder, C. and Kearney, V. (2002) *Drumcree: The Orange Order's Last Stand*. London: Methuen.


Samuel, R. (1994) *Theatres of Memory, Vol. 1: Past and Present in Contemporary Culture*. London: Verso.

Scarman Report (1972) *Violence and Civil Disturbances in Northern Ireland in 1969: Report of a Tribunal of Inquiry* (Cmnd. 566). London: HMSO.

Schaar, J. H. (1984) 'Legitimacy and the modern state', in W. Connolly (ed.), *Legitimacy and the State*. New York: New York University Press.

Scott, J. (1985) *Weapons of the Weak: Everyday Forms of Peasant Resistance*. New Haven, CT: Yale University Press.

Scott, J. (1990) *Domination and the Arts of Resistance: Hidden Transcripts*. New Haven, CT: Yale University Press.

Scraton, P. (2004) 'From deceit to disclosure: the politics of official inquiries in the United Kingdom', in G. Gilligan and J. Pratt (eds), *Crime, Truth and Justice: Official Inquiry, Discourse, Knowledge*. Cullompton: Willan.

Scraton, P. (ed.) (2002) *Beyond September 11: An Anthology of Dissent*. London: Pluto.

Shaw, M. (2002) *Crime and Policing in Post-Apartheid South Africa: Transforming Under Fire*. Bloomington, IN: Indiana University Press.

Shearing, C. (2000) ' "A New Beginning" for policing', *Journal of Law and Society*, 27(3): 386–93.

Shearing, C. (2001) 'A nodal conception of governance: thoughts on a policing commission', *Policing and Society*, 11(3–4): 259–72.

Sherman, L. W. (1978) *Scandal and Reform*. Berkeley, CA: University of California Press.

Sherman, L.W. (1983) 'Reducing gun use: critical events, administrative policy, and organizational change', in M. Punch (ed.), *Control in the Police Organization*. Cambridge, MA: MIT Press.

Shirlow, P. and McGovern, M. (eds) (1997) *Who are the People? Unionism, Protestantism and Loyalism in Northern Ireland*. London: Pluto.

Silke, A. and Taylor, M. (2000) 'War without end: comparing IRA and loyalist vigilantism in Northern Ireland', *Howard Journal of Criminal Justice*, 39(3): 249–66.

Sim, J., Scraton, P. and Gordon, P. (1987) 'Introduction: crime, the state and critical analysis', in P. Scraton (ed.), *Law, Order and the Authoritarian State*. Milton Keynes: Open University Press.

Simmons, A. J. (2001) *Justification and Legitimacy*. Cambridge: Cambridge University Press.

Sinclair, R. J. K. and Scully, F. J. M. (1982) *Arresting Memories: Captured Moments in Constabulary Life*. Coleraine: RUC Diamond Jubilee Committee.

Sinn Féin (1996) *Policing in Transition: A Legacy of Repression, An Opportunity for Justice*. Dublin: Sinn Féin.

Sinn Féin (1997) *'An Appalling Vista' – Collusion: British Military Intelligence and Brian Nelson*. Belfast: Sinn Féin.

Sinn Féin (2002) *A Police Service Representative of the Community as a Whole*. Dublin: Sinn Féin.

Sinn Féin (2003) *Transfer of Policing and Justice Powers*. Dublin: Sinn Féin.

Skolnick, J. H. (1993) *Justice Without Trial: Law Enforcement in a Democratic Society* (3rd edn). New York: Macmillan.

Skolnick, J. H. and Bayley, D. L. (1986) *The New Blue Line: Police Innovation in Six Cities*. New York: Free Press.

Skolnick, J. H. and Fyfe, J. F. (1993) *Above the Law: Police and the Excessive Use of Force*. New York: Free Press.

Sluka, J. (1989) *Hearts and Minds, Water and Fish: Support for the IRA and INLA in a Northern Irish Ghetto*. Greenwich, CT: JAI Press.

Smyth, J. (2002a) 'Symbolic power and police legitimacy: the Royal Ulster Constabulary', *Crime, Law and Social Change*, 38(3): 295–310.

Smyth, J. (2002b) 'Community policing and the reform of the Royal Ulster Constabulary', *Policing*, 25(1): 110–24.

Smyth, M. and Fay, M.-T. (eds) (2000) *Personal Accounts from Northern Ireland's Troubles: Public Conflict, Private Loss*. London: Pluto.

Social Democratic and Labour Party (1975) *The Northern Ireland Police Service*. Belfast: SDLP.

Social Democratic and Labour Party (1995) *Policing in Northern Ireland*. Belfast: SDLP.

Social Democratic and Labour Party (1999) *Independent Commission on Policing for Northern Ireland*. Belfast: SDLP.

Social Democratic and Labour Party (2003) *Policing: Freedom from Intimidation and Harassment*. Belfast: SDLP.

Sparks, R. (1992) *Television and the Drama of Crime: Moral Tales and the Place of Crime in Public Life*. Buckingham: Open University Press.

Spurr, D. (1993) *The Rhetoric of Empire*. Durham, NC: Duke University Press.

Stalker, J. (1988) *The Stalker Affair*. London: Penguin.

Statewatch (2000) 'Patten's radical model of policing is emasculated in Police (Northern Ireland) Bill', *Statewatch News Online*. See: http://www.statewatch.org/news/jun00/07patten1a.htm.

Stenson, K. (1998) 'Beyond histories of the present', *Economy and Society*, 27(4): 333–52.

Stevens, Sir John. (2003) *Stevens Enquiry 3: Overview and Recommendations*. See: http://www.cain.ulst.ac.uk/issues/collusion/stevens3/stevens3summary.pdf.

Stewart, A. T. Q. (1989) *The Narrow Ground* (rev. edn). London: Faber & Faber.

Sutton, M. (2001) *Bear in Mind These Dead: An Index of Deaths from the Conflict in Ireland*. Online database available at: http://www.cain.ulst.ac.uk/sutton/index.html.

Taylor, P. (1980) *Beating the Terrorists? Interrogation in Omagh, Gough and Castlereagh*. Harmondsworth: Penguin.

Taylor, P. (1987) *Stalker*. London: Faber.

Taylor, P. (1997) *Provos: The IRA and Sinn Fein*. London: Bloomsbury.

Taylor, P. (1999) *Loyalists*. London: Bloomsbury.

Taylor, P. (2001) *Brits: The War Against the IRA*. London: Bloomsbury.

Teitel, R. (2000) *Transitional Justice*. Oxford: Oxford University Press.

Thompson, J. (1990) *Ideology and Modern Culture*. Cambridge: Polity.

Tilley, N. (2003) 'Community policing, problem-oriented policing, and intelligence-led policing', in T. Newburn (ed.), *Handbook of Policing*. Cullompton: Willan.

Tomlinson, M. (1980) 'Reforming repression', in L. O'Dowd, B. Rolston and M. Tomlinson (eds), *Northern Ireland: Between Civil Rights and Civil War*. London: CSE Books.

Tomlinson, M. (1993) 'Policing the new Europe: the Northern Ireland factor', in T. Bunyan (ed.), *Statewatching the New Europe*. London: Statewatch.

Tomlinson, M. (2000) 'Frustrating Patten: commentary on the Patten Report', *Irish Journal of Sociology*, 10(1): 103–9.

Turner, V. (1974) *Fields, Dramas and Metaphors: Symbolic Action in Human Society*. Ithaca, NY: Cornell University Press.

Tyler, T. (2004) 'Enhancing police legitimacy', *Annals of the American Association of Political and Social Sciences*, 593: 84–99.

United Nations (1998) *Special Report of the Rapporteur on the Independence of the Judiciary and Lawyers*. Submitted by Param Cumaraswamy pursuant to UN Resolution 1997/23. Geneva: United Nations.

Urban, M. (1992) *Big Boys' Rules: The Secret Struggle Against the IRA*. London: Faber & Faber.

Van Maanen, J. (1978) 'Observations on the making of policemen', in P. Manning and J. Van Maanen (eds), *Policing*. Santa Monica, CA: Goodyear.

Waddington, P. A. J. (1999) 'Police (canteen) sub-culture: an appreciation', *British Journal of Criminology*, 39(2): 286–309.

Walden, K. (1982) *Visions of Order: The Canadian Mounties in Symbol and Myth*. Toronto: Butterworth.

Walker, B. (1996) *Dancing to History's Tune: History, Myth and Politics in Ireland*. Belfast: Institute for Irish Studies.

Walker, C. (1990) 'Police and community in Northern Ireland', *Northern Ireland Legal Quarterly*, 41: 105–41.

Walker, C. (2001) 'The Patten Report and post-sovereignty policing in Northern Ireland', in R. Wilford (ed.), *Aspects of the Belfast Agreement*. Oxford: Oxford University Press.

Walker, N. (2003) 'The pattern of transnational policing', in T. Newburn (ed.), *Handbook of Policing*. Cullompton: Willan.

Walsh, D. (1988) 'The Royal Ulster Constabulary: a law unto themselves?', in M. Tomlinson, T. Varley and C. McCullagh (eds), *Whose Law and Order?* Belfast: Sociological Association of Ireland.

Weber, M. (1946) *From Max Weber*, eds and trans. H. H. Gerth and C. Wright Mills. New York: Oxford University Press.

Weitzer, R. (1990) *Transforming Settler States: Communal Conflict and Internal Security in Zimbabwe and Northern Ireland*. Berkeley, CA: University of California Press.

Weitzer, R. (1992) 'Northern Ireland's police liaison committees', *Policing and Society*, 2(3): 233–43.

Weitzer, R. (1995) *Policing Under Fire: Ethnic Conflict and Police-Community Relations in Northern Ireland*. Albany, NY: SUNY Press.

Whyte, J. (1990) *Interpreting Northern Ireland*. Oxford: Clarendon Press.

Wilford, R. (ed.) (2001) *Aspects of the Belfast Agreement*. Oxford: Oxford University Press.

Wilson, C. (2000) *Cop Knowledge: Police Power and Cultural Narrative in Twentieth-Century America*. Chicago: University of Chicago Press.

Wright, J. and Bryett, K. (2000) *Policing and Conflict in Northern Ireland*. Basingstoke: Macmillan.

Young, J. (1993) *The Texture of Memory: Holocaust Memorials and Meaning*. New Haven, CT: Yale University Press.

Young, M. (1991) *An Inside Job: Policing and Police Culture in Britain*. Oxford: Oxford University Press.

# Index